Game On

W9-CCJ-146

WITHDRAWN

WITHDRAWN

Game On

Energize Your Business with Social Media Games

Jon Radoff

WILEY

Wiley Publishing, Inc.

Game On: Energize Your Business with Social Media Games

Published by
Wiley Publishing, Inc.
10475 Crosspoint Boulevard
Indianapolis, IN 46256
www.wiley.com

Copyright © 2011 by Wiley Publishing, Inc., Indianapolis, Indiana

Published simultaneously in Canada

ISBN: 978-0-470-93626-9

ISBN: 978-1-118-08932-3 (ebk)

ISBN: 978-1-118-08930-9 (ebk)

ISBN: 978-1-118-08931-6 (ebk)

Manufactured in the United States of America

10 9 8 7 6 5 4 3 2 1

No part of this publication may be reproduced, stored in a retrieval system or transmitted in any form or by any means, electronic, mechanical, photocopying, recording, scanning or otherwise, except as permitted under Sections 107 or 108 of the 1976 United States Copyright Act, without either the prior written permission of the Publisher, or authorization through payment of the appropriate per-copy fee to the Copyright Clearance Center, 222 Rosewood Drive, Danvers, MA 01923, (978) 750-8400, fax (978) 646-8600. Requests to the Publisher for permission should be addressed to the Permissions Department, John Wiley & Sons, Inc., 111 River Street, Hoboken, NJ 07030, (201) 748-6011, fax (201) 748-6008, or online at http://www.wiley.com/go/permissions.

Limit of Liability/Disclaimer of Warranty: The publisher and the author make no representations or warranties with respect to the accuracy or completeness of the contents of this work and specifically disclaim all warranties, including without limitation warranties of fitness for a particular purpose. No warranty may be created or extended by sales or promotional materials. The advice and strategies contained herein may not be suitable for every situation. This work is sold with the understanding that the publisher is not engaged in rendering legal, accounting, or other professional services. If professional assistance is required, the services of a competent professional person should be sought. Neither the publisher nor the author shall be liable for damages arising herefrom. The fact that an organization or Web site is referred to in this work as a citation and/or a potential source of further information does not mean that the author or the publisher endorses the information the organization or website may provide or recommendations it may make. Further, readers should be aware that Internet websites listed in this work may have changed or disappeared between when this work was written and when it is read.

For general information on our other products and services please contact our Customer Care Department within the United States at (877) 762-2974, outside the United States at (317) 572-3993 or fax (317) 572-4002.

Wiley also publishes its books in a variety of electronic formats. Some content that appears in print may not be available in electronic books.

Library of Congress Control Number: 2011921776

Trademarks: Wiley and the Wiley logo are trademarks or registered trademarks of John Wiley & Sons, Inc. and/or its affiliates, in the United States and other countries, and may not be used without written permission. Disruptor Beam is a trademark of Disruptor Beam, Inc. All other trademarks are the property of their respective owners. Wiley Publishing, Inc. is not associated with any product or vendor mentioned in this book.

This book is dedicated to my parents,

Steve and Anna Radoff,

who always encouraged me to play.

ABOUT THE AUTHOR

on Radoff is an entrepreneur focused on the intersection of the Internet, entertainment and social communities. In 1992, he started NovaLink, an online game publisher that created *Legends of Future Past*, distributed commercially on the CompuServe network. *Legends* became one of the first independent, commercial game products on the Internet. In 1997, Jon founded Eprise, the creator of a content management system that was a forerunner of modern blog and wiki technology. At Eprise, Jon raised venture capital, established product strategy, and recruited a management team that succeeded in taking Eprise into Fortune 500 customers, culminating in a public offering on NASDAQ in 2000. In 2006, Jon started GamerDNA, a venture-capital funded social media company that built products driven by real-time gamer behavior. GamerDNA's advertising product reached over 10 million unique users per month and counted top-tier game publishers including Blizzard/Activision, Electronic Arts, Namco, and Turbine amongst its customers. GamerDNA merged with another gaming media venture in 2009 to become GamerDNA Media.

Jon's new startup, Disruptor Beam, is a social game developer that is disrupting the current social game landscape by leveraging Jon's experience with software platforms, analytics and online communities. Disruptor Beam develops its own social game products, and also partners with publishers and media companies to bring new social game ideas to life.

ABOUT THE TECHNICAL EDITOR

than Kidhardt is a Technology Specialist living in sunny San Diego and has been a writer and reviewer for MMORPG's for over 10 years, working closely with developers and publishers to produce the strategy guides that you buy in the stores. Ethan has written extensively for games such as *Dark Age of Camelot*, *Asherons Call 2*, *Anarchy Online*, *Everquest 2*, *Lineage*, *Final Fantasy XI*, *Star Wars Galaxies*, *City of Heroes*, *The Matrix Online*, and *D&D Online*. Ethan met the author during one of his online forays, and in finding a kindred spirit, has worked and played together off and on ever since. Ethan brings a wealth of expertise in the areas of design, strategy and critical analysis. When not embedded in the world of technology, you can find him teaching Spanish, volunteering, and dancing Salsa throughout San Diego.

CREDITS

Executive Editor
Carol Long

Project Editor
Maureen Spears

Technical Editor
Ethan Kidhardt

Senior Production Editor
Debra Banninger

Copy Editor
San Dee Phillips

Editorial Director
Robyn B. Siesky

Editorial Manager
Mary Beth Wakefield

Freelancer Editorial Manager
Rosemarie Graham

Associate Director of Marketing
Ashley Zurcher

Production Manager
Tim Tate

Vice President and Executive Group Publisher
Richard Swadley

Vice President and Executive Publisher
Barry Pruett

Associate Publisher
Jim Minatel

Project Coordinator, Cover
Katie Crocker

Compositor
Maureen Forys,
Happenstance Type-O-Rama

Proofreader
Nancy Carrasco

Indexer
Robert Swanson

Cover Image
© Colin Anderson / Getty Images

Cover Designer
Ryan Sneed

CONTENTS AT A GLANCE

CONTENTS

FOREWORD

Imagine you have a secret power that could completely change the way you do business. With this power, you'd earn more customers, make existing customers more loyal, and attract more talented employees. How would this change your life?

I've learned that whenever you make people feel special, you win them over. It's one of the things I'm always telling people to do. It really works, because it is a universal law that people want to feel important. Customers want to feel valued. And customers that feel special become your fans. They love what you do and help you attract even more customers.

The revolution in social media has shown the world how important this is. Call it social status, call it bragging, call it sharing your experiences—human beings are deeply concerned with what other people are doing and thinking. Everyone loves to share their successes and seek comfort from friends when facing the tough challenges in life.

A well-executed game makes people feel special because games are an age-old way to reach someone's heart and mind. Let's take sports for example. I began leading the Philadelphia 76ers in 1996, when they were in last place. Fueled by vision, passion, and determination, we made it to the NBA Championship Finals by 2001. When the 76ers began winning, we retook our place as an important part of Philadelphia culture. Once again our fans felt special about being part of the 76ers story. The team became enormously popular, and the stadium seats began to fill. This success was all about making people, in this case Philadelphians, feel special, making them know in their bones that they could be their best and that dreams do come true. Any type of game can make people feel this way—not just sports. Games can make people feel like they are part of something amazing.

There is nothing new about games. People have been playing games for as long as cavemen hit rocks with clubs. Yet so many people seem surprised whenever games jump to the forefront of the latest technology and business news. In retrospect, it is no surprise at all that games have become so popular on social networks. Social networks—where people desperately want to connect with each other and make their mark on the world—are a natural fit for games.

Let me give you another example of how games can capture your heart.

Ever since I saw Errol Flynn in the film *Captain Blood*, I've had a passion for pirates from the Golden Age of Pirates—the drama, the swashbuckling, the lifestyle, the history. I've collected an amazing cache of rare artifacts—like one of only two Jolly Roger black flags in the world and the only authentic pirate treasure chest in existence—and started a museum in St. Augustine to introduce other people to the magic of this historical time. However, reading and watching movies and visiting museums can get you only so far; I wanted to give people a real taste of what it would be like to live life as a pirate.

Fortunately, I was introduced to Jon Radoff—an expert on both games as well as the World Wide Web. His crew from Disruptor Beam came down to Philadelphia to help me realize my vision of creating a pirate game for the burgeoning world of social media. I explained how I have been fascinated with pirates, rogue stories, and buccaneer legends for as long as I can remember. That was not enough for them.

Jon's crew wanted to probe deep. They wanted to feel what I had felt. They really got it when I shared a very personal bit of memorabilia from my childhood. You see, when I was a child I attended a school ruled by nuns. They tried to subdue my insolence by using a twelve-inch ruler over my knuckles. Instead of subduing me, they just stoked my rebelliousness. I carved a skull and crossbones into the very ruler they tried to use to squelch my individuality. I still have this ruler, locked away in a safe. When I showed it to Jon, he got it: the spirit of freedom, anti-authority, and rebellion against rules. Our game was born: *True Pirates. No Rules, No Mercy.*

Games are about feelings. Whether it is sports, or a childhood dream about pirates, or the genius that has gone into the competitive reviews on Amazon.com—games all have a story to tell. But games are more than that: They grab you and take you inside the story. Games are about cooperation and competition; teamwork and victory; recognition and bragging rights.

You hold in your hands a special book. It is about finding out the stories within your customers and turning them into business advantages. If you're bold enough and determined enough to use the secrets contained here, you'll be on your way to creating that special feeling inside everyone you sell to and work with.

Attack!

—Pat Croce
Villanova, Pennsylvania
January 2011

ACKNOWLEDGMENTS

want to thank the numerous people who have influenced me, contributed directly to this book through conversations or editing, or otherwise made this book possible.

First and foremost is my wife, Angela Bull Radoff, who I met in an online game and has truly made my life an adventure. Angela helped steadfastly, looking at each of my chapters before anyone else—and contributed many of the great ideas that made it into this book.

The team at Disruptor Beam was invaluable with both conversations and actual edits to the manuscript. In particular, Tim Crosby, Athena Z Peters, and Jason Callina deserve special mention. Maria Picasso is a splendid artist who we're fortunate to have on our team, and created the designs for several of the icons used in the book, as well as the "History of Social Games" chart that originally appeared in my blog, and now in this book. Melissa Kelt also assisted with several of the technical illustrations.

Likewise, I want to thank the many business partners at Disruptor Beam who have made it possible for us to create the games: Doug Levin of Ayeah Games; Tug Yourgrau of Powderhouse; Pat Croce of Pirate Soul (who was also kind enough to share a Foreword); Jonathan Strause of I-Race; Jim Jonsin; Sam Rogatinsky; Trapper Markelz of MeYouHealth (who was also my right-hand at GamerDNA, where he helped me assemble and lead an incredible team of social media developers); and Peter Blacklow and the whole team at GSN Digital.

A number of people were kind enough to have conversations with me, or review some of the materials in the book: D. Yvette Wohn, for reviewing some of the game design and social psychology comments; Tom Snyder of Emotion Mining for commenting on my neuroscience and psychology content; and Daniel Cook for very helpful conversations about game development processes. Any shortcomings that endured in any of these areas are entirely my responsibility.

I draw inspiration from other social media entrepreneurs and writers, especially those who are fighting the good fight out here in the Northeast: Seth Godin, Chris Brogan, C.C. Chapman, Dharmesh Shah of Hubspot, and Darius Kazemi (lead analyst at Blue Fang Games, but a major force behind the IGDA and Boston Post Mortem); Marshall McLuhan and Jenry Jenkins for taking popular media and games seriously; Jim Gilmore and Joe Pine for their work on the experience economy;

Charles Stross, Bruce Sterling, Arthur C. Clarke and Vernor Vinge for expanding my dreams.

Thank you to the team at Wiley for backing this book: Carol Long for having the outstanding good taste in choosing me as author for this project, and then persuading me to do it—and Maureen Spears, my project editor, for her incredible patience and tireless editing of the manuscript. Ethan Kidhart, who I originally met as "Esis" in Asheron's Call 2, worked as technical editor—and offered numerous improvements to the text.

Finally, thank you to everyone who has made it their life's work to create games.

INTRODUCTION

I'm stepping off a plane in California and I'm about to meet the woman who will change my life. In the months previous, I'd braved battle and hardship, and fended off other would-be suitors. I'd won the girl.

Her name was Angela, and I had seen her photos, and so I knew what she looked like. She's standing at the gate (it would be years before airport security would change forever) and I tentatively approach. My heart is beating so hard that I can feel it in my ears and her cinnamon-laced perfume fills my nostrils. We touch hands in greeting, and a spark leaps between us that had first ignited from across thousands of miles of space and kindled within the wild realms of imagination.

Angela and I had met in a world called Elanthia, a realm constructed entirely of electrons and dreams. I was a wizard named Lythe, and she was an elven dark temptress named Kaoti. Elanthia was the setting of a game called *Gemstone*. It was a social game, where people from around the world met to go on adventures, have fiery romances, and cross blades in combat. The game was played on an online service called GEnie, one of the social networks of the nineties—although that term wouldn't be established for another decade.

Angela and I not only met in an online game, and came together romantically, we also discovered our shared passion for the art and business of games. We felt in our marrow that we could make great games, and so we did: launching our own *Legends of Future Past* on the Internet and the CompuServe network. The game won a couple of awards and launched the careers of several people who went on to create successful games in the industry.

Thousands of people played *Gemstone* and *Legends of Future Past* in the early nineties. Today, millions play the descendants of these games. Although the technology has changed, the essential essence of what makes games work has not. Games have been an enduring part of humanity for millennia, and the craft of making games is as old as the story of civilization.

The Things You Remember Best

Between the salad days of early online games and today, I've had the good fortune to form and launch a range of companies both in and outside of entertainment.

Each experience has shown me something different about how people interact with technology and each other. At Eprise, a company that created software for managing websites—a precursor to the concept of wikis—I learned how people have an innate hunger to interact and share information with each other. At GamerDNA, a social network for gamers, I learned of countless other people who had similar experiences to Angela and me. It turns out that the world was catching up to us—games had made a profound imprint on people, and their lives have been changed as a result.

As I write this, I've returned to my original passion: entertaining the world through online games. At Disruptor Beam, the new company Angela and I have created, I knew that I wanted to do more than build games. I want to help people rethink what games can be. I want to refine the special magic of games into an elixir that can make the world a better, more fun place to be.

It turns out I'm not alone.

At some point during 2010, a curious new term emerged: *gamification*. The idea is that you can take certain features that exist in games,and power up a business by sprinkling them in any business or software application. You could add a leaderboard to a website to spark competition or give people badges to reward the behaviors you want.

Something was missing from all this talk about gamification.

Angela and I didn't meet because of a leaderboard, or a badge system, or a point system. We met because of emotion and imagination. Our shared experiences in games inspired strong emotions, our dreams, and imaginations. Yes, points are important. Badges can be helpful. Leaderboards are compelling. But these are simply the tools of game design; they don't tell you what makes games actually work.

This book is about social games: the type of games that people play with each other. This book is also an adventure story, with you as the hero—because you'll learn techniques to transform your own business by using some of the magic of games within your own work. Leaderboards, points, and badges are explained because they're important. But I'll also try to get to the heart of what makes things fun, by discussing how human beings relate to each other, and how the universe of social media is an ideal frontier for the delivery of these experiences.

Myths, storytelling, brainstorming ideas are covered to help you think about your business in new ways. This book also discusses new ways to look at elements of your online presence, such as user interfaces—not simply as a set of gadgets on a computer screen but as a doorway into a world you craft for your customers.

So start your journey.

What Is a Social Game?

A *social game* is a game that people play with each other. Such games have existed throughout recorded history.

In recent years, the term social game is usually used to refer to a particular class of games: the games that have exploded on social networks. These social network games have grown from almost nothing to millions of players around the world in a short period of time, earning companies such as Zynga and Playdom massive chests of gold. It's a market that is frequently misunderstood, even by experts in the computer game industry, who sometimes insist that its games aren't even games at all.

It's a new market, with new customers and few expectations, but it's also a rapidly growing market, and everyone is still learning exactly what makes it work. This book discusses why it works, and why these games share properties that are both different and similar to well-known types of games.

However, social games are also much broader than these new social network games. Others have emerged over the last decade, including massively multiplayer games such as *World of Warcraft*, or the real-time strategy game *League of Legends*. These games have every right to be called social games, so they are discussed side-by-side with games such as *Mafia Wars* and *FarmVille*, and Disruptor Beam's own products such as *True Pirates* and *Gods of Rock*—identifying similarities and differences.

Many social media sites have taken on several of the properties of games: Youtube, LinkedIn, and Facebook are three examples that use some of the same elements that make games work so well. Amazon has reinvented electronic commerce by incorporating social and game elements. You can adapt similar techniques to create your own social media games that deliver business results, harnessing the power of social relationships and emotion.

What if Anything Could Be a Game?

Many of you have never read a book about game design before and have probably never thought about your business as a game. For those of you, I'm going to propose a simple game that you can play while reading this book: Imagine your business as if it is a game. Imagine that your customers are players, and they're coming to you for fun. How does this change the way you think about them?

Fun isn't a panacea. It isn't appropriate 100 percent of the time. The world is often a serious place, and many of the things you have to do simply aren't fun. But if you allow yourself to indulge in the thought experiment, you might find yourself thinking about your problems in an entirely new way.

If at times I speak about your game or your players, keep in mind that I'm not simply talking about a hypothetical game you might make. I'm referring to your business, whatever it might be. If you can master this metaphor, you can unlock a great deal of the value this book offers.

Who Should Read This Book?

This book is for anyone who would like to learn how to capture some of the magic of social games so that it can be put to work in a business. This includes the following:

- **Marketers** who would like to learn how games can help find and keep customers.
- **Product designers** who want to create experiences that enchant customers, leaving them with lasting memories.
- **Website designers** who want to use fun to increase engagement and visitor retention.
- **Executives** who want to inject fun into their enterprise, leading to the profit that comes from increasing customer joy.
- **Game designers** and enthusiasts who want to understand more about what makes a social game tick.

What's In this Book?

So how do we go about the business of gamification—the idea that non-business applications could increase engagement by incorporating elements of fun? As discussed, effective games are about stories and worlds and this book arms you with tools to energize your own business with games. The following sections outline this book's content.

Part I: Understanding Social Games

This part covers all the ins and outs of what defines social games. You'll learn about gaming theory, how to develop games, how to think of your customers as players and what makes games fun.

- **Chapter 1, "How to Play This Book,"** discusses the factors that contribute to interest in social games, how to relate your interests to this book's content and how quizzes can uncover customer motivations.
- **Chapter 2, "Games Have Changed the Business Playfield,"** explores why games are popular today, the common themes of games through the ages and how cultural trends drive social game as well as the type of people who should be curious about the impact of games.
- **Chapter 3, "Developing Social Media Games,"** shows you the differences between social games, traditional games, and non-game software development, what skills and people you need on your social media game project and the player-centered design process for managing your project.
- **Chapter 4, "Customers as Players,"** explores how thinking of your customers as players helps you positively transform your business relationships. You also discover the power of myth as a creative tool to explore customer belief as well as how to classify different types of customers using various methods.
- **Chapter 5 "Fungineering,"** you're shown why things are fun from the standpoint of game psychology, the sixteen basic motivations behind the things you like, the power of emotion, the forty-two features that people love and how brainstorming helps you develop fun ideas for your own game.
- **Chapter 6, "Turning Work into Fun,"** explores the opportunities and risks of gamification, how games make tasks more fun, how to apply the techniques of social games to non-gaming experiences to make them fun and rewarding, as well as how to critically evaluate the content of games and social media experiences.

Part II: Designing Social Games

This part goes in depth into how to design your very own social games and covers how you can introduce the various principals of gaming into your own business model.

You'll learn the art of storytelling, how to make your customer return to your site again and again as well as how to design the perfect game interface complete with virtual goods.

- **Chapter 7, "Anatomy of a Social Game,"** illustrates how social games work with Facebook, what features make a game social, the three life-cycle phases that social game players experience, and how social games spread through social channels.

- **Chapter 8, "Understanding Social Game Business Models,"** discusses how to keep a player's attention, the approaches that social games use to monetize players, and the techniques for acquiring players. You explore the metrics for measuring player acquisition, attention, and revenue; and how to create a spreadsheet that captures your game's business model. You also learn the different modes of testing you can use to design, develop, and operate your game, as well as the risks and benefits for different methods of testing.

- **Chapter 9, "Using Storytelling to Understand Your Design Objectives,"** explores how to create player narratives that capture the essence of fun in your game, how to use the tools of myths to enhance your games, how to extract lists of goals and feature from abstract ideas and suggestions for brainstorming and refining your stories.

- **Chapter 10, "Creating Compelling Game Systems,"** shows how flow and pace work to make a game compelling, how to design game systems that result in compulsive interaction, and how to deepen your own game design skills while having fun.

- **Chapter 11, "Designing Game Interfaces,"** discusses how different user interfaces address different challenges in game design as well as how they convey your story. You also discover ways to take your player narrative and user stories and turn them into an interaction map.

- **Chapter 12, "Designing for Virtual Goods,"** explores who is buying virtual goods and what they're buying, how to manage the risks of a virtual economy, and techniques for selling virtual goods in your game.

- **Chapter 13, "Coda,"** is a brief summary of what you learn in the book, and touches upon the future of social games.

Part III: Glossary, Resources, and More

Part III gives you valuable resources that are cited throughout the book but are discussed in great detail here. You also are presented with a handy glossary and ending thoughts from the author.

- **Appendix A, "Glossary,"** gives you a handy list of terms that are covered in this book. This is invaluable to people reading this book who are new to the gaming arena.
- **Appendix B, "Resource Guide,"** gives more details on the various resources touched on throughout the book.
- **Appendix C, "Book References,"** lists the various notes associated with each chapter of the book as well as a list of references.

How to Read this Book

Although the content of this book is designed around a linear reading experience, as the outline of the last section showed, the book is segmented into two parts—one that is heavy on game theory and the other on game design. Obviously, if you're more interested in the mechanics of games or the design of games, your attention may be more drawn to one part over another.

To help you get the most out of your reading experience, the following is a list of book features of which you need to be aware.

Book Icons

You'll encounter three types of icons in this book, each specific to your personality type. To determine your personality type, take the test in the section "Quiz: Who Are You?" in Chapter 1. After taking the test, you can easily determine your predominant personality type. Then, it's just a matter of looking for your personal icon throughout the book to find notes specifically geared to you.

 IMPRESARIO In this book, these are the people who focus on the business aspect of games, including how to produce, market, and distribute them.

ARTISAN In this book, artisans are more concerned with the craft of game design, including what makes it tick and how it works.

 OTAKU In this book, these are individuals who are genuinely passionate about gaming and all its aspects, including a history of the game, past and present; the major game designers of our times; and gaming forums and events.

Finding Your Own Path in This Book

At the end of each chapter, you'll also find helpful sections that help steer you to areas that you might find of particular interest. These include:

- **Chapter in Review:** These sections review the chapter and its content including all the ideas and concepts.
- **Choose Your Path:** These sections show you content in other chapters that is related to whatever you're reading in the current chapter. For example, if you enjoyed the quiz and the discussion of the Impresario, Artisan, and Otaku personality types, the "Choose Your Path" section will direct you to Chapter 4, which discusses the way games classify player types. A "Choose Your Path" section is included in this introduction so you can get started!

Choose Your Path

Games are about decisions. In that spirit, enjoy this book by taking your own path through it. The natural way is to read it one chapter at a time, but many people like to pick up a book like this and jump from section to section. As mentioned, at the end of each chapter, you can find some suggestions on where you can turn to next.

In that light, the following list gives areas of the book you might want to visit next.

- If you'd like to continue in order, the next subject covered is instructions on how to play this book. That's right, this book is also a game! You'll take a short quiz to figure out what sort of reader you are, which points you to certain signposts throughout the text. If you're ready to discover a bit about yourself, turn the page to Chapter 1.

- If you'd like to learn more about the history of games, and how games have changed business, turn to Chapter 2.
- If you want to dive right into the nuts and bolts of a social game, including how they function within Facebook, you can go all the way to Chapter 7.
- If you'd like to interact in a community of people who are trying to learn to use social gaming techniques, then you can also go online to the book's website at www.game-on-book.com.

Or turn to any page you like. It's your adventure.

Game On

Understanding Social Games

1 How to Play This Book

n this chapter, you'll learn:

- What factors contribute to your interest in social games
- How you can relate your specific interests and motivations to the content of this book
- How you can use quizzes to uncover customer motivations

In *FarmVille*, your role is clear—you're pretending to be a farmer. In a fantasy roleplaying game like *World of Warcraft*, you can be a healer, protector or a damage-dealing spellcaster. Even in the more abstract game of chess, you can become a military strategist. Understanding the role of your customer is important for games, and it is also key for you to understand why different people interact with your business. You'll learn more about this in Chapter 4 when you read about personas, but for now you can learn more about this concept by seeing how it applies to the book.

As you progress through this chapter, you explore what interests you about games and how that information relates to the content of the book. Learning how to explore roles can give you a better way to understand your customers. More important, this can also be a form of self-enlightenment: People often enjoy learning things about themselves. This information can be surprising, self-validating, or serve as a tool to help you navigate an unfamiliar landscape.

Quiz: Who Are You?

You are at the start of a journey. If you're a gamer, some of this will be familiar to you. But if you're approaching games for the first time, then think of yourself as a cultural anthropologist: Throw yourself into the tribe, and learn how games work.

You'll soon learn that gamers aren't really a separate tribe at all—the aspects that make games fun work on all of us. One of the reasons social games are successful is that millions of people who hadn't previously thought of themselves as gamers found games to be so compelling. These are your customers!

Later in this book I'll discuss how important it is to understand your customer. You can begin by starting to learn a bit more about yourself, and why you've chosen to read this book. If you learn something new about yourself, imagine how much you'll discover about your customers by formulating your own questions.

Taking the Test

For each of the questions, pick the option (A, B, or C) that you feel best reflects your own answer. If something is close but not exact, you should choose that option. If you think two choices are equally true, it is fine to mark each one. If you think that none of the answers fit you, skip to the next question. After you answer or skip each question, you learn how to score your responses.

1. When considering a new game, you're most curious about…
   A. The game's business model and how much money it will earn.
   B. What decisions the game designers made when they created the rules for the game.
   C. Whether the game will be fun to play.
2. When deciding to try a new game, you're most likely to be influenced by…
   A. Games you've read about on business blogs, such as TechCrunch, Inside Social Games, or ReadWriteWeb.
   B. Games that have been discussed on game design blogs.
   C. The games your friends play or plan to play.
3. You are interested in games because…
   A. Games are the hottest part of the media industry.
   B. Games are the great new art form of our time.
   C. Games are fun.
4. When talking to other people about games…
   A. You're most often talking about business issues, such as virtual economies, business models, customer acquisition programs, or ways that games can be adapted to experiences outside the game industry.
   B. You discuss the design of the games and focus on the artwork, rules, and structures that make them work.
   C. It's usually your friends and online acquaintances, and you discuss the games you actively play (or plan to play) in the future.

5. You are reading this because…
   A. You're looking for new ways to make a company more innovative by involving customers in more engaging experiences.
   B. You'd like to understand techniques that can be used to design experiences to be more fun.
   C. You just enjoy learning anything about games.

6. Most of the books you've purchased recently are…
   A. Business books, such as marketing, social media, management, and so on.
   B. Technical, design, or other nonfiction books (not including business).
   C. Fiction.

7. In business meetings, you are most likely to be…
   A. Leading and organizing.
   B. Contributing creative ideas.
   C. Daydreaming about playing a game with your friends.

8. If you have an idea for a game, you are most likely to turn to…
   A. Excel, PowerPoint, or some other office productivity tool to capture the concept and business ideas.
   B. A prototyping or design tool to help sketch out the way the idea might actually play out.
   C. A gaming forum to talk to other game fans about things that would be nice to see in games.

9. The biggest potential benefit to structure a business as a game is that…
   A. The customers might spend more money.
   B. You can stand out in the minds of your customers.
   C. You'll have a legitimate excuse for "analyzing" games at work.

10. You are most likely to attend…
    A. Business networking events that talk about new businesses or help make connections with other people in your industry.
    B. Design networking events that focus on engineering, design, or scientific issues related to your career.
    C. Informal meetups with people you meet online, or fan conventions around games (such as Penny Arcade or Dragon*Con).

11. When purchasing a new mobile computing device, you are most likely to be influenced by…
    A. The product that you think will keep you most connected to your coworkers.

    B.   The product with the most elegant design.

    C.   The product with the most entertaining games and applications.

12.   Do you prefer pirates or ninjas?

    A.   Pirates: The lifestyle, freedom, financial upside, and fundamental capital efficiency of their business model is an example for us all.

    B.   Ninjas: Their dedication to craft, tradition, and constant self-improvement is enviable and admirable.

    C.   You like either pirates or ninjas more than the other but not for the reasons indicated.

Scoring Your Results

Now that you've taken the quiz, it is time to score your results. Remember, it was okay if you skipped some answers or gave multiple answers to one question.

Go through each question to find the total number of times you gave A as an answer, and then repeat for B and C. Next, identify which answer you gave the most and then the second most. Each type of answer correlates to a particular type of reader personality: A is an *impresario*, B is an *artisan* and C is an *otaku*, which are explained in a moment. Your overall type is a combination of two categories; whichever you answered is your primary category, and whichever you answered second-most is your secondary category. For example, if you answered A 7 times, B 4 times, and C once, you are an impresario-artisan.

What Your Results Say about You

Throughout the book, you'll see things that might be of special interest to you. Just look for the icons related to your personality categories next to various sections of the book, and you can find things that you might think are particularly interesting—think of them as signposts for quickly skimming or navigating areas of the book.

 ARTISAN The artisan is mostly concerned about the art and craft of game design. The focus here isn't on the money-making potential of a game but on what makes a game tick. Artisans may never have created actual games at any time in their life, but they are aficionados of the game creating craft and have a wealth of thoughts on the subject.

IMPRESARIO In the 19th century, impresarios were originally the financiers or organizers of theatrical productions. Today, the term is still sometimes used in the entertainment industry to refer to people who organize things such as concerts and events. The term is extended here to include people who produce or organize games for people to enjoy, with a particular focus on those who are interested in the business aspects of games: either how to produce, market, and distribute traditional games or incorporate game-like qualities into other areas of business. The various impresario notes scattered through the book point out interesting facts and information for business people.

 OTAKU William Gibson, the father of cyberpunk, has called the otaku (pronounced oh-tah-coo) a "passionate obsessive, the information age's embodiment of the connoisseur." It's a Japanese word for someone who is a serious fan of some facet of popular culture; it can be vintage cars, baseball cards, kitchen appliances, lawn gnomes, or whatever. If you're an otaku according to the quiz, it means you probably have a genuine passion for games. The otaku icon highlights anything of particular interest to game fans, game historians, and cultural anthropologists.

Do You Have a Combination Personality?

In the "Scoring Your Results" section, you recorded not only the category in which you scored the most points, but also the second-most. That's because most people probably express a little bit of each category. With three basic categories, and allowing for both a primary and secondary interest, you can have six total combinations:

- Artisan-otaku
- Artisan-impresario
- Impresario-artisan
- Impresario-otaku
- Otaku-artisan
- Otaku-impresario

COMBINATIONS AND PERMUTATIONS

Combinations are an important concept in game design because they can give you an indication of how complex your system is. If only a few basic outcomes occur, people might become bored. On the other hand, it is significantly harder for you to balance and comprehend your own system as you add more and more combinations to the mix.

When the order of a combination is important (such as occurs when you draw a sequence of cards in certain card games), it's more properly called a *permutation* (which was the case of the simple list of three categories that became six combination categories).

It's quite easy to sketch out the permutations of three categories, but it quickly becomes overwhelming for larger numbers. The mathematical formula to calculate the number of permutations follows:

$$\frac{n!}{(n-k)!}$$

where *n* is the total number of items that you can select from, and *k* is the number of items you want in each ordered group. The *!* is a symbol for a factorial, which simply means to count from 1 up to the number, multiplying each item along the way. In the simple case of the three personality categories with two ordered items, this equation works out to *3!/(3-2)!* Or (1)(2)(3)/(1), which is 6. If you add only one more category, you'd be up to 12 permutations. If you have a standard pack of playing cards (52 cards), there are 311,875,200 unique ways the first five cards can be dealt. In games that include rules that limit the type of combinations that are valid—such as the number of possible chess board permutations—the math becomes a lot more complicated, but the numbers can reach truly staggering values. Recent studies of chess show that the number of valid chess board permutations might be as high as a number 47 digits long.

For each of the categories, you can read a brief description of how everyone can fit into them. A famous individual is included in each category who represents it; although some of these people might not be gamers, these are the categories they'd end up in if they decided to apply games to their areas of expertise.

Artisan-Otaku

The art and science of game design fascinates you. Fueled by a passion for games born from your own firsthand experience of playing them, you're intrigued by the social gaming phenomena. Perhaps it is the large number of people who play social games, or perhaps it is the idea that social networks provide a unique environment for trying new forms of game design, but you're interested in using social games as a form of artistic expression, reflecting your own tastes in games.

- **Famous artisan-otakus:** Andy Warhol, American pop-culture artist; Todd McFarlane, creator of Spawn; R. A. Salvatore, fantasy author.
- **Read on to learn:** How to combine social technology and game mechanics to make compelling experiences that your customers will love.

Artisan-Impresario

Like most who are interested in game design, you've played enough games to know what you like, but your real passion is figuring out how to translate your artistic interest in games into commercial success. It's great to make things that are fun, but you want to make them fun and profitable.

- **Famous artisan-impresario:** Walt Disney, animator and entrepreneur who founded the eponymous entertainment behemoth.
- **Read on to learn:** How to create commercially successful businesses that use the magic of games to produce memorable, remarkable experiences.

Impresario-Artisan

Business is ultimately about satisfying customer needs and building the relationships you'll need to do so. Human motivations, psychology, and business models fascinate you. You want an environment in which creative designers can provide a more engaging, fun experience for your customers.

- **Famous impresario-artisan:** Steve Jobs, co-founder and CEO of Apple.
- **Read on to learn:** How to create high-growth businesses by leveraging the power of social games.

Impresario-Otaku

It always seems to you that the world could use a little more joy in it. If you could bring the fun of games to more people, maybe you'd leave the world a better place—and also create a great business in the process.

> **Famous impresario-otaku:** Quentin Tarantino, who began as a video store clerk known for his encyclopedic knowledge of cinema and who went on to create *Pulp Fiction*, *Kill Bill*, and *Inglorious Basterds*.

> **Read on to learn:** How to turn your passion for games into a business.

Otaku-Artisan

You've played a lot of games and have strong opinions on what works and what doesn't. You know how you'd change games to make them better. You have an interest in making games, but you'd also like to explain to other game creators how they could make their products even better.

> **Famous otaku-artisans:** Minh Le and Jess Cliffe, who began by hacking around with a copy of *Half-Life* for fun—eventually modified it to create *Counter-Strike*, which sold millions of copies.

> **Read on to learn:** What makes social games tick, how they might be improved, and what role they play in our culture.

Otaku-Impresario

You're driven by a genuine passion for fun, but you want it to be more than a hobby. You may have ideas for certain games or strong artistic and design skills, but your real passion is to take the fun you've had and share it with the world.

> **Famous otaku-impresarios:** Joss Whedon, a lifelong fan of comic books, turned his passion for pop culture into television hits like Buffy the Vampire Slayer; Jerry Holkins and Mike Krakulik, founders of Penny Arcade.

> **Read on to learn:** Why social games are the hottest part of the social media industry today, and why they're transforming social media.

What Is the Use of a Quiz?

There are plenty of criticisms that can be leveled at a quiz like this. First, it isn't scientific. It's possible that some of the factors are quite a bit more important than others. You haven't done any factor analyses or tried to weigh the results based on certain critical answers. For example, maybe people who answered "pirate" for question 12 are such strong impresarios that the answer should be calculated as having more weight than anything else.

Furthermore, the categories and answers are all fairly speculative. Although the intended audience for this book was considered, people weren't studied in a lab to determine their motivations. Because this is a dynamic marketplace which changes all the time, intuition was used.

Yet another critique is that the quiz contains some false dilemmas (or more technically speaking, false trichotomies). In reality, more than three reasonable answers to each question can exist, yet you had to pick from only three. This was softened by saying it was okay to skip questions or to answer more than once, but you might still have felt constrained by the answer set.

With all that criticism, what is the purpose of creating a quiz like this? Consider the following answers:

- **Most people think quizzes are fun.** They are fun for the same reason some people find horoscopes to be fun—they give people positive feedback about who they are. They're experiences; as you'll learn in the next chapter, experiences are central to the success of games.
- **People enjoy becoming part of groups.** When you join a category, you're not just gaining a label—you're part of a social group that reflects your own interests. Aren't you a bit curious about what you might share in common with someone like Steve Jobs, Quentin Tarantino, or one of the other famous people included in the list of reader categories?
- **Being part of a group makes it easier for you to be directed to the places you might find the most fun.** That's the point of the iconic signposts for impresarios, otakus, and artisans. Good games are excellent at giving you a great degree of control—or at least the illusion of control—and showing you ways that your choices can be pursued.

Quizzes are just one way that you can assist people in becoming part of a group. Another method is for all people to self-enroll in the group by providing merchandise, badges, or other symbols that signal their affiliations—think of all the emblems that people enjoy sharing in everything from Boy Scouts to our armed forces to political parties. Allowing people to "win" their way into certain groups is another valid scenario.

Maybe you're willing to accept that quizzes are fun. What about the earlier critique about how decisions are limited? Although most of us cherish freedom and liberty, game designers made an important discovery long ago: Experiences can be made more entertaining by limiting choice. These days, people are faced with a constant flurry of anxiety-producing decisions. In games however, designers can offer the luxury of easy packaged decisions divided into simple structures—the choice is often between only a few options. Games aren't intended to mirror real life. Games are intended to be fun. Often, the choices made by a game designer are to identify a few fun branches and get people to focus on them.

Often, fewer choices are more enjoyable than a large number of options. Too many options can result in confusion and resentment. Consider google.com, which presents you with the option to search for web pages and little more. The iPhone is popular for the same reason. The beauty of these products isn't that they're packed with unlimited options, but that designers made smart choices that addressed what the majority of customers needed to do.

Barry Schwartz is a professor of psychology and economics who has studied happiness and choice in our modern society—and has concluded that the huge number of choices that we as consumers face might actually be making us miserable. "As the number of choices we face increases, freedom of choice eventually becomes a tyranny of choice. Routine decisions take so much time and attention that it becomes difficult to get through the day," he writes in *The Paradox of Choice*. Think of all the decisions you need to make every day. Really, wouldn't it be far easier if some of these were already made for you?

Good games grow along with you, eventually satisfying your hunger for challenge and complexity. Like games, the iPhone and Google can grow more complex. You can add applications to each, you can travel down new paths, and you can customize them. In game design (and philosophy), this is called *emergent complexity*—the idea that complex systems can grow out of simple ones (in contrast to *inherent complexity*, in which things are complicated to begin with).

Chapter in Review

The quiz you've taken in this chapter demonstrates several ideas within game design. The quiz enables you to take on a role and use that role as a means to navigate a complex landscape. It also illustrates the principle of creating limited, focused options. All these ideas are explored in later chapters.

 OTAKU The signposts in the book also represent a form of power-leveling. You can skim through the book quickly. Look for the otaku, impresario, and artisan signposts. Before long, you'll slurp down a series of facts and trivia sure to help you command authority in any conversation about games.

Choose Your Path

The following list gives areas of the book you might want to visit next.

- If you'd like to learn more about the history and background of games and how they can impact culture, continue to the next chapter, which explores how games have the power to transform business.
- To learn more about how quizzes, roles, and "personas" can become a tool for understanding your customers better, you can jump forward to Chapter 4, to explore the ways games have classified player types.
- If you'd like to read about what makes games fun, skip over to Chapter 5, "Fungineering," which explains many other features in games that make them enjoyable.

2 Games Have Changed the Business Playfield

n this chapter, you'll learn:

- Why games are popular today
- The common themes that emerge from thousands of years of games
- Cultural trends that are driving social gameplay
- The types of people who should be curious about the impact of games

Once upon a time, there were gamers and nongamers—and then things changed. Those who had grown up with microcomputers, *Dungeons & Dragons*, Nintendos, and Ataris started to have their own families, and their children began playing games.

In the fall of 2008, the Pew Research Center surveyed American teens from age 12 to 17 and learned that more than 97 percent of teens play games. Meanwhile, some of us who grew up playing games had become engineers, marketers, and business leaders. There were entire populations of people who missed out on games, which were now created for new audiences—women, families, and retirees—who had been overlooked by the game industry. The result was the social game market, one of the fastest-growing industries in history. By the middle of 2010, Zynga, the largest company in this new industry, had reached more than a quarter billion users per month in only three years of operations.

If a social game is defined as a game that people play with their friends, social games have existed for thousands of years—so what combination of social, cultural, and economic factors have converged to make them so popular *now*? This chapter discusses some of the changes happening around the world and why games—and things such as work-like games—are essential for every business leader.

The story of games in the modern era begins with a subtle but pervasive change away from things and toward experiences.

The Power of Experience

I was raised in a home heavy in experiences: traveling and camping, music and building—and games. I was exposed to many ways of thinking, perhaps because my parents came from vastly different religious and professional backgrounds. My father, an engineer, taught me the joys of tinkering and learning, whereas my mother imbued me with a love of stories that sparked my imagination.

My memories of the holiday season are a rich tapestry of two religions—Judaism, the religion I was raised with—and my mother's Lutheranism; holidays were a mixture of the family menorah and dreidels, Christmas trees and rice pudding. What I remember best are the sights and feelings of the experiences, the memories that made me who I am.

It so happens that some of those holiday memories are tied to games. The Jewish tradition of the dreidel dates back to the medieval German gambling game of *totum*, which involved spinning a top to win various proportions of your bet. Likewise, my mother taught us the Norwegian yuletide tradition of placing an almond in a bowl of rice pudding—whoever found the almond would win a marzipan pig.

The Evolving Experience Economy

Luck. Anticipation. Surprise. Reward. Stories. Experience—all these facets combine to create enduring memories. It is no wonder that games are at the forefront of our evolving *experience economy*, to reuse a term from Harvard Business School researchers James Gilmore and B. Joseph Pine, who have argued that many of us, exhausted by the overload of material junk that crams our homes, garages, and attics—are finding greater reward in the memories and transformation that are the true "products" of an experience.

It is more than an idealistic theory. Mounting evidence supports the notion that it is experiences that give us the most happiness. Leaf Van Boven and Thomas Gilovich are research psychologists who wanted to know whether there's any truth to Aristotle's ancient claim that leisure alone—and not external goods—is the source of happiness. Their data, summarized in Figure 2-1, illustrates the effect of material goods on happiness at different income levels. The vertical axis shows the relative (percentage) increase in happiness that occurs along with spending, and the horizontal axis shows varying income levels. The data shows that for purchases of material goods, happiness reaches a point of diminishing returns as someone's income increases, whereas experiences such as going skiing, dining out, or going to a concert can continue to lead to further increases.

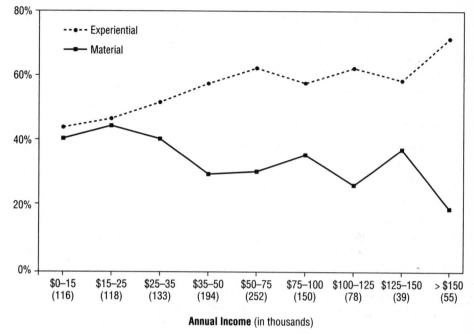

Leaf Van Boven and Thomas Gilovich. "To Do or to Have? That Is the Question," American Psychological Association 85.6 (2003): 1198. Reprinted with permission.

Figure 2-1: Spending versus Happiness

More recently, Thomas DeLeire and Ariel Kalil conducted an economic survey of retirees, the people who generally have the free time to do as they choose. After categorizing all forms of consumption, they found that only one category—leisure consumption—had a significant relation to happiness. Even essentials such as housing and health care or feel-good behaviors such as charitable donations couldn't compare.

Granted, there are possible critiques of the theory that experiences lead to happiness. For example, maybe happy people are the ones most likely to seek out new experiences in the first place. Perhaps the studies also understate the extent to which certain material goods provide the preconditions for positive experiences. Although reasonable criticisms are likely to continue for some time, it seems more than plausible to explain the increasing revenue being collected by the experience industries as the direct result of the happiness people are experiencing from their choices.

The media industry is largely about packaging and delivering experiences; however, one sector of the industry stands out: games. In the first decade of the new millennium, games have pulled ahead of other media industries such as movie box office sales, music, and DVD sales.

Why is it that the experiences games provide are in such high demand today? Can you expect it to continue? How are games changing the business landscape, and how can you learn from their success? You'll now explore the answers to these questions.

The Real Game Machine

It is helpful to begin a discussion of games by considering the machinery that media technology runs on. This does not include computers or telecommunications equipment, which are just examples of delivery technology. Media operates within the human brain, a most complex machine: with more than a hundred billion neurons, supported by perhaps another trillion cells in supporting roles, interconnected by hundreds of trillions of interconnections. The mathematics of the human brain quickly becomes incomprehensible in all but the most abstract terms. As if these numbers were not high enough to defy comprehension, each individual brain cell contains duplicate copies of three billion genetic instructions, each operating in intricate ways based on its unique expression and combination of proteins.

That's one hell of a machine to design for—yet there's one more level of complexity to consider: media, particularly social media that exist between networks of people. Not only do you need to consider how the individual person interacts with media, but also the subtle network of social relationships existing between consumers.

The content of experiences delivered by the media of games and the techniques used to deliver them successfully is the subject of most of this book. For now, try to keep in mind that no single thing makes a game work well—there is no Grand Unifying Theory of Fun. To try to reduce a game to a single feature would be to deny the complexity of the neural and social machinery upon which games operate. Nevertheless, you can identify several of the factors that contribute to making games work well. Start by thinking about why games—at this particular point in time, at the dawn of the third millennium—have become such a popular form of media.

The Evolution of Mass Media

In 1814, the *Times of London* had just taken shipment of an amazing new device: a printing press capable of churning out more than a thousand pages per hour. Built from precision parts and driven by the new technology of the steam engine, it heralded a new age in media—one driven by the capability to distribute information on an industrial scale. Coupled with other business innovations, such as printing on both sides of a single sheet, the cost of newspapers dropped dramatically. Newspapers were consumed not only in the heart of factory-laden cities, but also in every corner of every industrializing nation where railroads brought cheap information into the hands of millions.

I like to think of 1814 as the inaugural date for the First Era of Mass Media. The novel wasn't new—many consider *Cervantes's Don Quixote*, published between 1605 and 1615, to be the first modern novel—but by 1814 people like Charles Dickens could create popular fiction for mass consumption. Although the technology of mass production was essential to this success, it was evolving culture, business models, and consumer tastes that made the *Pickwick Papers* and *Oliver Twist* so successful. Newspapers contributed directly to at least three important factors:

- The increase in literacy assisted by widespread access to cheap, written content.
- One suspects, regular access to complex real-world stories of politics and culture might have helped prepare people for novels.
- The business innovation of serialized publication, made it possible for people to amortize the cost of purchasing a Dickens story over several episodes. If you consider that people were actually buying access to Dickens' imagination a story at a time—and not really buying the paper and ink—perhaps these serialized novels prefigured the modern notion of "virtual goods."

How is 19th-century literature relevant to understanding why games are popular today? It shows that although technology is an essential enabler for any new media, it is the complex interrelationship of culture, education, work, and home life that makes any form of media important in a given era. Games are no different.

Just as the news existed before the industrial production of newspapers, games existed long before the modern game. Games are one of the earliest forms of art that human civilization has produced. The reason games are growing in popularity today is a combination of the ancient features of human psychology and neurobiology along with recent cultural changes converging to make games the most important new media of our time. By understanding the cultural underpinnings that make games so important today, you can be better equipped to understand the forces shaping your economy, your lives, and your evolving tastes.

The Evolving Media Landscape

Table 2-1 describes some of the major changes that have altered culture across the different ages of media. The First Era of Mass Media was characterized by increasing literacy and the economic infrastructure that made it possible not only to produce massive quantities of media, but also to distribute media products far and wide. The compression of geography continued into the Second Age, when it became possible to transport dramatic images directly into homes. Today, you can connect with friends and coworkers across any distance at nearly instantaneous speeds, making distance irrelevant—and even shattering many political boundaries.

Table 2-1: Three Eras of Mass Media

	First: Novels	**Second: Film**	**Third: Age of Games**
When	**19th Century**	**20th Century**	**21st Century**
Economic force	Industrial	Bureaucracy	Creativity
Time	Highly scheduled	Scheduled	Asynchronous
Space	Wide distribution of goods	Expansion of business and leisure travel; telephones shrink the world	Teleworking, "World Is Flat," geographic disintegration
Center of the home	Kitchen	Living room	Digital
Social center of work	Lunch break	Water cooler	Email, blogs
Form of new media	Printed word	Visual	Interactive, social, experiences
Customers	Consumers	Consumers with more choices	Participatory

No table can accurately contain the full set of enormous changes that human society has experienced over the last several centuries, but you can begin to appreciate the incredible trajectory that media and economies have been on. The following sections will explore some of these trends in greater depth.

Compression of Time and Space

At the beginning of the First Era of Mass Media, the cycle of the sun was still adequate for timekeeping throughout most of the world. But by the end of this era, the network of railroads had expanded to make the world smaller, and the widespread availability of cheap clocks had conspired to consign time to slots. Suddenly one's time became allotted into strict divisions of hours set aside for work, home, and sleep. Railroads and factories aspired to run like clockwork. Large quantities of goods could be transported over long distances. A newspaper could be printed in one place and distributed in a faraway city where it soon informed and entertained.

This trend toward space-time compression continued unabated into the Second Era and hardly requires comment now in the Third. These days not only can you connect with others through blogs, social networks, electronic commerce, and games, but it's also often the only way you can connect in the time allotted. Today, with concerns over the cost of energy and transportation, people look for better ways to get more done from home or through their mobile devices.

Ironically, although many social and multiplayer games provide interaction between players across vast distances, many parts of the game industry continue to rely on traditional retail distribution channels and therefore are geographically bound. NPD reported in October 2010, that 79 percent of retail game sales occurred through physical distribution channels. For all the opportunity that exists to simplify people's lives through digital distribution, old channels take a while to die. The cracks in the dam are beginning to emerge, however: Companies like Blizzard now make all of their new games available through downloads, and the Steam platform created by Valve enables the distribution of a wide range of games from multiple developers directly to your desktop.

The role of physical places is slowly but inexorably changing. It isn't enough for retail locations to be places with shelves for the temporary storage of products between a creator and a customer. Physical places are transforming into venues for experiences—and in that way, are becoming more like games. Similarly, it isn't enough for websites to be piles of bits and bytes; they need to learn from successful physical spaces and fill the human desires for social contact and unique spaces.

 IMPRESARIO If you're in a business heavily dependent on physical locations, how can you become a locus for social interaction and experiences? If you aren't dependent on a physical location—such as a web-based business—what can you do to give your customers the experience of being in a "place?"

As concepts of time and space became compressed, so have ideas such as what *on-demand* means. Before the First Era, the concept of any pastime being available on-demand was reserved for the wealthy elite. Even then, ideas of what kind of entertainment could be obtained on demand were limited, perhaps to a cup of tea brought by a servant or a tune played or sung by a talented family member in the parlor. On-demand was also a reason why artists had patrons, enabling the wealthy to buy access to the type of art they desired.

By the end of the First Era, newspapers were about as close as one could get to on-demand entertainment. The industrial revolution enabled papers to be written in one place, printed in another, and distributed while still relevant. Their on-demand nature came not only from their easy availability, but also because people could fold up a paper and take it with them to be consumed on-demand, whenever they wanted—the industrial-age version of an iPod or a *save game* feature.

Well into the Second Era, people had to wait until Sunday for certain content, such as the comics or funnies in color ink or the famous New York Times crossword. Perhaps it shouldn't surprise anyone that one of the most popular features of early mass media was a game?

In the Second Era, as television dominated the days of homemakers and the evenings and nights of everyone else, the concept of on-demand arrived in the form of VCRs, but even then, people had to wait their turn for the latest releases at the local video rental outlet.

The Third Era reduced the distribution network to the flow of electrons streaming across the Internet. On-demand is nearly equivalent to *now*. Many companies are already creating predictive technologies so that on-demand may someday mean the capability of our media delivery networks to anticipate what you want—even before you know you want it.

Tyranny of the Clock

At work, you might often face immovable deadlines. If you're a parent, you're often hostage to the schedules of work, school, soccer games, or extracurricular activities. Students are usually stuck with certain class schedules. With all that scheduled activity, it's hard to keep up with any other forms of entertainment that happen on a clock. Television shows used to demand that you show up at a certain time; and playing sit-down board games with friends and family required significant coordination.

Because today you're less restricted by geography than you were at any previous time in human history, another subtle, but perhaps more pervasive, change has been at work for the past decade or so. It's something you take part in whenever you glance at an email between work assignments, steal a few minutes to place some moves in *Mafia Wars*, record a television show on TiVo, or stream an on-demand movie from Netflix. Thanks to the decreased importance of *where* the bits of entertainment are flowing from, the logical extension is that time you'd also want to choose *when* you engage in entertainment—and several companies have risen to the challenge.

Asynchronous gameplay refers to the idea that certain games can be played by multiple participants simultaneously, and that everyone can choose to place their moves when they feel like it. Nobody else is blocked by needing to place each move in an exact order. Most social games are asynchronous in that you play alongside many other people, but you can choose when you'd like to play—and you don't need to wait for anyone else to finish their moves. This raises a number of interesting challenges because most games have been designed with a specific order in mind. Take chess for example: You can't make your move until your opponent has finished.

When you choose to watch an episode of television, you tend to watch a series in order—but the time you choose to watch it in is up to you. You didn't need to coordinate your viewing schedule with the network programmers. That's another form of asynchronous entertainment.

Emails arrive in your in-box, and you can decide when you get to them. If you're like me, you check them often and between lots of other activities. (I just checked my email between writing the last paragraph and starting this one.) That's a form of asynchronous work. Another is happening around the entire revolution in software development called *open source*. In open source development, volunteer programmers work on large projects in which they contribute enhancements when and where they feel like it. The open source "release schedule" isn't usually blocked by their individual components.

Stock markets are asynchronous. You don't need to show up at a specific time or place to sell some shares of a stock. Markets match buyers and sellers together any time the market is open.

Mounting evidence shows that people aren't good at multitasking; neuro-imaging data shows that for most activities, people can think about two tasks at a time. The answer, then, is a system that enables people to set aside their work and play, returning again and again when convenient. Asynchronous technologies have stepped in to enable people to handle more tasks without having to think of them at the same time. In the world of entertainment and games, it's about having fun when and where you want, without needing to worry about when everyone else chooses to play.

> **IMPRESARIO** The lives of your customers are overscheduled. How can you make it so they can interact with you when and where they want? Make a list of the things you normally require customers to do at a certain time or in a specific sequence, and see if you can think of a way to reorganize them asynchronously. Your customers will adore you!

The Power of Creativity

In the First Age, creativity was mostly limited to only a few entrepreneurs, artists, and scientists. In the Second Age, the number of these people as a percentage of our society expanded dramatically. The Second Age primed our culture to embrace creativity because it led to huge improvements in our standard of living. Richard Florida, a researcher who studies the economics of creativity, has estimated that the creative class had grown to represent more than 30 percent of the workforce.

Just as the number of creative workers has increased in the Third Era, creativity has been embraced as a positive value for everyone. It is promoted in schools, rewarded in numerous lines of work, and flourishes online in the form of user-generated content such as blogs, wiki pages, and Facebook wall posts. Meanwhile, the number of choices and customization options offered by companies has increased, enabling you to express your own creativity and individualization through product selection.

There are different forms of creativity:

- **Unstructured creativity**: This is when there are few boundaries beyond the person's imagination and the inherent limitations of their medium.
- **Structured creativity**: Includes cases where there are significant limits on the choices available, yet you have the option to combine elements together in a unique way that reflects your values.
- **Emergent creativity**: Here, the creativity is highly unstructured yet heavily dependent on a platform provided by someone else.

Table 2-2 compares examples of each form of creativity.

Table 2-2: Unstructured, Structured, and Emergent Creativity

Unstructured	Structured	Emergent
Blog posts	Blog comments	Blog mashups
3D graphic modeling	Customizing an avatar	Designing extensions to an avatar system (such as is possible in *Second Life*)
Facebook wall posts	Facebook wall comments	Facebook memes
Designing a game	Creating a character in a game	Creating movies (machinima) and comics from in-game characters
Knitting a toy bear	Build-a-Bear Workshop	Playing with toy bears

Many people want to be creative but lack the dedication or time to do so. In other cases, they are creative in certain ways but not others. That's the power of structured creativity and part of why many games are possible: They give people the ability to choose, individualize, and express themselves within a structured process that facilitates their creativity.

 ARTISAN Choice is at the heart of structured creativity. Although choice is a powerful tool—and games are all fundamentally about choices—too many choices can be overwhelming to a game player. What are some ways your customers might like to be more creative, and how can you match that to systems that make it easy for them to do so?

The Digital Living Room

During the First Age, most interaction within families happened around meals; interaction was face-to-face and personal. By the close of the Second Age, family entertainment had come to revolve around television, a change seeded with the advent of radio and the reordering of entertainment away from expensive concerts and performances. Because most families had one television and most shows were scheduled, families came together to watch and be entertained at the same time. Interactions started to include a third-person element, where one could involve the presence of characters brought about by media into the conversations at home.

Now that technologies have emerged that enable the consumption of content on-demand, the scheduled nature of television has changed. People began watching when and where they wanted. Meanwhile, the number of screens exploded. The living room became less important. Technology has reduced much of our direct interpersonal communication, allowing our interactions to occur in virtual spaces instead.

People have talked about the *digital living room* as a place containing physical products: game consoles, video-on-demand, and HD televisions. All those things exist, but the reality is that the digital living room is no longer a physical place. It has become digital itself. We "live" on places such as blogs and Facebook, exchange messages with our families, and enjoy time with each other within online games. Indeed, long before Facebook, people used language such as "virtual communities" to describe the loci of social interaction on the Web. With families now flung across wide areas, social technology enables people to stay more engaged and better connected.

Given that the digital living room has expanded to encompass anywhere in the world that you can plug-in, how can you bring families together in new and rewarding ways?

The Social Nexus at Work

Like the digital living room, the places of social interaction at work are also evolving. The vast majority of business still occurs in physical locations, be it an office or a factory—but something else has changed. The water cooler is alive and well, and you still meet coworkers for lunch, but *where* you interact socially has slowly shifted toward somewhere else: online.

The change began with email and included mailing lists used by coworkers to coordinate activities. From there, it grew to blogs and Facebook as people became comfortable with maintaining connections to each other online. Facebook has blurred the lines of social and professional work relationships unlike anything that existed before it.

The integration of social networks within the work environment has created a new set of challenges that have yet to be resolved. For example, many people feel pressured to accept friend connections from coworkers and bosses. For others, the blurring of these boundaries in the online world offers a chance for many people to deepen their relationships with each other. Businesses have even found that there are large, quantifiable benefits to integrating social technology into the workplace. Consider Pfizer, the world's largest research-based pharmaceutical company; by using telecommunication technology and instant messaging, they've been able to save over $30 million per year.

Given the investments that so many companies make in parties, events, corporate offsites, and other means of connecting employees with each other, might social games offer an even lower-cost means of promoting teamwork and camaraderie?

Participatory Culture

With the increase in overall creative outlets and ability, combined with the technology to locate and communicate with kindred spirits on the Internet, fandom has flourished. Fans appear when there are products that are so experiential or transformative that they move from being simple customers to becoming celebrants. They promote, persuade their friends, and enjoy the sense of community they gain when hanging out with others who "get it."

It seems that the experience industries are best at creating fans. Indeed, becoming a fan can be a transformative experience. Fans create blogs, write fan-fiction, go to conventions, and urge others to share their joy. Would you like to have some fans? Then create experiences that people love.

The Changing Nature of Social Media

The term *social media* was coined to refer to blogs, social networks, and other online technology that enables people to create content and interact socially with each other. Of course, social media already existed before this definition: Bulletin board systems, forums, and older online services such as America Online shared many of the same features before the mass-market expansion of Internet usage. Before that, numerous forms of nonelectronic social media existed—ranging from Letters to the Editor to graffiti to citizen debates in the *Forum Romanum*.

Even forms of media that you don't think of as "social" are important parts of your social lives. When you watch a popular movie, the act of viewing it isn't particularly social but the discussions you have with friends about it are. Popular culture provides a set of shared memories, experiences, and stories that provide you with ways to connect with each other.

Social media is not simply a product of the Third Era: It is a reaction to the social vacuum that might have otherwise been left behind by the isolating impact of technology. Social networks such as Facebook provide a venue for social interaction, often replacing the physical meeting places you once relied upon. Unlike physical meeting places, they can be accessed asynchronously, enabling you to satisfy your need for social contact whenever you want.

Social Status as Currency

During the height of the dotcom boom, management guru Peter Drucker predicted that money was no longer going to be enough to satisfy the needs of modern workers. Perhaps he had already detected the change that was at work, the shift toward a desire for experiences over things. He characterized the system of paying people as amounting to "bribing" knowledge workers and said that "When this can no longer be done by satisfying knowledge workers' greed, as we are now trying to do, it will have to be done by satisfying their values, and by giving them social recognition and social power."

A decade into the Third Era has shown us that social recognition alone is a huge motivator that shapes and directs peoples' behavior, not only in the world of work but also in all aspects of life. It's a large reason why people contribute their time—for no financial compensation—to open source software projects and wikis. It seems likely that social status is also a major motivation behind philanthropy.

Social media works because it taps into society's changing values—one that regards social status as more important than many material products. Andy Warhol said everyone would be famous for 15 minutes, which seems mathematically improbable, but on social networks, you can be famous among your friends.

Why Are Social Games So Popular?

In the early days of Facebook, it described itself as a *social utility*, which sounds helpful but not particularly fun. More recently, the home page for Facebook.com says that it "helps you connect and share with the people in your life." This begs the question, Share what?

Many things shared by people on Facebook are experiences. Photos and stories are the artifacts of people's experiences; messages and schedules are used to coordinate future experiences.

However, the common denominator for all that content is that it was originally dependent on experiences that occurred outside Facebook. Games changed everything in Facebook because they provided experiences that happen *inside* Facebook, making it not only a place for talking about the outside world, but also an actual "place" where social experiences happen. This leads to a number of observations:

- **Games, especially social games, facilitate human contact.** Humans hunger for social contact. Unlike other forms of media, in which the social interaction is limited to the communication that happens around the content, games depend on social interaction as integral to the experience itself. Now that social technology exists to help facilitate and maintain social contact, games provide the principal experiential content of the Third Era. One of the major questions of the Third Age is whether the digital world will be sufficient to satisfy our biological need for social interaction; will it be the endpoint in our evolution, or a new way to facilitate ways to bring us back to the "real world?" Already, games that people play on mobile devices seem to cross both boundaries.

- **Games are popular because they are enjoyable experiences.** Why experiences are so important has already been discussed, but not much has been said about the content of the experiences. Like movies, music, and books, games convey not only information but also emotion. Emotion is like the mental glue that attaches your memories to your behaviors. This is why games create such lasting impressions for so many players.

- **Games use rules to recruit the learning machinery of the brain.** What separates games from other forms of media is the presence of rules—a set of options that define unambiguous consequences for your actions. (Although ambiguity might often exist in the mind of a player.) The brain is incredibly powerful at things such as creating abstractions, recognizing patterns, and uncovering rules. The same neural structures that provoke a child to ask why the sky is blue or a physicist to question the nature of black holes leads people to uncover the rules that exist within games.

- **Games engage creativity.** In the Third Era, people seek not only to consume, but also to contribute, create, and express themselves. As players uncover the rules that govern a game, their experience often deepens with the game: They begin to develop strategies to apply rules in novel ways or learn of ways to express their unique identity through the game.

- **Games can be consumed anywhere because of digital technology.** Although games have existed for longer than recorded history, the industry of games today owes a large debt to digital technology. Even early computer games depended on some amount of physical distribution. As on-demand, digital distribution of games has expanded, games transformed from a necessarily physical product to one that may be delivered anywhere.

- **Games are uniquely suited to asynchronous consumption.** Although many forms of media in the Third Era enable you to consume a bit at a time— an article here, a digitally downloaded episode there—with games there's a unique opportunity to create experiences that unfold over long spans of time yet require only minimal amounts of participation at each step along the way. Although most games are still played in an order-dependent and time-consuming way, a large part of the success of the new wave of games on social networks is their compatibility with the increasingly asynchronous manner that you access the online world.

Games as High-Value Experiences

Just as newspapers expanded in popularity during the 19th century in large part due to their lower cost, it can't be denied that games now offer one of the most high-value entertainment experiences, as illustrated in Table 2-3:

Table 2-3: United States Entertainment Costs per Hour, 2000–2010

Entertainment Experience	Cost
Borrowing a book from library	Free (taxpayer supported)
Playing a freemium/social game	Free to pennies/hour
Cable television ($71/month, 153 hours/person/month, 2.54 people/household)	$0.18/hour/person
Playing *World of Warcraft* 10 hours per week per subscription	$0.35/hour
Seeing a 2-hour movie for $7.95	$3.98/hour per person
Upper Bleachers Red Sox ticket ($12) for a 3-hour game	$4.00/hour per person
Average U.S. family vacation (AAA data: $250 per day):	$10.41/hour
2-hour Broadway show	$50–$150 per hour
Reading a thrilling book on social games	Priceless

Major Trends in Five Thousand Years of Social Games

Games are dramatic models of our psychological lives, providing release of particular tensions. They are collective and popular art forms with strict conventions. Ancient and non-literate societies naturally regarded games as live dramatic models of the universe or of the outer cosmic drama.

MARSHALL McLUHAN, "GAMES: THE EXTENSIONS OF MAN"

In the 1920s, Leonard Woolley trekked for weeks by steamship and then across the hot deserts of Iraq to reach a seemingly empty patch of land. Beneath it was the Royal Tombs of Ur, a burial ground of the Sumerian civilization, constructed nearly five thousand years ago.

During years of excavation, Woolley uncovered tombs containing servants and soldiers, their copper weapons still intact. Art depicted scenes of Sumerian life, and there was jewelry of lapis lazuli and gold, and everyday objects such as obsidian bowls and pottery. One of the items removed from a tomb was the Royal Game of Ur, as shown in Figure 2-2.

Figure 2-2: Royal Game of Ur

Archaeologists have learned the rules of the Royal Game of Ur by studying similar games and cuneiform tablets that described their rules. In essence, the Royal Game of Ur was a race between two players that combines elements of luck (by rolling dice) along with making tactical choices about where to place and move pieces.

Because ancient Sumerians buried their kings with an intricately carved and painted game tells us a great deal about the importance that ancient people placed on them.

>
> **OTAKU** You can play the Royal Game of Ur online. The British Museum, which houses the artifact, has made a Web-playable version on its Mesopotamia website at `http://www.mesopotamia.co.uk`.

Figure 2-3 shows a set of games that illustrate some of the core influences through the ages. Here, you can be less concerned with "firsts" and more concerned with those games that seemed to have the greatest impact on the growth of gaming as an art form and an industry.

Tracing the influences of games throughout history reveal a number of themes: the importance of art within games; their correlation to evolving human thought; and their role as social activities. The games trade began with skilled craftsmen to become a burgeoning commercial industry that today leads the way with innovative business models. Now consider some of these themes in greater detail, beginning with the role of art within games.

Games as Art

You need to look at the Royal Game of Ur to appreciate the craftsmanship that went into it. It's likely that the game could have been played with stones and scratches in the earth, but the ancient designers chose instead to make it permanent and adorn it with ornaments. This is because games are experiences, and the form of the game is often as important as the substance of the game. Today, the largest games employ hundreds of artists to craft the game's sensory experience, but even simple games can make an artistic statement, reinforce a brand, or convey an emotion. Games are an art of experience.

Architecture is an engineering discipline, but it is also an art. The shape of a building conveys feeling: Imagine the grandeur of a cathedral, designed to overwhelm you with its scale, drawing your eye upward toward the heavens. Three-dimensional games are art in the way that architecture is art, except that the game designer also has power over virtual earth, sky, and space. Games of fewer visual dimensions also play with space, creating architectures and geographies that exist within the mind. Games are an art of space.

Dance, theater, and music provide opportunities for performers to express themselves artistically, by interpreting and re-interpreting the content for an audience. Within the forking paths of games, it is the player who is the performer, as the painter and lifelong chess player Marcel Duchamp said, "I have come to the personal conclusion that while all artists are not chess players, all chess players are artists." The tools of expression for the player are strategy, tactics, and the synthesis of whatever creative palette is offered by the game. Games are an art of performance.

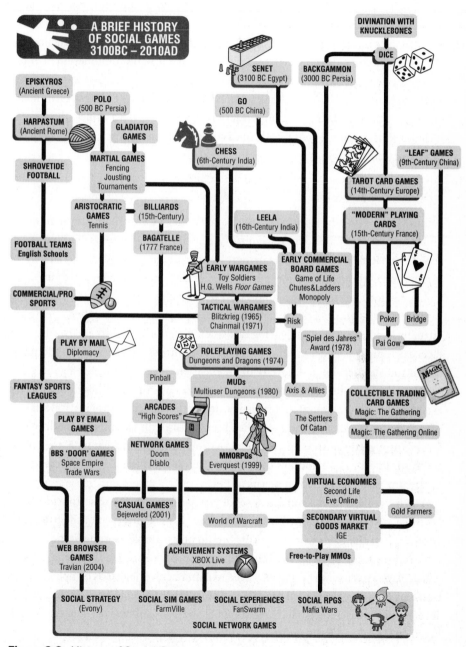

Figure 2-3: History of Social Games

In 1941, Jorge Luis Borges wrote "The Garden of Forking Paths," in which he imagined a book that could tell different stories depending on the paths you take. Games tell stories like that: In chess, you are a feudal lord, and the moves you make determine whether your tale ends with victory or your ignominious capture. Modern role-playing games have added to this by adding in elements of character, theme, and plot; and in other cases, the artistry is rooted in the unique combination of rules. Every storytelling medium excels at different aspect of fiction: With text, it is your ability to enter the mind of a character or narrator; and films enable you to enter a dreamlike state in which action and reaction is observed. With games, the artistry includes all these things, but it is the decision making that is the unique tool of the game storyteller. Games are an art of forking paths.

Games and Rules

Some of the oldest games, including the Royal Game of Ur and backgammon, which it may have inspired, had a mystical quality, drawing upon concepts of divine intervention and luck. Dice, one of the earliest features of many board games, share a lot in common with prehistoric forms of divination such as casting knucklebones.

Long before tarot cards became associated with the occult, they were used in games. By 15th-century France, tarot decks used for games had morphed into a form virtually identical to modern playing cards, complete with the suits and royalty. Like dice, cards provide a means of introducing randomness into a game. Randomness can introduce surprise and novelty to an experience, yet the rules of a good game require the player to learn about probability, which is the likelihood that certain events will occur with a certain frequency. Before the modern mathematical analysis of probability, the ancient mind was already grappling with the complex math behind "luck" through the abstraction of games. As you'll explore in Chapter 5, the reason for this is likely to be evolution because our minds are obsessed with deciphering, organizing, and recognizing patterns.

The laws of luck and a consistent set of play patterns are the basis for *rules*—the laws that govern how a game works. When you play a game, part of the fun is discovering how the rules work. The rules could be as simple as understanding how a die roll works or as complex as the fully open economy of Eve Online, a game in which players gather everything they need to manufacture objects as complex as giant starships. The development of probability into mathematical formalism occurred in 1656, when physicist Christian Huygens published *On Reasoning in Games of Chance*, based on Pascal and Fermat's research into gambling.

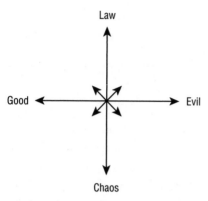

Figure 2-4: The Moral Axes of
Dungeons & Dragons

Rules need not be mathematical in nature; they may also be concerned with the social rules that govern human behavior. In the 16th-century India, the game of Leela was considered a model for teaching moral values. Benjamin Franklin wrote an essay in which he applauded the ability of chess to teach virtues such as caution, honesty, civility, and respect. More recently, role-playing games have opened up the exploration of all the dimensions of human character, such as the moral axes of *Dungeons & Dragons* illustrated in Figure 2-4. In this sense, human social behavior is sometimes not only the context, but also the very content of the game experience.

Games as a Social Activity

Throughout history, most games have been social in nature. Although there are exceptions such as solitaire and single-player computer games, for the most part games have facilitated social contact. This is further revealed by looking at many of the games throughout history, beginning with the most ancient to those in the modern day.

The Royal Game of Ur and backgammon were games that pit two opponents against each other. Later games, such as chess, built upon this tradition.

Meanwhile, a parallel track of development was unfolding: sports. Polo was originally conceived as a form of military training in ancient Persia. Later, the Greeks played a violent ball game called *episkyros*, which may have morphed through the Romans into a form called *harpastum*, finally emerging as shrovetide football in the middle ages. In shrovetide football, two mobs of people, often from competing villages, would attempt to move a ball from the town square into a particular landmark where they'd score a goal. There was no rule on the number of people you could recruit to your team, which shares a striking similarity to *Mafia Wars* and the player-versus-player aspects of massively multiplayer online role-playing games (MMORPGs). It's possible that this game lead to the creation of association football (that is, soccer) that is now the world's most popular sport. Association football and other commercial sports are social in at least two ways: first, as a game played between multiple people and second, as the social event that arises out of spectating.

Not content with the strict limitations of games such as chess, others created open-ended games around battle. H. G. Wells published *Floor Games*, which described a set of rules for engaging in war games with friends, using toy soldiers. War games became further formalized, and by the middle of the 20th century, commercially produced games such as *Diplomacy* and *Axis & Allies* became popular with a large and growing gaming market.

People had an interest in playing games with each other across long distances way before the advent of communication technology. Chess was played through correspondence as early as the 9th century, and *Diplomacy* became a popular play-by-mail game in the 1960s. Later, this gave way to play-by-email versions of the same and new games.

As war games grew in popularity through clubs and play-by-mail formats, designers began experimenting with battles from different time periods. Gary Gygax and Dave Arneson created *Chainmail* in 1971, a game of medieval combat. When they realized that the game could incorporate storytelling and character development, *Chainmail* had morphed into *Dungeons & Dragons* by 1974. An intensely social game, *D&D* remains popular to this day, providing the mental platform for epic struggles, heroic confrontations, and tales of magic and steel.

Like war games, a problem with *D&D* was one of time and space: It's difficult to get a group together for a game, especially after people enter college or start to work. Unlike war games, there are too many important moves and conversation to turn it into a slow, play-by-mail (or even email) format. Perhaps that partially inspired Richard Bartle and Roy Trubshaw to invent the first multiuser dungeon, or MUD, at Essex University between 1978 and 1980. A MUD enabled players to enter a virtual world from a distance, enjoying adventures and storytelling that would have previously required face-to-face interaction. A screen from *MUD1* is shown in Figure 2-5.

```
JWizTerm
unless you had a parachute.
*s
Waterfall.
Before you is an awe-inspiring sight; a waterfall plummets over a cliff and
explodes in a dazzling crescendo of rainbow colour on the menacing rocks
below.
*n
Cliff.
A sturdy ox lumbers past you nearby.
Karnifex is here, carrying nothing
*who
Karnifex is playing
Siggy the legend is playing
Tarinth is playing
*
Karnifex says "Hello, Tarinth!"
*
A distant neighing noise reaches your ears.
*
The Ox has just left.
*
```

Figure 2-5: *MUD1*, the First Multiuser Dungeon

Even before the Internet became available to the everyday person, MUDs made their way onto bulletin boards that were accessed by modems. However, most early bulletin boards were operated by hobbyists with only a single phone line, meaning that the games they offered needed a new feature: the capability for people to place moves separately, without blocking each other—asynchronous play. These bulletin board games, also known as door games contained gameplay patterns that reemerged in the form of Web-based games.

By the 1990s, designers added graphic interfaces to MUDs, creating a new and much larger market for MMORPG games. These games are "massive" because thousands of players can interact with each other within the same server, and players can form groups of up to dozens of players who can enjoy adventures together. One of the first was called *Ultima Online*, which featured an isomorphic interface. (A game that looks three-dimensional but is only viewable from one particular overhead position.) Later, as 3D technology improved, it became possible to place players within fully rendered environments, such as that shown in Figure 2-6.; *Everquest* was the first large commercial success in this market, blazing the trail for the creation of *World of Warcraft*, which rapidly became the leader, growing to 12 million subscribers by 2010.

Figure 2-6: Two Players in *World of Warcraft*

Emergence of Virtual Goods

When someone threatens to quit a *Dungeons & Dragons* group, there's often someone ready to make a sarcastic (or sometimes serious) retort, "Can I have your stuff?" The stuff they're referring to, of course, is the items "belonging" to the character of the player who is quitting. Even imaginary items are valuable to people.

Richard Garfield is a mathematician who realized that you could combine the scarcity of trading cards with the strategy of a game, and the result was a collectible trading card game named *Magic: The Gathering*. Thousands of collectible cards exist, with varying rarity—many with lush artwork. Although rarity is often correlated with the power of the cards, the demand for cards is mostly driven by market perception of powerfulness. Just as with nongaming trading cards, a secondary market emerged for players to buy and sell *MTG* cards. People continue to pay significant amounts—in some cases, thousands of dollars—to amass collections of cards needed for the decks they want to play with. Although the physical product has little tangible value (it's just ink on a piece of heavy paper), players perceive significant real-world value in them, not unlike their desire to amass imaginary treasures in *D&D*.

The desire to acquire wealth in *D&D*, and the emergence of a secondary market in *MTG*, prefigured what happened after the launch of games such as *Everquest*: As players found rare items, they acquired a real-world value, trading them on eBay for significant amounts of cash. *WoW* attempted to prevent this by limiting item exchanges between players, but many players began trading "gold" (its virtual currency) for real money instead. The virtual gold trade was so great that companies such as Internet Gaming Entertainment (IGE) attracted millions of dollars of venture capital investment, despite its blatant disregard for terms of service contracts presented by the game.

Although *WoW* got a lot better at restricting real-money transactions—sometimes banning thousands of accounts at a time involved in such trades—the real challenge to companies such as IGE was the emergence of new online games that, ironically, were informed by this consumer interest in exchanging money for virtual goods. Free-to-play (F2P) online games such as Nexon's *MapleStory* emerged that enabled players to join for free and pay for items that improved their experience or characters. *Second Life*, a virtual world platform in which people craft all types of experiences and games, features a real-money economy in which participants create and sell content to each other.

Given the poor performance of the advertising market and the unlikelihood of players paying large one-time fees or subscriptions for games embedded in social networks, the virtual goods model became the solution that enabled companies such as Zynga and Playdom to launch profitable and fast-growing ventures—a rarity within the dotcom industry. Chapter 12 offers a focused discussion on virtual goods.

Social Network Games

Because social games have existed for a long time, the current crop of games on places such as Facebook might be more properly termed social network games. Their primary feature is that they use the social relationships you have within the social network and typically monetize with advertising and virtual goods (with the latter providing the lion's share of potential revenue). The popular social network game *FrontierVille* is shown in Figure 2-7.

Figure 2-7: A Scene from Zynga's *FrontierVille*

These games fall into four broad categories:

- **Social role-playing games (or social RPGs):** Games in which you play a particular character in a virtual universe. Examples include games such as *Mafia Wars*, *Sorority Life*, or *True Pirates*.
- **Social sim games:** Focus on the management and development of environments rather than a character: farms, restaurants, zoos, and such. Examples include *FarmVille*, *Café World*, and *Zoo Kingdom*.
- **Social experience games:** Include games (such as puzzles or other action games) that have been repackaged for delivery on social networks and other experiences that have adopted game-like features to enhance engagement. Examples include *Bejewelled Blitz*, Flixster, and MeYou Health.
- **Social strategy games:** Focus on the decisions made during gameplay, drawing upon traditions in board games, real-time strategy games, and the like. Examples include *Evony* and *Kingdoms of Camelot*.

Because the social gaming market is growing so rapidly, it's likely that these categories will become strained over time. Over the coming years, new categories reflecting the rapid pace of innovation and revenues will pour into the market.

What Social Games Mean for Your Business

New distribution channels change who the customers are. They change not only how customers buy but also what they buy. They change consumer behavior, savings patterns, industry structure—in short, the entire economy.

—Peter Drucker, "Beyond the Information Revolution"

Social networks are redefining how you interact with friends, how you consume information, and how you think about space and time. Media and business is reshuffled to accommodate our new psychogeography. Some might suggest it has been for the worse: making us more narcissistic, more interrupt-driven, and leaving us with shorter attention spans and fewer real friends.

Social networks are not the singular driving force behind these changes. Along with cheap transportation, our families and friendships have fragmented far and wide in geographic space. Today, as I write this from Massachusetts, I have a sister in Washington, another who is traveling in South America, and parents who live in Florida—I am hardly alone. Social networks provide a means to stay connected with family and friends across intervening space enabling us to transcend physical limitations on friendships just as electronic commerce freed us from dependence on local retailers.

I admit that I sometimes feel a twinge of longing for the local shops, for the closeness of friends, for a return to sitting around a table and playing games in the flesh, before incompatible schedules conspired to disintegrate them. However, I have memories from the online world that are just as potent as any from real life: moments of adrenalin, moments of intimacy, and moments of community. Even though they're only taking their first baby steps into the market, it's clear that social network games have enormous potential to connect and inspire us.

We live in an experience economy. Social networks are where many of these experiences will happen, and not only will your customer desire an experience, they're also going to expect one. Like the experiences inherent to social networks, games can show you how to rethink the way you relate to customers.

Chapter in Review

This chapter presented a case for the changing nature of the economy: one in which experiences will become more important. In the presence of social networks, it is games that will define the experiences you have there.

Social games have existed through history, characterized by diverse rules, art, and interaction. Social network games are the most-recent version of this, offering new gameplay experiences that use social network relationships.

By learning the techniques of social game design, you can be prepared to energize your business by creating more engaging and rewarding experiences for customers, which is the topic that will occupy the remainder of this book.

Choose Your Path

The following list gives areas of the book you might want to visit next.

- If you'd like to start understanding what goes into building a social game, continue to Chapter 3, "Developing Your Social Media Game."
- To learn more about the business issues pertaining to virtual goods that were briefly touched upon in this chapter, you can skip ahead to Chapter 12, "Designing for Virtual Goods."
- If you want to understand the psychology of fun so that you can brainstorm ways it could work for you, then jump ahead to Chapter 5, "Fungineering."

3 Developing Social Media Games

 In this chapter, you'll learn:

- The differences between social game, traditional game, and nongame software development
- The skills and team members you need for a social media game project
- The player-centered design process for managing your project

Social Media Game Development Is Different

One of the challenges of social media games is the unique set of skills and methodologies that they require. Social media games draw upon the experiences of both agile web development and traditional game development, sharing properties of both.

The average cost of developing a single-platform console game in 2010 was $10 million dollars, with multiplatform games costing more than double. It comes as no surprise that many traditional game developers have had difficulty adapting to the realities of social game development, which has had huge successes with small teams that create products in a matter of months. The approaches to project management in console and PC game releases, built in response to their long cycles and high production values, doesn't scale-down to the frenetic pace of short-window, agile development employed within most social media game endeavors.

Website development teams often include the people most accustomed to smaller, more agile projects. However, many teams that have tried to tackle social games from a web-development mindset have run into a separate batch of problems, discovering that games are unlike any other type of project they've worked on before.

A quick breakdown of the founders of four of the top social game startups can tell you a great deal about the uniqueness of social game development:

- **Zynga:** Founded by Mark Pincus, a serial entrepreneur, who previously founded a social network, a support software company, and a web-based push technology company
- **Playdom:** Founded by a trio of entrepreneurs with a heavy background in math and analytics: Dan Yue, who studied economics and physics, worked at an advertising network company; Ling Xiao, who was a Ph.D. candidate focused on dataset analyses; and Chris Wang, who was a Google engineer with a Ph.D. in computer science
- **Crowdstar:** Founded by Suren Markosian, an engineer originally trained as a physicist, who worked at email marketing, forum software, and IT security firms; and Jeffrey Tseng, who built traditional console games at Secret Level, a company he previously co-founded
- **Playfish:** Founded by Kristian Segerstrale and Sebastien de Halleux. Segerstrale attended the University of Cambridge, where he studied economics. Between that and starting Playfish, he was with Glu Mobile, a creator of mobile games. De Halleux was educated as a civil engineer and worked on both mobile advertising technology at Nokia and mobile gaming at a company later acquired by Glu.

The first fact to observe about all these people is just how different they all are. Although some had gaming backgrounds, one company was created by a business-school-trained serial entrepreneur, another by some hardcore science and math types, and another by a web engineer. Does this give you a sense of the new territory you're entering in this field? For me, this is the exciting thing about social games: Everyone is figuring out so many new things, and everything is changing so rapidly. This can give you some inspiration that your own unique set of skills, which might not have come from a background in web development or games, might have an important role to play.

Although a lot of differences exist between the people who founded the outlined social game startups, there's also an important area of consistency: Most of them are people who are comfortable with numbers: economics, physics, and mathematics. Numbers are important to social games, just as they are in many areas of web development. Numbers can tell you what features people spend the most time on, the ways they spend their money, and the efficacy of your outreach programs.

IMPRESARIO Until recently, social games were limited to those that were played separately from social networks–*World of Warcraft* being the most commercially successful. Social media games took off after Facebook introduced its developer platform in 2007. As of 2010, nearly 60 million Americans—that's nearly one out of five–have played a social game.

Agile Development

Agile development is an approach to building software that has reshaped how games and websites have been built. It's about creating software through a series of rapid iterations performed by self-organizing and teams. The Agile Manifesto sums up the principal goals:

- **Individuals and interactions** over processes and tools.
- **Working software** over comprehensive documentation.
- **Customer collaboration** over contract negotiation.
- **Responding to change** over following a plan.

Goals of Agile Development

Although both games and websites have applied agile techniques, there are big differences between how website developers and game developers have instituted these techniques in practice. After coverage of the goals of agile development, you return to these differences and explain the implications for social game development.

Individuals and Interactions

Agile development teams tend to enable individual developers to make key decisions about the form for a solution; as long as the product solves the customer's problem, everyone is happy. This is in contrast with other development approaches that prescribe more of the details of how a particular solution is to be implemented. The benefit of this approach is that you involve more of the individual developers' creativity and also increase their level of ownership and responsibility for delivering a solution; they can't claim that the software failed because they were following orders.

Self-organizing teams adapt well to this model because the people who are best suited to a particular aspect of the development project emerge from the team, rather than being assigned based on an imposed hierarchy. For such teams to work, good communication is essential. Communication techniques, such as clearly visible boards that display current work in the queue, where it can be monitored or rearranged based on priorities, are essential. Many methodologies require a "daily standup," a meeting where everyone gets together to discuss progress and identify problems—and aren't allowed to sit down until the conversation is over. In practice, I find that some of these rigid processes wane as a team works together over time—instead, because of the focus on person-to-person interactions, each team also self-organizes the best communication systems that work for them. The key is that everyone, and especially management, need to be committed to open and honest communication through the course of the project.

Working Software

Rather than creating PowerPoint decks showing ideas of how something might look, agile development teams create functional live wireframes and working web pages. Rather than creating extensive documentation, agile teams work toward functional programs and self-documenting code.

Years ago, software development managers would have scoffed at the idea of diving into the coding of a project so far in advance. However, the benefits are clear in many cases: Customers react only to working software, not ideas. How many times have you seen a PowerPoint deck and been excited about the concept you're hearing about—only to be disappointed in the actual product? That's because our imaginations are so powerful, and we often imagine the world as we'd like it to be. Things become real only when you can see, touch, and taste a real product.

Fortunately, software is so fluid in its form that it's possible to make changes to it—you can't remake the engine of a car while someone is driving it, but you can do exactly that with software. Although writing software is a science, it is also a craft—more so than most other forms of engineering. To make a great piece of software often requires a few false starts and failures. If you aren't making failures, you aren't taking enough risks. That's the essence of making working software as part of the agile development process: to build products early and often, and evolve them based on what you learn.

Customer Collaboration

Product evolution also requires feedback. Web developers have two huge advantages over many other types of software development, which is why agile practices have become so common among web programmers

- Websites are almost always created with the intent of being enhanced over time, which means that important features and enhancements can always be backlogged beyond the initial release of the site.

- Websites can be analyzed down to the smallest details: which pages some-one uses, where someone makes a purchase, how long someone is present. Analysis of this data can lead to large improvements in a website after its launch.

Not only can the data help guide development, it's essential to have a customer present at product reviews. In cases where the actual customer isn't available (say, for a consumer product targeted at millions of people), the customer advocate could be a product manager, marketer, or even the CEO—who can be armed with real data about how the actual customer is using the product This person's role is to make the decisions about priorities in the project because it is inevitable that tradeoffs will need to be made in any project based on available resources.

Responding to Change

Markets change, customers change, and requirements change. A problem with long-running software projects is that it is nearly impossible to predict what the market will be like years in advance. In some cases in the game industry where less-than-agile methods were used, the game's graphics engine was antiquated by the time the game was released. A benefit of creating working software over many iterations—as opposed to following the software development world's equivalent of a Soviet five-year plan—is that it adapts to change as the world changes.

Change is a huge risk in any business venture. Given how costly software development can become, mitigating this risk is one of the largest advantages of agile development. By involving customers in the development process and making course-corrections to address these changes, agile development teams focus on what matters: creating products that people care about.

Social Media Games versus Traditional Games

It was previously pointed out how important numbers and analyses are to social game development and also how a data-driven approach to building software can power up an agile development process.

Numbers are also used in traditional game development. Large amounts of effort are expended by game publishers to determine potential retail sell-through, long-term franchise value, unit production costs, and development costs. Numbers are also used by the developers to decide which parts of the game are being used most. For example, in the development of *Halo 3*, Bungie built an extensive lab that recorded every second of gameplay for its testers, including a synchronized video recording so it could match play experiences with facial expressions. As people played, all this information was injected into databases the developers used to create reports for each level, showing where people moved, got stuck, or got killed. They tracked players' satisfaction with each level and made continuous improvements until it was perfect.

 ARTISAN There's a debate within social game development regarding the value of some metrics over the long term. Some would argue that when one looks at numbers only from the standpoint of monetizing a customer as quickly as possible, you do so at the expense of creating a long-term customer. It isn't known what will win out over the long-run, but if the social media game market ever evolves similarly to the traditional game market, it will begin caring more about the nonquantitative measurements of satisfaction as time marches on.

In most traditional game development projects, testing and numeric analyses happen before the product is released. After it is out the door and people buy it and reviewers critique it, it's too late to make big changes. One exception: Massively multiplayer online game companies (think of *World of Warcraft*) track numerous variables such as quest completion rates, abandonment at certain points in the game, popularity of items, and abilities. However, *WoW* is a type of social game—and like its cousins within the social media universe, it takes constant measurements and makes ongoing improvements because its revenue is tied to everyone's long-term enjoyment. This is in contrast to games such as *Halo 3*, where most of the revenue that will ever be collected on the game has already happened before the player boots up the game for the first time.

Because of the more static nature of traditional game development, developers are mostly focused on fixing big problems in gameplay or correcting bugs. Most game developers want people to enjoy their products. They do this because they want customers to think warm thoughts when it comes time to buy an expansion, sequel, or another product from their publisher. I also believe that the majority of hard-working game developers have a great sense of pride in their work and simply want people to love their products. However, their business models just don't support the high frequency of updates, improvements, and changes that accompany any sort of social game in which the revenue will be derived from long-term engagement. The vast majority of sales for a traditional game occur in the weeks (if not days) following the commercial release. Thus, the development practices are tied to performing infrequent, larger builds focused on correcting problems rather than extending engagement. Lack of adequate ongoing revenue following release too often constrains the ability to make products as good as they can be.

Many traditional game companies practice agile development. Clinton Keith wrote an excellent book on the subject and any perusal of the job postings at major game developers like Bungie (the developer of *Halo*), Valve (*Half-Life, Left 4 Dead*) and Bioware (*Mass Effect, Knights of the Old Republic*) reveals that agile development has taken hold within the creation of entertainment software.

Game companies are among some of the earliest adopters of agile methodology. Even before the term *agile* came into fashion, Valve had formed what it called cabals in the late '90s. The purpose of cabals was to bring together cross-functional teams of experts (engineers, level designers, writers, animators) who could co-design important aspects of the game—increasing communication between members, preventing technologies from being created that would never get used, and producing better experiences. As early as the development of *Half-Life* (released in 1998), Valve involved extensive customer feedback in the process by having cabal members observe players interacting with the game—a task that would have probably landed in the lap of a quality assurance engineer at many other companies.

Agile methodologies can work well in game development, but following are several important differences:

- **Iteration does not replace vison:** Iteration can be a helpful tool in the early stages of a game's concept-creation stage, as designers play with different ideas for interactions and sources of fun. However, after the key decisions are made about the brand and the fun in the game, the team needs to stick to it; agile methods are not a replacement for vision, and if you wait too long to figure these things out, you won't iterate your way into a fun experience.

- **Success mean involving everyone:** Agile methodologies are focused on software engineers, and it is engineers that are currently best-trained to apply their principles. Artists, writers, and designers don't have as immediate or direct an impact on the deliverable as an engineer and sometimes get left behind. Overcoming this requires a strong coach who mentors and involves everyone, not just engineers. Sometimes this may mean creating or acquiring tools to give non-engineering team members a more direct impact on the deliverable.

- **Some parts of agile aren't always necessary for every aspect of game development:** Games are hierarchical and can sometimes contain a huge number of content and graphical assets. When it has been decided what assets are needed in a game, the assets need to be produced on a production schedule that's sometimes closer to non-agile processes. (Although the assembly of these assets into levels and experiences might be highly agile, as was the case in the level iterations used in *Halo 3*).

Social Media Games versus Websites

Only a tiny fraction of web development projects approach the budgets seen within traditional game development, and millions of websites are in production at any given moment. This has been an amazing digital petri dish for the refinement of agile methods within website development.

Because of their reliance on data-driven customer feedback and agile methods, many web development teams feel they're well equipped to tackle a social game project. Indeed, if you look at many of the successful social game companies, including those mentioned earlier, you'll find teams with extensive web development but little game development expertise. However, many web development teams have found profound differences from what they're used to:

- **Finding the fun within a game isn't quite the same as maximizing a business metric.** Although engagement metrics are a good way to measure whether you've succeeded, too many teams think of "fun" as another thing they can iterate late, only to find that they've gone too far without solving the fundamental problem of any game: identifying what will be fun.
- **Getting useful customer feedback is hard when you're still figuring out what is fun in the game.** Teams need to find the best ways to get market feedback even when you don't have a fully fleshed-out game demo to show to potential customers. Focus groups can sometimes be helpful, which is an unfamiliar process to many agile teams.
- **Many game experiences depend on a unique look-and-feel, an innovative interface, or a particular brand.** Many agile teams make the mistake of shunning these aspects as a form of debt. However, the unique flavor and experience of a game comes from these elements—not simply the programming—and agile teams need to become accustomed to incorporating nonprogrammers into the team.

Table 3-1 compares traditional game development, web development, and social media game development:

Table 3-1: Comparison of Traditional Game, Website, and Social Media Game Development

	Traditional Game	Website Project	Social Media Game
Example products	*Halo, Half-Life*	Amazon, LinkedIn	*Bejewelled Blitz, Mafia Wars*
Frequency of post-release changes	Usually limited to a few bug-fix patches	Up to daily	Up to daily
When metrics are used	Mostly prerelease	Post-release	Post-release
When the fun is identified	Before production	Happens at any time	During the first prototypes
Voice of the customer	Product visionary, playtesters	Customer interviews, website analytics	Game analytics
Hierarchical inter-dependencies	Massive amounts due to content needs	Typically few	Could be few or many
Minimum viable product	Expensive, due to market expectations of product values	Often small, due to simplicity of many initial website projects	Relatively small and inexpensive but rising as customer expectations increase

Teams

Not many people have a resume packed with a list of social media game development credentials. Producing a social media game depends on your ability to draw talented people from within your organization and from people who come from traditional game or website development backgrounds. However, this is where the cross-functional team that arises in agile game development can be so helpful.

Team Skills

Rather than focus on specific job descriptions, you need to find people with the right combination of skills to get your project done. Table 3-2 shows some of the things that most social game development teams need:

NOTE This book, helps you gain an understanding of several of the following areas, helping you identify what you'll be good at and what you'll need help with.

Table 3-2: Social Game Development Team Requirements

Requirement	Description
Game design skills	Expertise in creating point systems, badges, and leaderboards; understands emotion and how to create fun. Good game designers are also great communicators, capable of expressing themselves and conveying rules and systems to other designers. Depending on the complexity of a game, there can be multiple subdomains of game design: item designers, story writers, level designers, puzzle designers, and economy designers.
Data analysis	Skills with analytical tools including spreadsheets and databases. Experience with website analysis tools can be extremely helpful, especially for the construction of customized database-driven systems for measuring conversions, purchases, and engagement.
User experience design	The ability to turn the hopes and dreams of your players and game designer into stories, storyboards, wireframes, prototypes, and aesthetically pleasing interfaces.
Artists	Depending on the project, may include not only the typical website art developers, but also illustrators and pixel artists (who create icons and grid-based art assets a pixel at a time)—and some projects could even use 3D modelers and animators.
Front-end programming	The ability to use front-end technologies like HTML, Flash, and Unity to create functional interfaces for players to experience the game with.
Back-end programming	Expertise working with databases, application servers, and web-development languages. (Ruby on Rails, PHP, and Flex are among the most common in social media game development.)
Project management	Someone to act as an agile coach and producer who can help manage assets and deliverables, help coordinate, facilitate communication, and tend to infrastructure, such as issue-tracking systems.
Quality assurance	Intuitive hands-on testers are more valuable than people who depend on heavily scripted test environments, given the frequency of change within social media game projects.

Team Interests

In my experience, great game design teams consist of people with a wide range of interests. Just as the team is cross-functional, individual team members also tend to be multifaceted. The people who founded some of the most successful social gaming startups shared an interest in games, but their experiences mostly came from outside the game industry.

 ARTISAN Ken Birdwell, one of Valve's first engineers—and the person who shared the cabal strategy with the world—was a developer who had worked on artificial intelligence, medical technology, and electrical engineering systems. Ken had also pursued a degree in fine arts and has said that it's the art training that made the biggest difference in his career.

On my own teams, I look for people who have a combination of a deep level of expertise in a particular domain—for example, writing software to create sophisticated user interfaces, using the latest and greatest technologies—but I also look for a secondary set of interests that will help broaden the expertise of the team. If they're mostly technically oriented, I look for secondary interests in literature, theater, and art. If they'll be focusing on art and the more human aspects of game development, I like to find people with a curiosity about human behavior, thinking, and numbers.

Game development is both a left-brain and a right-brain endeavor; the more your team and your individual team members reflect that reality, the more capable you'll be of delivering great products.

Team Formation

Bruce Tuckman is a psychologist who started his career in a think tank within the U.S. Navy, where he analyzed more than fifty papers detailing the way small groups turn into effective teams. His model, which has come to be known as Tuckman's stages of group development, contains four stages: forming, storming, norming, and performing. His model has been helpful in understanding everything from the way teams work on naval vessels—as well as management teams, product development teams, and creative collaborators. Because so many agile development teams are going to be new, you may find it helpful to think about the formation of your own team in the context of the stages presented in Table 3-3.

Table 3-3: Game Development Stages

Stage	Description
Forming	People are concerned with understanding the rules under which the group will operate. People will try to learn a lot about what the others have to offer but they might not offer much information. If you're forming an agile development team, this is a great time to make sure people understand what exactly agile development is. Sharing this chapter with them would be a good start!
Storming	Personal egos will emerge at this stage as people choose to express what they're good at—sometimes taking center stage. Emotions can run high, and arguments can break out. Remember that this is a normal part of the team formation process. This stage is also when know-it-alls—often game developers who think they're God's gift to gaming, or developers with prior experience with agile techniques—might try to dominate the process. One-on-one coaching is helpful here. Remind everyone that some amount of conflict is normal but that you're also doing something new: Although everyone is an expert in their domain, as a group you haven't created a social game, and things will be different this time. You can point out some of the things already covered about what's a bit different in social game development versus traditional web and game development.
Norming	People have come to know each others' personalities. Most team members focus on harmony above anything else. However, the group's desire for harmony shouldn't override the requirement to produce a great product: This is where the use of outside, analytical data is extremely helpful—data can show how people use the product and can eliminate egos from the group dynamic while keeping people focused on goals. During this stage, the team should start confiding in each other, and saying "we" and "our" a lot more. It's also a good time for team members to recognize areas in which others could help them develop further—for example, teaming game designers more closely with interface designers, so each can benefit from each other's knowledge.
Performing	The politics of the group have become known, and the group has a strong understanding of what each group participant has to offer to the team. The team becomes an effective tool for delegating tasks, identifying the best person to get the job done, and refining new ideas. If you've done a good job with keeping the team focused on business results—which data and analytics can be invaluable for— then the team can make pragmatic decisions. If the game design and vision have worked well, the team will rally behind it, looking for ways to bolster it—and if it isn't working, consider ways it can be changed or even consider completely new approaches.

Tools for Team Collaboration

Because agile processes emphasize communication and interaction over documentation, you need to work at creating the systems that get people talking to each other. Software can assist you in managing a team that will be producing social media games in an agile manner.

One of the more common forms of software for team collaboration is a wiki, which enables anyone on your team to contribute and edit documents. We use wikis at Disruptor Beam for all our projects. However, after several years of working with wikis, I've concluded that while they're great for capturing and storing knowledge, they aren't that great at facilitating interaction or creativity. The reason is that many people participate in a project who simply don't have a natural reason to get involved in the wiki on a frequent-enough basis to benefit from the conversations and changes happening there. By all means, use wikis; they certainly beat the snot out of a shared file directory—and can breathe life into a set of design documents that might otherwise gather dust over the course of a project—but don't expect them to act as the communication glue within your teams.

The best tools are those where designers and developers work together on an interactive basis to create the artifacts that actually make it into the product. These work because they're part of someone's natural work process. A good example is a product called Protoshare, which we use at Disruptor Beam to enable everyone in the brainstorming, wireframing, and user interface development effort to participate in the creation and commenting. We take the output directly from Protoshare and use it for building out production interfaces. Protoshare and a few other products of this type are included in the "Creativity Tools" section of Appendix B.

Another invaluable tool used at Disruptor Beam is Skype. Several of our developers are located out of the main studio, which means activities need to be coordinated all over the world. Everyone should feel like they're part of the team, and part of the conversations going on throughout the company. Skype enables us to maintain chat threads between multiple participants—and we make use of multiuser video teleconferences for our equivalent of the standup meetings.

If you've got a distributed team, you need to go to extra lengths to make sure everyone communicates. Although telecommuting has many benefits, it is actually more management overhead—not less.

Working with an Outside Team

As you consider what skills you might need to add to your team to tackle a social game development project, it might be a bit intimidating. An alternative is to work with a studio with expertise in social game development; that's exactly what we do at Disruptor Beam, and I've included some other studios that are open to working with partners in Appendix B. An advantage of taking this approach is that you'll work with developers who've tackled many of the challenges presented in this book already. You can also use the experience as a means of absorbing a great deal of knowledge about social game development into your company.

When you think about engaging an outside development team to help you create a social game, the following are some questions you should ask yourself:

- Does the team you're considering have experience building games, websites—or both? Social games require a crossover of skillsets from both website and game development.
- Does the team have a process for understanding your unique interests and requirements, and transforming it into a plan of action?
- Can the team tackle the entire set of development challenges, from the high-level design down to the ongoing operation of servers?
- Will the team collaborate with you closely so that you're deeply involved?

Player–Centered Design

Over the years, product design—particularly in software—has focused increasingly on various forms of customer-centered design. The intent of these approaches is noble: to focus more on what customers want to get out of a product, rather than what the product designers want to build. However, many product teams have found that they've applied techniques from customer-centered design and still ended up with products that don't deliver value.

If you're a game designer, you might find that these techniques may provide some additional tools for thinking about game design. If you aren't a game designer, you can learn some secrets that might inject some added fun or engagement into your products.

Traditional customer-centered product design has involved six steps:

- Innovate to arrive at a general idea for solving a business problem.
- Develop personas, which are descriptions of customers based on interviews, research, or intuition.
- Develop use cases (stories that explain how customers want to use the product).

- Develop user interfaces that enable the use cases. Designers create proto-types to test the interfaces with users and iterate until the interfaces work as expected.
- Developers create software that delivers an actual product. The product is tested with customers until it works as intended.
- Managers collect information on how the finished product is used in the wild and use it to inform subsequent iterations of the overall process.

The player-centered design methods revealed are based in part on traditional customer-centered design techniques but are focused on the unique needs of games—products that need to make things fun. Figure 3-1 illustrates the overall flow for the player-centered design process.

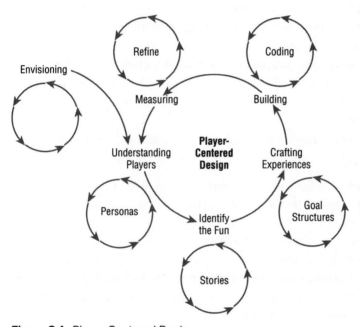

Figure 3-1: Player Centered Design

Envisioning Your Game Concept

Any game needs a visionary behind it: a CEO, product leader, lead game designer, or producer that has an idea for what they want to do. Few successful games are created out of committees.

The purpose of envisioning is to determine what the game is fundamentally about. You might not know exactly who the customer is, or have certainty over what will make it fun, or even what the content of the game is. Nevertheless, knowing what the game is about can provide you with clarity as you move forward with the process. It's helpful if you force yourself to create a statement that begins, "A game about..." such as these:

- A game about becoming a mafia kingpin
- A game about making your lifestyle more environmentally friendly
- A game about designing cities and making certain decisions about their management
- A game about learning ways to become healthier, where you actually change behavior over time and become healthier
- A game about solving puzzles of increasing difficulty, with a distinct brand motif based on gemstones
- A game about playing with the folding structure of proteins, enabling players to make actual scientific contributions
- A game about real-life celebrities in which the player needs to predict things that happen in the news
- A game about imagining yourself as a fantasy character locked in an epic struggle against an opposite faction that wants to conquer your world

Beyond an "about" statement, the purpose of the envisioning stage is to come up with some of the broad narratives and key experiences that can guide the development of your game.

Sometimes there is a strong vision statement for a game even before it begins, but at other times the vision statement needs some tuning and deeper exploration before it's appropriate to engage a team on the project. To help you think about the creation of these stories, you can invoke techniques from brainstorming, storytelling, and myths—a subject covered in Chapter 9.

Understanding Players

When you know what the game is about, you need to think about your players—the customers who want to have fun experiences and are willing to pay for it. The purpose of this stage is to learn everything you can about them—particularly the motivations they have that relate to what your game is about. The particular methodology explained for this process is the creation of player personas, which are motivation-oriented descriptions of the people who will be playing your game, as covered in Chapter 4.

Identifying the Fun

If you know what motivates your players, you're ready to think about what the source of fun will be in the game.

This is where many games go wrong; they know who their customers are, and they're creating a game "universe" in that there's an environment to play in, but there haven't been clear decisions about exactly what will make the game fun. Chapter 5 discusses various theories of fun, and Chapter 9 touches on how to use storytelling as a way to identify some of the most enjoyable experiences in a game. These are helpful tools in identifying the potential fun in the game, but at some point you'll need to say to yourself, "that's it. This is the type of fun we're going to stick with."

How do you know you've really hit on the fun of the game? The first gut-check is whether it is fun for you. There's no end to the number of disastrous game development projects where all the developers knew in their hearts that it wasn't really fun. Unless the team is passionate about the game they're creating, it is extraordinarily unlikely that the game will be fun. That said, good games are made for large markets—not simply for the developers themselves—and customer feedback is helpful in the process. In Chapter 8 you'll read about some engagement metrics and playtesting methods to validate that the fun you're feeling is shared by the market at large.

Crafting Experiences

At this stage, a number of attempts are made to determine the right way to deliver fun to the players. This involves thinking about what memories the players will take away from the game, how they might explain it to a friend—down to the details of what interfaces and goals they should be given and what will drive compulsive engagement.

This phase often includes a significant amount of rapid iteration, usually in individual cycles measured in days. Whenever possible, prototypes are created that enable people to interact with facets of the game. Based on the reaction to prototypes, the team might return to the previous phase (because sometimes the source of fun isn't quite as fun as they hoped) or reiterate (because the fun is right, but the means of delivery isn't).

This is often when big decisions are made about funding the remainder of the project; if potential players aren't responding as hoped, and the team feels they've tried enough different approaches to the problem, it might make sense to abandon the idea. Otherwise, the project gets the green light and moves forward to the next stage.

Building Software

As games reach a later stage of development, they tend to become more of a hierarchical development process. Funding requirements typically increase as more developers become committed to the project, so you want to make sure the game idea has endured some amount of testing. The purpose of previous stages is intended to minimize the risk that you're building the wrong things, but you should still expect to discover and solve big problems at this point.

Rapid iteration continues during this stage of development, often on weekly increments; certain user interfaces and product components are still being developed based on the designs arrived at during previous phases but will continue to need customer testing and feedback. The content of the product, which tends to be hierarchical, is also being developed at this stage, and due to the interlocking dependencies that tend to occur in games, it might be somewhat less iterative in nature.

This is not a programming book, so not a lot of time is spent on software development issues. Instead, the book discusses ways that your development team should be involved in your process, starting with the collaborative and agile development techniques proposed in this chapter.

Measuring Success

After the game is "in the wild" with real customers, the goal of measurement is to quantitatively analyze how players interact with the game. At this stage, you use information to learn more about players, refine interfaces to improve performance, and identify opportunities for game improvement. Depending on what you learn, you might continue to reengage developers at any of the previous phases, which is covered in Chapter 8.

Chapter in Review

This chapter discussed what sorts of teams have tackled social game development projects, pointing to the huge successes enjoyed by people with a numbers-oriented but often nongaming background. It presented some thoughts on the type of people who can assist in your game development project, suggesting that you look for multitalented people with a combination of game, website, and analytical skills.

This chapter discussed the benefits of agile development, which is about making products customers love by focusing on customer collaboration through small iterations that are responsive to changes in the business environment. It also discussed how games and websites have benefited from agile development in different ways; for example, major retail game releases have largely used it to get products ready before they ship—whereas websites and social games apply agile techniques to continue to evolve products after they've shipped.

Finally, this chapter presented a particular design methodology used at Disruptor Beam and which is called player-centered design: a process intended to establish vision, understand players, identify the fun, craft experiences, and then build and measure social game products. Most of the rest of this book focuses on various elements of this methodology.

Choose Your Path

The following list gives areas of the book you might want to visit next.

- If you get into the heads of your customers by thinking about them as game players, you can uncover new ways to motivate and engage them. If this intrigues you, continue to Chapter 4.
- If you'd like to understand more about what makes something fun, which can help you envision products and start you on the path to identifying the fun of a game, turn to Chapter 5.
- If you're ready to start thinking about the design of a social game product, move on to Chapter 7.
- If you came from page 137, you have fallen through a trapdoor and you are now lost in the Plane of Infinitely Iterative Software Development. Roll a 12-sided die to see which chapter you should continue to next.

4 Customers as Players

n this Chapter, you'll learn:

- How thinking of customers as "players" can help you transform your business relationships for the better
- How to use the power of myth as a creative tool to explore customer beliefs
- Methods online games use to classify different players
- How to create a player persona to guide your development efforts

What if there was a way you could think of your customer in a fresh, new way—one that reveals their deepest hopes, dreams, and desires? Part of this transformation requires a little bit of magic, so I'll share a simple incantation you can use. Repeat it to yourself from time to time to help you reframe how you think about your customer: *My customer is a player.*

A *player persona* is a fictional character that attempts to capture the personality, attitudes, and attributes of the real-life customers who play your game. A player persona enables you to prioritize product features based on what customers have the most fun with—which can lead to greater engagement and more profitable relationships. This chapter will equip you with a set of tools for constructing these personas, including interviewing techniques, motivational psychology and mythical archetypes.

The process of creating a persona includes the following steps:

- Identifying your best customers
- Collecting information about customers through research and interviews
- Organizing information into descriptions, motivations and goals
- Repeating as necessary based on what you learn, or to fill-in gaps in your knowledge

After you've developed one or more personas, you'll have an idea about which experiences will make your customers most happy.

Describing Customers with Player Personas

The first step in creating a player persona is to speak to people you think are potential customers. You'll want to find people you think represent the different types of people with whom you do business, because the next step of this process will involve asking questions to learn more about what makes them tick.

If you can meet them face-to-face, that's best because you can watch people closely and observe subtle facial expressions that might convey surprise, irritation, or skepticism that can be helpful for you in asking good questions. To connect with some of the people you'll learn from, you could:

- **Invite communication:** Invite potential customers to communicate with you by setting up an online community using a blog or Facebook fan page.
- **Utilize online venues:** Engage in conversations with people in online forums, Twitter, or social groups on Facebook.
- **Online ads:** Place online ads that target keywords relevant to your product, channeling people towards your online community.
- **Ask customers:** Approach customers who have had previous contact with your company and ask them what they think. Most people will respond very favorably when they feel their feedback has a real impact.
- **Watch shoppers:** Observe the people who are shopping at a store that you think represents demographic. If you're feeling bold, you can even ask them a question or two.
- **Try a focus group:** If you've tried everything else and you need help, you could consider working with a market research company to assemble a focus group.

Once you've found a few people to talk to, the next step is to decide what you'll ask them.

What to Ask during a Customer Interview

Player personas are intended to help you gain insights about your customers. Unlike surveys, which are usually more formulaic, and may help you validate or weigh factors you already suspect are important, a customer interview is intended to help you learn and explore.

The starting questions you can ask people should be "what" and "where" questions that yield information about competitors, behaviors, and goals. For example:

- What do you think of...?
- Where do you usually buy...?
- Where do you go to find out about...?
- What level are you in *FarmVille*?
- What virtual gifts have you given people in *Zoo Kingdom*?

Of course, you'll need to tailor your questions to your exact business. Maybe your customers don't care about *FarmVille* or *Zoo Kingdom*, or maybe they don't think about games at all. Use these examples as inspiration for the specific questions you'll ask.

Some of the most useful information you'll gain at this stage of the interview is what people are doing with competitors' products—as well as the names of a few products you might not have known about. However, the best information you can collect is about motivations. Your job as an interviewer is to be incisive. After all, this isn't a survey, and you want to learn things that aren't obvious. To uncover motivations, ask a lot of questions that begin with why and how:

- Why don't you like giving gifts to people in *FarmVille*?
- How do you decide whether to share an achievement on your Facebook news feed?
- Why do you log in to Facebook only during your lunch break?
- Why don't you allow your coworkers to friend you?
- How would you feel if you didn't win any epic loot during a raid while playing *World of Warcraft*?
- Why did you stop using the online diet website after two weeks?

Remember, you're doing this to learn—not to persuade! Avoid introducing bias through the way you ask questions. Don't offer approval or agreement when the customer gives you what you feel are the right answers, or tell the customer what they "should" think. If you steer the conversation too much, you'll create a persona of yourself—rather than of the person you're talking to—and you'll miss out on a valuable opportunity to learn the nuances of how someone might interact with your business. Customers may even invite you to share your own opinions so that they can agree with you; let them know that you're very curious about what *they* think, and that you don't want to lead them toward particular answers. You can always offer to share your opinions with them at the conclusion of the interview.

If they'll let you, you should also watch your potential customers do the things they normally do. Watch them use Facebook, play online games, or use the products most similar to your own. The goal here is to learn exactly how they use the product.

Turning Research into Personas

After collecting your research about customers, try to arrange lists of interviews and information into buckets most like each other. If almost everyone is the same, you might need to create only one persona, but usually you have at least two or three distinct groups.

The most important thing at this stage is to resist the temptation to "average" all your results into one or two mythical customers. By speaking to people and arranging them into groups based on inherent similarity, you effectively go through a form of cluster analyses. In cluster analyses, statisticians try to plot groups of similar data together by plotting them on a grid and identifying the groups mathematically arranged closest together. Because most of your data is qualitative, you need to focus instead on your own judgment for what makes people similar.

Within your groupings, try to identify the person that you think is closest to representing the qualities of that group. It's fine to change some basic facts (especially to conceal your interviewee's identity) but again, it's best to avoid averaging them into someone that doesn't actually exist.

Collect these groups of information and turn them into simple descriptions. If you or someone on your team is graphically talented, it can be fun and helpful to turn them into posters that can be put on walls. Making them into posters can keep you focused on supplying the most important information. You can also simplify your descriptions into one-pagers that fit into a PowerPoint deck, a wiki page, or even an email summary.

A persona description should include the following:

- **Demographics:** Gender, age, marital status, job, education, income, and geographic location for a typical customer have a huge impact on how you market a product.
- **Motivations:** Why do they use similar products? What are their hopes and dreams? What do they want to get out of your product? How does a similar product make them feel?
- **Hero's Journey archetypes:** Which characters best describes your customers when they use your product? How does that compare to how they currently feel using alternative products?

- **Online identity:** How do they interact online? Do they prefer anonymity? How closely do they blend their real-life identity with who they are online or in games?
- **Frustrations:** What do they dislike about similar products?
- **Using similar products:** When do they usually use a similar product? And where do they usually buy or use those similar products?
- **Media consumption:** What websites, magazines, television, and so on do they enjoy?
- **Daily routines:** What activities do they do every day? Focus on the things that are most relevant to your product.

Naming Your Personas

Personas need a name that makes them memorable. It can help everyone in your company—marketing, design teams, and the CEO—to stay on the same page regarding who your customers are. Think of it as a helpful communication tool.

Sometimes alliteration can be helpful for remembering. When a previous company I ran developed GamerDNA.com, a community for core game players, three of the personas were Paul the Prover, Shawn the Sharer, and Don the Doer. These were shorthand names so that we could remember that these were players who cared about: (a) how powerful they were, (b) considered themselves information mavens and wanted to share their expertise with others, and (c) people who cared only about extracting immediate utility from the site (such as finding a new game to play).

Nine Pitfalls with Personas

There are some potential problems you should be aware of in the course of developing a persona. By keeping these concerns in mind, you'll create better interviews and eliminate inadequately detailed personas that might lead you to make the wrong decisions.

Designing for Users instead of Customers

Many companies design products for users rather than customers. *User* is a highly depersonalizing term that comes from a far more technically oriented stage of the software industry's origins when most engineers designed things for other engineers.

The other problem with the term user is that it isn't always someone who pays for something. A *customer* is someone who pays you for providing value. Reminding yourself that you serve customers and not users is a helpful way to reinforce the idea that you operate within a business model. A *player* is a type of customer who expects fun and is willing to pay for it.

NOTE Unfortunately, the term *user* is part of the vernacular of the software industry, so it will be used elsewhere in this book—particularly where it is part of phrases that are in common use. I do this to avoid confusion, but you can try to eliminate it from your own vocabulary whenever possible.

Failing to Address Your Business Model Early Enough

Like having a clear vision, understanding your business model early is a tool to sharpen the focus of your product. How customers pay has huge implications for how you ultimately position, package, and deliver a product. In games, the business model is intimately related to the way the game mechanics need to be designed; subscription-based games are completely different than those supported by virtual good transactions. Even if you aren't certain what your business model will be, you need some general ideas, and you can use your customer interviews to learn more about how your customers might be willing to pay for it.

Just as failing to think about a business model early can lead to an unfocused design process, it is just as painful to think about it in the wrong way. The right way is to stay focused on customers, and how they perceive value, and the methods and timing they are willing to use to pay for value. The wrong way is to enforce a business model because "That's how we always do it" or "That's how our competition does it."

The Henry Ford Faster Horses Fallacy

A popular quip is ascribed to Henry Ford in which he says that if he asked customers what they wanted, they'd have told him "faster horses." This is often interpreted to suggest that customers don't know what they actually need. It's true that customers often have difficulty envisioning the right solution to a problem; however, it wouldn't have taken many additional questions for Henry Ford to have figured out that the reason they wanted faster horses was to get to places faster.

When interviewing, customers often have a lot of their own ideas about solutions to problems. The job of the designer isn't to dismiss their thoughts as "faster horses" but to uncover the deeper motivations behind their ideas. One of the fantastic facts of games is that people *always* want to give an opinion of what they enjoy—which is yet another reason why games can be a powerful tool for any business to engage with customers.

When you think of your customers as a player, your customers expect fun. They know they want fun, and they're right. It's your job to determine how to deliver fun to them in a novel way.

Inadequate Focus on Motivations

The process of creating personas can often get overly focused on the specifics of a customer's goals. Make sure you also identify the motivations that drive customers toward their goals—perhaps before the goal was even realized. Motivations highlight why the goals are important, and may even allow you to identify a different set of goals that the customer should focus on instead.

Personas Crafted by Committee

Committees tend to create personas without adequate firsthand knowledge of the customer. Personas become an idealized view of the customer based on hopes and fictions rather than actual facts. Sometimes the committee uses data to guide decisions, but it picks and chooses data based on what it feels reinforces its beliefs rather than using it to challenge designs.

Often, these symptoms indicate a lack of adequate vision: The committee becomes a random walk through the market, looking for the right vision for the product. Sometimes it might also indicate the polar opposite: A vision that is too narrowly defined and therefore overrides the ability of designers to identify the best way to explore solutions.

Not Enough Personal Interaction

Customers are human beings, not revenue-generating units. Designers are also human beings capable of discerning subtle clues through interactions with customers. Survey data alone won't tell you enough about your customer. Exchanging messages through email or message boards is better; telephone conversations are better than that, and face-to-face interactions trump all.

It only takes a minimal effort for someone to respond to an online community and make customers feel valued, while also gleaning important insights. Despite the increase in social media, this practice remains underutilized. At a minimum, the people involved in designing personas need to communicate directly with customers through whatever electronic means are available—but why not also participate in local customer meetups (or tweetups) and networking groups?

Quantitative Analysis Paralysis

Quantitative data about customers is extremely helpful, but it's also the job of designers to take risks. If every decision is based on preexisting data, you'll become constrained by the data. It's okay to make some decisions based on qualitative data or even gut instinct.

Analysis paralysis is symptomatic of organizations that punish people for taking risks because the data becomes the best self-defense strategy. Often, this punishment is because the organization lacks structures for failing cheaply and moving forward.

Measurement can be a powerful tool in the course of delivering your game but can be more important when people can actually interact with it. Hold off on becoming overly quantitative at the early stages while you try to understand who your customer is.

Lack of Antipersonas

No product can be all things to all people. It's just as important to identify the customers you cannot serve as those that you can. Products that attempt to solve every possible customer type can become overwhelmingly complex and may have confusing interfaces, which will make no customer happy.

Twitter is a good example of a website that has never had confusion about the type of customer is serves: people who want to stay in touch through simple, impromptu messages. They know that different customers would probably take advantage of messaging services that offer much longer, more complex messages—and they're happy for customers that need those services to go elsewhere. Likewise, a social network game like *FarmVille* could incorporate a mathematically-intensive game for players who want a more true-to-life simulation experience, but that would alienate a huge number of other customers.

Failing to Consider Experiences

Chapter 2 discusses how important experiences are to the modern world economy. Often, product designers think about *customer experience* (or worse, *user experience*) too narrowly. When they use these terms, they talk about user interface, which is the graphical elements and widgets for interacting with information. Remember that an experience is either a memory or a transformation that the customer undergoes—what are the experiences you will leave someone with?

Failing to Account for Evolution

Players change over time. Someone who starts out as one persona might become more like another persona with enough exposure to the game. Likewise, entire communities might change as a game evolves. Personas are something that need to be revisited from time to time, and you also need to consider some of the paths that might lead players to change from one type to another.

Earlier, I mentioned how Twitter as a good example for sticking to a particular set of customer desires while intentionally not satisfying other desires. Although Twitter has stayed true to the idea that it exists for exchanging short messages, over time they've also learned that customers want more out of the service—and have added features like spotting trends and suggesting people to follow. This might have been too much if introduced early in the life of Twitter, but now that customers have *leveled-up* (to draw upon a gaming term), the added complexity makes sense.

The Hero's Journey

What if your customers weren't simply customers? What if you imagined them in a quest to defeat evil and return balance to the world? What would it mean if your customers were *heroes?* What if you could invoke the power of myths to help you brainstorm the elements of your player personas?

Psychologists and philosophers including Nietzsche, Jung, and Freud have noted certain recurring motifs in mythology and stories. Joseph Campbell synthesized these observations into a model he called the "Hero's Journey" in his seminal work, *The Hero with a Thousand Faces.* Mythical structures and characters—the hero, mentor, and princess—occur over and over within fiction and dreams. These structures have a deep resonance that stems from culture, and might even have a biological basis.

This section focuses on using the archetypal characters from mythology as a way to think of new questions to ask your customers (and yourself) in the course of developing your player personas.

NOTE You can read more about how these archetypes apply to the types of fun within games in Chapter 5. Later, in Chapter 9, you also learn how you can use the Hero's Journey as a tool for creating stories that describe the experiences in your game.

The Resonance of Myth

In the original Star Wars trilogy, Luke is ripped from his home to confront a terrible evil, save a princess, train under a succession of mentors that prepare him to face his ultimate nemesis, and eventually save the galaxy.

The Greek hero Perseus grows up as a poor fisherman's boy until events conspire to force him to rescue his mother from evil. After the gods prepared him with magical gifts, he slays Medusa, rescues a princess, and then becomes king.

In most story-driven games—and many movies and novels—a similar pattern emerges: A hero is cast into a dire situation, is prepared by mentors or equipment, faces a number of struggles, and then clashes with an ultimate adversary. The world is changed for better or worse depending on the choices the hero makes.

Since these characters resonate so much with humans in their lives, why not apply these archetypes to your customers? This not only facilitates identifying with your customer on a personal level, but it also helps to focus your product on the features and benefits that have the greatest chance of excitement, enlightenment and transformation.

The Mythmaking Game

The following is a list of 30 core character archetypes that frequently emerge within myth:

Table 4-1: Thirty Core Character Archetypes

Artist	King	Rebel
Avenger	Martyr	Shapeshifter
Child	Mentor	Storyteller
Clown	Messiah	Student
Conqueror	Monster	Temptress
Father	Mother	The Dark Lord
Gambler	Pioneer	The Shadow
Gatekeeper	Princess	Trickster
Healer	Prisoner	Warrior
Hero/Heroine	Puppet	Wizard

These are the archetypes that you can eventually apply to your customers. First, look at the list of characters, and ask yourself these questions:

- Which of the characters best personifies my customers when they use a competitor's product?
- Which of the characters best personify the way my customer would actually like to be if the product worked as well as it should?
- If I think of my own product as a type of character who could transform my customers into what they want to become, which character would personify it best?

Each archetype can inspire you to think of the personality traits that define your customers. Because these archetypes may mean different things to different people, you'll also want to record the specific traits you had in mind. For example, maybe the "Temptress" archetype makes you think of beauty, mischievousness and risk-taking. Jot down the answers to these questions (as well as the traits you've identified) so you can refer to them later—you'll use this information to assemble your player personas.

Visual Aids for Creativity

Brainstorming from a list of characters can help you kick start the creation of your player personas, but you'll find that your creativity is amplified when you use visual aids. Sharon Livingston, a psychologist who has studied mythical archetypes for use within clinical help, marketing, and creative enterprises, has expanded the list of archetypes into a deck of 94 Iconicards (a sample is shown in Figure 4-1).

Not only can these mythical symbols help enhance your own thought processes, but they are also great for collaborating with groups because pictures are an effective way to evoke creativity. You can also use them in discussions with customers, eliciting more revealing comments than you might get from a standard interview. Refer to the Resources in Appendix B for information on where you can obtain a set.

You can use Iconicards within the customer interviews you use to develop personas. This can inspire a whole new set of questions that might yield unexpected insights. Present the customer with the set of cards and ask questions such as the following:

- Which of these does [a competitor's product] make you feel like?
- Is there a character here that you want to become?

Figure 4-1: Iconicards

By incorporating techniques such as this into the interviewing process, you can make the interview a bit more like a game. Your customer will be more engaged and interested, and they may reveal things they otherwise wouldn't. This may help you identify the real hopes and motivations that drive them toward decisions—which are among the most valuable facts you can include in a persona.

Now that you've read about ways that stories and myths can inspire new ways to rethink the motivations and dreams of your customers, it is time to return to games, which provides another set of tools for categorizing customer motivations.

Different People, Different Fun

One of the first games I developed was a text-based role-playing game called *Legends of Future Past,* launched in 1992, in which people explored ancient ruins, battled terrifying enemies, and participated in live role-playing events.

Legends was part of a genre of games called multiuser dungeons, or MUDs, which I described back in Chapter 2. MUDs were fertile territory for experimentation; designers imagined every sort of world and a huge array of novel game mechanics. Although social games existed long before computers, MUDs were the original social games on the Internet. Much of what MUDs taught us is still applied today.

Most MUDs were free, run by students and hobbyists. A few, such as *Legends* and its contemporaries such as *Gemstone* charged an hourly fee for access. Although a fairly limited market of people existed who were willing to pay for text-based game products, the business model forced developers to learn exactly what customers wanted—and make sure that every minute they experienced was entertaining. The second they didn't have fun, they'd vanish!

Fortunately, a considerable amount of ethnographic research has been conducted on the players of social games, dating all the way back to some of these early MUDs. The benefit of this information is that you can put it to work for you. Even before you start your customer interviews, understanding some of the well-understood game motivations can help you frame potential player types and evolve your design ideas. During your actual customer interviews, you can also custom tailor your questions to explore which of the well-known player motivators are important to your customers.

Bartle's Four Types of Fun

One of the researchers who shared an interest in the ethnography of online game players was Richard Bartle, inventor of the MUD (see Chapter 3). Bartle observed a wide variety of play styles within MUDs and wanted to understand the motivations behind them. First, he observed that many players were interested in the world of the game, whereas others were more interested in the other players in the game. Furthermore, some players appeared to be more interested in "acting" (doing things to something or someone), whereas others were willing to "interact" (do things with something or someone). These interests can be plotted on a simple graph, as shown in Figure 4-2.

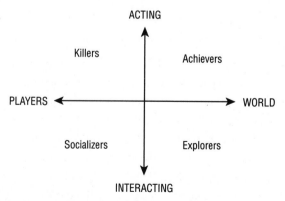

Figure 4-2: Bartle's Player Interests Graph

The result maps use four groups:

- **Achievers**: Players who act on the world
- **Explorers**: Players who interact with the world
- **Socializers**: Players who interact with players
- **Killers**: Players who act on other players

These are further outlined in Tables 4-2 through 4-5.

Table 4-2: Achievers

Description	Achievers are players who are motivated by a sense of mastery over the game world. They like the sense that they can become more powerful, making progress or advancing certain concrete goals.
Achievers like to:	<ul><li>Measure objectives, such as a level that increases as you advance through the game.</li><li>Watch progress bars that tell you whether you're advancing towards a new level.</li><li>Gain recognition for hard-to-perform actions, such as badges or achievements unlocked.</li><li>Collect objects that make you more powerful.</li><li>Complete collections of objects, badges, or events.</li><li>Acquire unique and rare objects.</li><li>Analyze and understanding game mechanics.</li></ul>
Real life über-achievers	**Colin Powell**, former secretary of state and four star general **Warren Buffet**, world-renowned investor **Steve Wynn**, casino-developer and art collector

Table 4-3: Explorers

Description	Explorers like to learn about their environment—which may map to a physical place (such as the virtual world within a MUD or MMORPG) and the story or information about the game.

Explorers like to:	• Find the best ways to get to places. • Learn about places that nobody else knows about. • Uncover the history and lore of the world. • Know secrets. • Create maps.
Real life explorers	**Jacques Cousteau**, scuba innovator and underwater explorer **V. S. Ramachandran**, explorer of the brain **Stephen Hawking**, explorer of the cosmos

Table 4-4: Socializers

Description	Socializers use games as a way to enjoy contact with other people.
Socializers like to:	• Be loved. • Gain friends and influence people. • Join or lead groups. • Get to know people. • Gain prestige. • Gossip. • Own places or locations frequented by other players. • Role-play. • Organize cooperative activities.
Real life socializers	**Ashton Kutcher**, actor with millions of Twitter followers **Oprah,** TV personality and owner of OWN **Almost any politician**

Table 4-5: Killers

Description	Originally, the killer in Bartle's model referred to people that mostly enjoy *griefing*, a form of play motivated by their ability to make others miserable. Although some players are motivated by this, the definition has evolved over time to encompass the idea of head-to-head competition. For many players, there's a big difference between winning against the environment of the game (referred to as player-versus-environment, or PvE) and beating other players of the game (player-versus-player, or PvP).

continues

Table 4-5: Killers *(continued)*

Killers like to:	• Be feared. • Dominate real people. • Appear at the top of leaderboards. • Feel the physical sensation of adrenaline. • Express pride.
Real life killers	(in the competitive sense, not in the life-ending or griefing sense) **Lance Armstrong**, multiple winner of the Tour de France **Michael Jordan**, dominant NBA player **Johnathan Wendel**, a top *Quake* player who goes by the moniker Fatal1ty

TAKING THE BARTLE TEST

There is a Bartle Test you can take online. It wasn't created by Richard Bartle, although it is based on his player motivation categories. More than 600,000 people have taken it as of October 2010, and many players of MMORPGs enjoy sharing their test results with each other. You can take the test by going to `http://game-on-book.com/bartle`.

Modernizing the Bartle Categories

The Bartle categories are a helpful model for thinking about the ways in which different players interact with social games. Many game companies use the categories as a way to think about the motivations of their customers, and some nongaming companies have started to think about it as a method to develop personas as part of a user experience design process.

The advantage of the Bartle categories is that they are relatively simple to understand. However, its categories suffer from a few problems. First, the idea of the "killer" as originally conceived was associating with griefing, which literally means the act of causing other players grief. Within normal competitive gameplay, losing is part of the experience; without winners and losers, many games don't even make sense.

However, if competition makes people unhappy instead of happy, there's a problem; that's not to say that individual losses aren't unpleasant but that the overall environment of competition needs to seem fair and balanced for players. When players are griefing, which is actually a form of exploiting a poorly designed system, it should be considered a bug that needs to be fixed.

It's safe to say that if a griefer category of player exists, it should be an antipersona. Therefore, instead of creating a product that appeals to these griefers, you should use this category to design a game system to make the game unsatisfying for them. Within social media, a griefer is often referred to as a *troll*, which is a person who shows up in the middle of conversations solely to excite anger by exhibiting antisocial behavior such as name-calling and belittling. Systems such as moderation, ratings, karma, and the like have been created to lessen a troll's impact because trolls are rarely welcome. Therefore, designing against trolls will ward them off and in turn pleases your other customers. The pros to this are to create satisfied and pleasant gamers, but the cons are losing the griefer customers. Statistics show, however, that the other three categories greatly outnumber the griefers, so in the long run, you will be coming out on top.

Another complication with the Bartle categories is that the four categories exclude a wide range of motivations. The concept of the explorer seems to overemphasize the idea of mapping out and literally exploring a landscape. Is the person who likes to click links on Wikipedia also an explorer because they like to explore knowledge? What about people that simply like to pretend and create stories within their mind? Are such people achievers because stories are an act of creation or socializers because the pretending happens alongside other people? These over-broad categories sometime complicate persona assignments and subsequent product creation.

Next, two of the approaches are outlined that have attempted to reconcile some of the underlying problems in the original Bartle classification system. Then we move on to consider my own synthesis that incorporates elements of each.

Implicit versus Explicit Play

Richard Bartle saw some of these problems in the underlying model, so he created an updated model of eight player types. His updated model adds a distinction between *implicit* (players who like to react as events unfold) versus *explicit* (players who like to plan ahead). When these two axes are added, it results in eight categories that are included in Table 4-6.

Table 4-6: Bartle's Eight Player Types

Category	Type	Description
Opportunists	Implicit achievers	People whose play is characterized by randomness. They are motivated by progress but need to be taken by the hand to be shown the next steps to take.
Hackers	Implicit explorers	People who are more motivated by discovering things through spontaneity.
Friends	Implicit socializers	People who tend to interact mostly with people they already know.
Griefers	Implicit killers	People who like to stomp on whoever gets in their way.
Planners	Explicit achievers	People who develop organized plans for how to achieve progress, such as working out their character on a spreadsheet or working out their *build* in advance.
Scientists	Explicit explorers	People with an organized plan to determine how the game works.
Networkers	Explicit socializers	People who form guilds, seek out new people to play with, and have a method for expanding their influence.
Politicians	Explicit killers	People who manipulate people.

Although you might find this formulation helpful in thinking about how different people might interact, this may be an example of an overcomplicated persona scheme. For example, is a politician actually a killer? It's just another dimension of social game-play, and manipulation doesn't have much to do with the adrenaline or competition involved with killers.

Bartle's updated model is helpful to recognize that many players progress through different player types. Bartle suggests that progression occurs from type to type, such as from implicit to explicit play.

Player Evolution

Players change over time as they engage with a game. Few people begin a game with an organized plan of how to succeed—that comes with experience and increasing interest. Most people start a game as something akin to Bartle's opportunist and then morph into a planner as they become acquainted with the rules.

However, an increasing willingness to learn rules and formulate plans is only one of the factors that changes over time as players enter later stages of the game. Players also seek ongoing novelty and increasing complexity. Many players become more interested in the social aspects of the game as they become more committed, whereas only single-player aspects of the game may have enticed them in the beginning.

Time is an important variable to account for when you develop your personas. Do you have personas to account for what happens after the player has been involved for a few minutes, a few hours, and a few months? I'll return to this subject below under "Evolution of Social Gameplay Motivations."

Rethinking Bartle

Nick Yee, a virtual worlds researcher at Palo Alto Research Center, has processed thousands of surveys from the players of massively multiplayer online games. Using factor-analysis techniques, he's reduced player motivation into three main components:

- **Achievement:** Shares some similarity to Bartle's original formulation of the Achiever. It includes everything related to "winning" the game, such as progress and measurable rewards, but also adds an interest in learning about game mechanics and competition.
- **Social gameplay:** Includes socializing (chit-chat and forming friendships), relationships, teamwork, and collaboration.
- **Immersion:** Encompasses Bartle's explorer but also adds the idea of becoming lost within the experience of a game—stories, role-playing, escapism, and customization.

Yee's updated model for gameplay is based on a ton of data, and in general it provides a much better way to think about social game players compared to Bartle's original four components. However, it is also tied to virtual world games and may not apply broadly to the wide variety of games that have emerged in the social game market.

Furthermore, human social behavior is complex, and creating only one "social" category to capture socially oriented gameplay isn't enough. Bartle's original idea with killers suggests at least a second category of social gameplay focused on competition.

Bartle and Yee's categories suggest the differing value systems from person to person, as well as the differences in how people wish to be perceived in their communities. The next section will attempt to align some of the motivational models into one system that you may be able to use within your person development.

Social Gameplay Motivations

Rather than thinking about social motivation as one particular category, consider refactoring Yee and Bartle's gameplay motivations categories into four (illustrated in Figure 4-3) that are more useful to analyze interactions within social games.

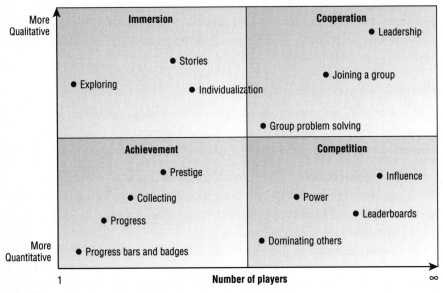

Figure 4-3: Social Gameplay Motivations

The horizontal axis represents motivations focused on the single-player experience, moving right toward more multiplayer experiences. The vertical axis considers motivations more clearly quantitative (such as a level that the player can measure) and moves toward the increasingly qualitative (such as a feeling of fulfillment). This enables the scattering of various motivations across the field of play, all of which can be generally captured by four quadrants:

- Achievement (single, quantitative)
- Immersion (single, qualitative)

- Competition (multi, quantitative)
- Cooperation (multi, quantitative)

Achievement

Achievement in social gameplay is anything that gives the player a sense of progress. You can measure this in many ways, including but not limited to collecting or owning things, gaining levels or badges, or earning prestige. For example, seeing a progress bar fill all the way up as you gain a level is a form of achievement, but you might also receive an additional payoff when your friends learn that you gained the level and congratulate you for it.

Immersion

Immersion is the sense of forming an enduring emotional connection to a game by feeling as if you're actually part of something. Immersion is satisfied by content to explore, stories to unravel, and secrets to learn. For real-time games (such as *World of Warcraft*) immersion often refers to a level of immediate absorption. For more asynchronous games (such as *FarmVille*), it is helpful to think of immersion as the features that enable the player to individualize, or to think of the game even when they aren't playing.

Competition

Many people are not satisfied with simply beating the computer; there's a special feeling associated with beating people you know are real people. This makes competition inherently social. Most of the time, *competition* is quantitative: If you beat someone, you know it and they know it. It can be reinforced through things such as competitive leaderboards, which increase the prestige of winning a competition. Competition also involves trying to win scarce resources, such as bidding for virtual goods in an auction house or convincing a talented player to join a guild.

Cooperation

Cooperative gameplay is when players interact with each other in a noncompetitive way. It includes teaming up to solve problems that might be hard or impossible to do alone, leading and forming groups, helping each other with information or gifts, or simply getting to know other players.

Evolution of Social Gameplay Motivations

As previously described, players change over time, evolving from one category to another. Evolution is a good way to think about this because players do not immediately discard everything associated with their past. They hang on to a lot of the original motivations, but now they're looking for more.

Players will be more focused on single-player experiences at first and then grow into the multiplayer experiences. You may find it helpful to think about how this progression might look. Starting with the more single-player-oriented categories previously described, the following sections describe how many players can change over time:

Achievement → Competition

Players who follow this pathway usually start out focused on how they can improve their gameplay. They tend to optimize the rate at which they progress through the game, increasing their level of planning along the way. As they become aware of the competitive elements to the game, they increasingly focus the form of their achievements on those they think can help them compete with other players. They begin testing themselves competitively, tentatively at first, but eventually become focused on ways they can beat other players.

Achievement → Immersion

This trajectory suggests players are less interested in interacting with other players. However, they still want the game to provide them with potent emotional experiences. After playing for a bit, they realize that simply moving along a leveling treadmill or winning badges isn't enough for them At this stage, they start looking for ways they can deepen their connection through stories and interesting content.

Achievement → Cooperation

Players who pursue this path begin encountering things that are too hard for them to do alone. They are motivated to form groups with other players to meet greater challenges within the game. However, be careful to make sure you know your players well. If people are truly seeking immersion (which they could have done on their own) and they feel forced to form groups or cooperate with others, they might be resentful. On the other hand, many players enjoy the camaraderie that comes with cooperative play. This is why thinking about personas as a dynamic, evolving process is important: Evolution is an opportunity to deepen the involvement of the player— or lose them.

Immersion → Cooperation

Players who play along this pathway are less interested in measurable forms of achievement. What they like is the content, stories, and environment of the game. Their "progress" through the game will be based upon the novelty of new experiences they have within it, as measured by themselves. As they continue to experience the game, they can find new dimensions of the game to be experienced if they work with other players. In addition, they seek a deeper emotional connection to the game. This connection can form when they feel that they are not only part of a world, but also part of a group of real people within that world.

Immersion → Competition

These players seek the game as a form of escape and learn that the players who have the most impact are those who can dominate other players. However, as they shift toward a more competitive form of play, they won't abandon their roots. For them, competition becomes a new way to make the game experience more "real."

Immersion → Achievement

Initially intrigued by the content of the game, these players become increasingly interested in the game mechanics. For them, it may be that they feel they're missing something until they start to uncover the secrets hidden within the inner operations of the game. The best way for them to continue their deep engagement within the game is to learn how the game works, as measured by levels, badges, and so on. For these players, it is also helpful to provide a schema of badges and achievements because it serves not only as a motivator, but also as a form of documentation for things they can do within the game.

Should You Focus on Multiple-Player Personas?

It isn't necessary to map out a social game that fulfills every type of the four types of social gamers. Many games fail because they lose focus, attempting to be too many things for too many different people.

Ultimately, it is the progression through new experiences that defines the staying power of a particular game. If you create a game mostly focused on achievement, you need to provide a lot of novelty along the way. If you want to make multiplayer interactions an important part of the game experience, you may need to decide whether competition or cooperation is the emphasis. It's perfectly fine to choose one over the other and even eliminate one category of play entirely. It's better to have a simple game that starts out focused on achievement and grows into a fantastic multiplayer

competitive experience than one that becomes a mediocre combination of both cooperation and competition.

Next, let's examine a specific case from *Magic: the Gathering*, a game that gives
players the opportunity to enjoy a fun experience with their friends, uniting friendly
competition along with creative expression.

Case Study: Magic: the Gathering

In *Magic: The Gathering* players purchase packs containing a random assortment of
cards. Different cards have different rules on them, which players use to assemble
into decks of cards. Once each player has assembled what they think is an effective
deck of cards, all with individual values and effects, they face off. Each takes turns
drawing cards from their decks until one player loses a certain amount of health,
and the other wins. Some cards are monsters that a player summons to attack the
other's health, others are spells that can affect a player directly, and others provide
the player with resources that power their abilities. Across the thousands of unique
cards that have been released, there are hundreds of distinct rules.

People enjoy *MTG* for several reasons. Mark Rosewater, one of the early members
of the *MTG* research and development team, created a system over several years for
defining and naming the different players based on the behaviors he had observed
among players. Following is a summary of the actual classification system that
Rosewater used to describe *MTG* players.

MTG Personas: Timmy, Johnny and Spike

Rosewater's personas for *MTG* are based on three principal types:

- Those who want to have fun (Timmy)
- Those who want to express themselves (Johnny
- Those who want to prove something (Spike)

Enjoying the Game: Timmy

Timmy is a player who enjoys the game for the game's sake. Rosewater says that
Timmy plays to "have a good time," which isn't helpful on its own but suggests
that Timmy likes the things inherent in the actual process of playing, rather than
anything that happens before, after, or around the game. Rosewater identifies four
subtypes of Timmy:

- **Power gamers:** Want to dominate the game by having the most powerful cards.

- **Social gamers:** Less concerned about winning or losing, and simply enjoy the idea of getting together with friends.
- **Diversity gamers:** Enjoy the huge variety of cards offered by *MTG*. They enjoy collecting, seeing the artwork, and playing with rare cards.
- **Adrenalin gamers:** Enjoy unpredictability, such as the thrill when an unlikely event turns the game around for them.

Expressing Yourself: Johnny

Second, is Johnny, a player who wants to express something. For these players, the game is a platform for their own creativity. They could be writing or playing a musical instrument but they've chosen *MTG* as one of the ways to express their uniqueness. The Johnny subtypes include the following:

- **Combo players:** Like to find powerful strategies that depend upon combinations between cards. Unlike Spike, this player is more concerned with strange and unexpected combinations more than winning for winning's sake.
- **Offbeat designers:** Motivated by strange themes, such as creating decks around a particular type of monster.
- **Deck artists:** Look to express an idea over a concept of winning. (I created an *MTG* deck around a red, white, and blue card called the Lightning Angel and declared that it represented the United States Air Force, so perhaps I'm a deck artist.)
- **Uber Johnnies:** Stubborn players who want to use weird cards that nobody else uses and show that they can make them work.

Proving Something: Spike

Finally, Spike represents players who enjoy the game because they want to prove something. Their pride is closely related to whether they win or lose, and they see the game as a mental or mathematical puzzle that they can solve. Subtypes of Spike include the following:

- **Innovators:** Look for ways to use newer cards in the game to overcome older strategies.
- **Tuners:** Look toward successful strategies applied by other players and then tweak them to attain slight statistical advantages over other opponents.
- **Analysts:** Focus on the meta-game; they're concerned about trends in gameplay occurring with other players. When the innovators develop a new deck

strategy that becomes popular, Analyst Spike attempts to play with decks designed to beat them.

- **Nuts and Bolts players:** Feel that improving their tactical gameplay—putting on a good poker-face and choosing the right actions during each round of play— is the key to winning.

Critique of Timmy, Johnny, and Spike

Wizards of the Coast has enjoyed years of benefits from guiding its game design process, and in that respect, the trio of Timmy, Johnny, and Spike is a success. Spike and Johnny are particularly well-designed personas, and the nuances presented in their subtypes strike me as subtle differences rather than entirely new types of characters.

Nevertheless, Timmy is strained by too many subtypes. It isn't enough to say that players enjoy playing the game for the fun of it because all gameplay is ultimately about fun. The Adrenalin Timmy and the Power-Gamer Timmy appear to be closely related; they are players focused on the inherent game mechanics, like to win, but don't want to invest a lot of effort in trying to win over everything else. The motivation for Social Timmy seems quite different; he likes to organize events and get people together and looks at *MTG* more as an opportunity to gather with others—he'd probably be just as happy playing another game, except that the popularity of *MTG* makes it easier for him to interest people in a group activity. Finally, the Diversity Timmy might be best renamed to Collector Timmy, who is more interested in rarity, completing collections, and having things that others don't. Perhaps the following five categories would be a simpler, motivation-centered list of personas:

- **Timmy, the power gamer:** Enjoys winning but not tinkering with game mechanics. He prefers simpler cards that don't require as much deck building.
- **Tommy, the organizer:** Enjoys hanging out with friends.
- **Tammy, the collector:** Enjoys collecting cards; rarer and older cards make her gasp with delight.
- **Spike, the tournament player:** Cares mostly about winning; he's the most likely to show up at tournaments that pit him against other hardened players.
- **Johnny, the maestro:** Enjoys composing decks into cool combinations which express his creative genius.

Most people probably start out as Timmy or Tommy and morph into the other categories over time, becoming hybrids but never quite abandoning their original motivators. Thus, Timmy might become a Spike. Over time, as he learns more about game mechanics, he becomes increasingly interested in winning and begins to focus on the things that provide a statistical advantage. Likewise, Tommy might become a Johnny because a large part of the reward that comes from creative expression is the ability to share it with friends. This evolution is not unlike how a business person could cultivate an interest in game design to create more enjoyable experiences, or how a software engineer might want to learn some graphic techniques for building better interfaces.

Like the other tools presented in this chapter, the case of Timmy, Johnny, and Spike is intended to help you consider the different motivations that players have, as well as the ways different people wish to be perceived. This will help you develop a set of questioning techniques for learning what your customers really care about—which is the subject of the next section.

Turning Motivators into Questions

Now that you understand a lot more about online game motivation, you're prepared to improve your persona interviews by asking questions oriented around some of the motivational categories discussed previously. You need to vary your question-and-answer format a bit, but one recommendation is to ask negative questions: In other words, rather than asking potential customers if they'd like a particular feature in your game, ask them how they'd feel if a certain feature were removed. For example, how would people feel if Facebook didn't allow photo uploads?

Similarly, you can ask them why they haven't used certain features. These types of questions can reveal a lot about your customers and the way you'll want to think about your experience design later.

The examples used in this chapter draw from the motivational models that exist within games. However, many of the same motivations work well in social media websites and other technology products. Competition drives people to win points (and friends); cooperation leads people to form social connections with each other by helping each other out. Posting content and sharing messages is a form of creativity, and earning recognition is both a form of achievement and socialization. Whenever possible, try and compare the motivations that exist in games—because the answers to what people enjoy in games may suggest particular motivations that will lead to features in almost any product. Remember the mantra of this chapter: Your customer is a player. Your goal is to determine how they'd like to play your product.

The following sections include some sample questions that you can adapt to create questions for your own game. Naturally, these won't all be applicable to your situation, but with a little creativity, you can get to the heart of what your customers care about.

Cooperation

Questions about cooperation should focus on identifying the things that players do or don't do pertaining to social game play—mostly things related to their ability to work with their friends to accomplish goals, or to deepen their sense of social contact:

- How long were you playing before you attempted a feature that required help from your friends?
- Do you like features in which you can team up to complete big challenges that can be finished only with help from your friends?
- How would you feel about a collecting feature in which any of your friends could contribute toward a shared collection?
- Do you like the idea of forming your own guild or team within the game?
- How do you feel about expanding your land in *FarmVille* by asking your friends to become neighbors?
- Why haven't you used the feature of *Castle Age* in which you can add your friends to an Elite Guard, helping you complete hard quests?
- Would it be fun if everyone in your friend list could win a special badge if you all agreed to reduce your carbon emissions by 20 percent?
- Would you be willing to ask your friends to play the game?

Competition

Questions about competition should be focused on the parts of the game that enable players to confront each other directly (such as a head-to-head battle) or indirectly (by comparison, such as leaderboards or competition for scarce resources).

- Would you like it if the game included a chart that showed which players have been defeated by other players?
- Are you more interested in leaderboards that show how you are doing compared to your own friends?
- How do you feel when you see a friend in *Bejeweled Blitz* who is only a few points ahead of you?

- Would you be comfortable if players could challenge you directly in the game? What if they could unilaterally decide to attack you?
- Why don't you use the feature in *Mafia Wars* that lets you attack other gangsters?
- Would you be interested in a feature in which certain ultra-unique items were added to the game, but you had to outbid other players?

Achievement

Achievement-oriented questions should focus on the things that give the player a sense of accomplishment, fulfillment, or completion:

- How would you feel if *Mafia Wars* had no levels in it?
- Why did you complete so many collections in *Castle Age*?
- Would you post something on your wall if we gave you a badge for completing a real-life challenge involving improving your physical fitness?
- Why don't you like to share the badges you've received with other players?
- Why have you completed so many world-event achievements in *World of Warcraft*?
- How long did you have less than 100 percent profile completion on LinkedIn?
- Would you alter your play style to use the game at unusual hours to gain special benefits?

NOTE You'll notice that the above questions are all centered around the relationship between feelings and experience. The opportunity is to reinforce certain behaviors with positive emotions—while also uncovering why your customer avoids certain actions.

Immersion

Immersion questions are some of the trickiest and most varied. This is where you can find out how much the player is customizing, inventing, learning, and "living" in your game. They are important because they reveal opportunities for you to create memories in the mind of your customer—which is the real product of any experience

- What do you think about your animals in *Zoo Kingdom* when you aren't playing?

- At what point during *FarmVille* did you get more concerned about how pretty your farm looked?
- Have you read any of the background stories about the various races in *World of Warcraft*?
- Would you use a feature in which you get to design how your character looks in precise detail?
- Do you feel that seeing a person's real avatar from Facebook while playing a game takes you out of the experience?
- Do you lose the sense of time on Wikipedia, traveling from one article to the next?

Interpreting Answers

You've done a bunch of work learning about your customers. What do you do with all this information?

Personas won't do you any good unless you act upon what you've learned. Even before you make a game, you can make simple changes in your business. For example, consider a few changes you could make if you learn that customers are interested in…

- **Cooperation:** In a game, this might include features where players work together to take down powerful opponents—but you can also find cooperative elements in many places outside of games; for example, reviewing and commenting on books on Amazon.com is an example of bringing cooperation into a commercial experience.
- **Competition:** Games can have leaderboards and head-to-head battles between players. Returning to the Amazon.com example, this includes things like ranking all the reviewers based on who's made the most helpful contributions. An important thing to keep in mind is that everyone needs to have a sense that they could eventually "win" over others—if your system doesn't offer an opportunity to rise to the top, then it isn't really a competition.
- **Achievement:** Utilize systems that communicate exactly what the person has achieved. Games use systems like levels, badges, and awards to recognize achievements.
- **Immersion:** Include elements that reinforce the memory and uniqueness of the experience. The best games offer unique experiences. The real world can take advantage of this too; consider how each Apple Store completely immerses each visitor in the world of Apple products, complete with their Genius Bars, uniformed staff, and consistent look-and-feel.

In the chapters that follow, you'll learn about different types of fun—and the game systems that appeal to different people.

AMAZON.COM'S COMPETITIVE REVIEWS

At the start of 2010, the top Amazon.com reviewer was Harriet Klausner, who had submitted more than 20,000 reviews. However, Amazon.com changed the formula to focus more on recent, high-quality reviews, which has made the system more dynamic. Someone with only a few hundred helpful, current reviews now has a chance to become #1. This is good game design for competitors because it makes it possible for new people to break-in—which may not have been possible under a system that just counted the number of reviews taken.

Differences in Real versus Online Identity

One of the things you need to be keenly aware of is that people who are online act in ways often quite different from their real-life behavior. As you get to know your customers, try to understand how they act within the online world, and realize that you need to address online behavior within your game. In particular, the high emotions that run within competitive games can tend to inspire the worst behavior among many players. The artists at Penny Arcade summed this up in a famous not-safe-for-work comic that you can find online by searching for "John Gabriel's Greater Internet Theory."

The Online Disinhibition Effect

Why is online behavior so different? John Suler, a psychologist with Rider University, has dubbed this the *online disinhibition effect*, the tendency of people to behave in a way they never would in the physical world.

First, in any environment in which players are anonymous, they won't feel that their reputation is on the line whenever they make a statement. In a 2008 study at Nagoya University, researchers asked subjects to play a game in which they had the opportunity to violate the rules and steal a monetary reward. When given the opportunity, only the anonymous participants violated the rules. In social networks such as Facebook, this is mitigated to some extent because people need to use their real names, but because many games obfuscate this identity, you may begin to see similar behaviors, such as the griefing style of play that Bartle was concerned about.

Online participants have sometimes exploited the weak user registration systems—most of which allow you to create as many accounts as you have email addresses—to create "sock puppets," fake accounts used entirely to post messages from an alternate identity. On Wikipedia, this is sometimes used to post articles that people don't want to have associated with their real name, or to prop up the number of votes involved in "deletionist versus inclusionist" squabbles (disagreements between people who want a particular Wikipedia article deleted or not). In games, people sometimes create alternative accounts in which they act in disruptive or hostile ways that vary from their "main" account. Think this is limited to crafty teenagers? Think again; the CEO of Whole Foods was caught posting messages under a sock puppet in an attempt to manipulate his and a competitor's stock price.

The implications of anonymity are something you need to carefully consider when you think about personas and motivators involved in your game.

Even among people who know each other, the absence of face-to-face communication such as body language—or even the subtle audible cues that might be present in a telephone conversation—can lead to an escalation of negative feelings. Messages intended as sarcasm or humor can quickly become misinterpreted, leading to nastiness. Emoticons such as J and L have appeared to help people convey some of the same emotional cues. Research indicates that people are overconfident about their ability to convey their emotional state through electronic messages. Perhaps things such as gifts, experiences, and the like are an opportunity for games to give online communities much better ways to communicate feelings—although they will have a long way to go.

The asynchronicity of most online communication—and social games in general—was addressed earlier and in Chapter 2. It's another thing to consider as part of online identity as well; the way in which people engage and disengage with conversations is much different from the way we normally develop our thoughts in a linear conversation. The extent to which this is changing our modes of communication is still being understood.

How comfortable are your particular customers with online messaging? Would they be receptive to sarcasm or irreverence that might be hard to deliver through text? How likely are they to exploit multiple user registration by creating sock puppets or other forms of "gaming" your game? These are all issues to consider when designing your personas as well as your game systems.

Is It All in Your Head?

Another phenomena observed by Suler is what he calls "solipsistic introjection," or the "It's All in My Head." Because text flows directly into the mind, without the other cognitive machinery that may be involved in oral communication, our mind fills in the blanks by imagining them as characters. Because they are characters, we might imagine ourselves in all sorts of emotionally charged situations (for example, romantic or aggressive). These feelings may lead us to do or say things with that person online that we wouldn't consider in a face-to-face context. It's possible that games amplify this effect: For example, a positive relationship with a person in a game might result in a sense of closeness to that person that would not have existed in real life.

What if people move in the opposite direction—thinking that the "characters" they envision people to be are less real? After all, if they are just characters, someone might feel that they can treat them in any way their imagination allows, leading to antisocial interactions. Games reinforce this by existing within fictional worlds; often, you'll hear a gamer rationalize an antisocial behavior by describing it as "only a game." On the other hand, games exist in part to separate us from our daily lives and enable us to explore things that we'd do only in a safe environment—so when this imagination can be channeled in a positive manner, it is often welcome. How will your different personas interact with other players and fictional characters you present in your game?

The Leveling Effect

Finally, online communities have a leveling effect. We're more comfortable saying and doing things without regard to whether someone is an authority figure. In many ways, this is an original advantage of games: to place people in cooperative and competitive situations in which the rules define the outcome, rather than any authority hierarchy. (Although authority figures have a duty not to exploit their position to gain advantage in a game, as with several of the Roman emperors who performed as gladiators.)

The implications of online behavior are complex: The best way to understand it better is to identify games and products closest to your own and closely observe the communication that occurs within the game, and in the communities and message boards that surround the game. As you learn how your particular customers interact with each other, you'll be able to refine your personas—which will allow you to channel behaviors and desires into positive outcomes for your business. For example, are your customers more likely to follow a few key opinion-leaders in the community—or are they more democratic? Do they prefer cooperation or competition? These motivations and preferences will have a profound impact on the type of features you'll include in your products.

Chapter in Review

Player personas can help your team understand the different categories of people who will play your game—as well as other products that would benefit from game-like qualities. Different tools including mythical archetypes, motivational models, and interviews can help you collect and refine information that you can use to design fun features for your customers. The Social Gameplay Motivations model—based on research pertaining to how people behave in online games—can help you identify elements of cooperation, competition, achievement, and immersion that might work for your product.

Personas are a tool for helping you make decisions. By understanding who your customers are and what motivates them, you're on your way to benefitting from the rest of the player-driven design process. Next, you'll use your personas to prioritize the experiences and features that will yield the greatest business results.

Choose Your Path

The following list gives areas of the book you might want to visit next.

- If you'd like to learn more about what makes things fun, continue on to Chapter 5, which looks at the psychology and neuroscience of fun and identifies 42 starting points you can consider to make a great game.
- If you were intrigued by the idea of the mythical archetypes discussed in "The Hero's Journey" section, you can skip forward to Chapter 9, which expands on this idea and shows how you can use it for both the narrative of the game and the customer stories that define their experiences.
- What sort of games do you like? If you'd like to go online and take a simple quiz that reveals whether you're mostly interested in cooperation, competition, achievement, or immersion, go to http://game-on-book.com/ and enter **quiz** in the secret code box.

5 Fungineering

n this chapter, you'll learn:

- Why things are fun—the neuroscience and psychology that make games work
- Sixteen basic motivations behind the things you like
- The power of emotion in games
- The importance of rules for having fun
- Forty-two different features that people love
- How to play a brainstorming game to develop more fun ideas of your own

At Disney, the experience designers are called imagineers, a blending of imagination and engineering. Like the theme park attractions crafted at Disney, games exist entirely in the landscape of the imagination—but games also involve you more interactively than a ride or movie. This chapter discusses aspects of games that make them "fun."

When you design an experience with fun as its goal, you increase engagement, involvement and memory. Anyone can do this—not just designers at a major entertainment company. You can call it *fungineering*.

Why Adults Never Outgrow Stickers

A year before I began this book, I set out to do one of the more challenging and rewarding jobs I've ever done: teaching a five year old child how to read. When I saw that she understood how to read a new word, it was an exhilarating feeling—that I had successfully passed knowledge on to a new generation. To succeed, I needed to figure out how to make it fun for her.

I turned to one of the time-honored reward techniques known by kindergarten teachers around the world: stickers. Kids love stickers. They love the way they look, they love the recognition, and they love showing other people that they've succeeded. Stickers are great because you can get a ton of them for almost no money, they don't cause tooth decay, and only a few of them will go a long way.

As our "reading game" evolved, I started using stickers in new ways. I turned them into a currency: After accumulating enough stickers, my student could turn a complete set in for another reward, such as a game from the toy store. Beyond their initial value as a collectible and a visible form of recognition, the stickers started acquiring a perceived value. When earned, she wanted to get more—and the knowledge that a certain amount would translate into additional rewards served as specific goals. She started thinking of the stickers as an investment.

Adults love stickers, too, although we call them by different names. When I was a kid, the Green Stamps system was popular: You would "earn" stamps by making purchases at participating grocery stores, gas stations, and other merchants. When you collect enough stamps, you could exchange them for catalog items. Although Green Stamps are no longer as pervasive as they were in the 1980s, they've been replaced by a plethora of new reward programs: frequent-flyer miles from your airline, point-reward programs on your credit card, and hotel frequent-stayer programs. A company called Upromise has even turned the concept into a college-savings program for online purchases.

 IMPRESARIO Remember that a major theme of this book is to pretend that your business is a game; think through all the aspects of marketing, product design, and customer service and consider whether they could be made better by reconceptualizing them as game features, comparing them against the motivators that game designers might use.

Endowment Effect and Loss Aversion

Why do reward programs work so well? One explanation is that they play upon a basic psychological principle that behavioral economists call *endowment effect*, the tendency for someone to value something they already own more than they'd be willing to pay to purchase a new but equivalent object. The twin to this principle is *loss aversion*, the tendency for people to dislike losing what they've already gained. These compulsions are so strong that most of us would prefer to avoid any risk to what we've earned before we'd worry about gaining anything more. When you earn reward points, you hate the thought of letting them lapse, or diluting them with a competitor's program. Although it's irrational, you're often willing to pay a little more to stay loyal.

Endowment effect and loss aversion explain not only the allegiance to rewards programs, but also a wide range of other behaviors. It explains why investors sell their winning stocks and hold onto their losers, often resulting in disastrous long-term performance. In the gaming world, these effects explain why numerous MMORPG developers find it so difficult to compete with *World of Warcraft*: People place great value on the characters they've invested in and the equipment they've earned. The longer they continue to play, all the while gaining more levels and equipment, the more loyal they become.

It turns out that these tendencies—like all the other motivators you learn about in this chapter—are rooted in our biology. In your brain is a small, almond-shaped structure called the amygdala, which is responsible for the emotion of fear. The amydala evolved to help us deal with fight-or-flight situations in the primeval forest. Should we climb up the tree to get away from the tiger, or is our only option to fight? When you experience a fight-or-flight reaction, you might breathe harder, feel your heartbeat race, or break-out in a sweat. It's your brain's way to prepare you for a life-and-death struggle. However, the neural circuitry that evolved to save your lives hasn't kept pace with the rapid development of technology and modern culture—the amygdala leaves you with primitive responses to things such as the stock market, loyalty programs, and computer games.

We know that the amygdala is responsible for loss-aversion behavior because researchers have found that individuals who suffer damage to their amygdala can actually make better investing decisions in controlled experiments. Neuroscientists at Stanford University, Carnegie Mellon, and the University of Iowa collaborated on an experiment in which individuals were initially given $20. During each round of play, each participant was asked whether they'd like to "invest" $1 in a chance (determined by a simple coin toss) to win $2.50. If they lost the coin toss, they'd lose the dollar. In mathematical terms, the correct decision would be to always invest because the expected outcome of each round (weighted by probability) is to walk away with an average of $1.25. Intellectually, most people recognize that a 25 percent rate of return is quite good. However, most people would rather keep the money they already have rather than risk the loss—except that people who suffered damage to their amygdala had a much higher rate of return because they made unemotional decisions.

Although some games, such as a survival horror genre, focus on the emotion of fear, there's a lot more that goes into a loyalty system to make it effective. After all, you need to make the experience of acquiring reward points (or stickers, stamps, or badges) fun. In game terms, a reward points system is a type of collecting game. Collecting is inherently fun for other reasons that you learn more about as you read this chapter.

In the sections that follow, you'll explore the basic motivations that drive most people—all of which are rooted in evolutionary biology. From there, you can identify specific types of game mechanics that leverage these basic motivations—all of which you can use to create social games that can energize any business experience.

This Is Your Brain on Games

Whenever considering what makes games fun, remind yourself that the brain is an incredibly complex system—the most complex system that science is currently aware of! The amygdala, which can be implicated within the role of fear and loss, is only one part. The brain includes structures for reward and pleasure, such as the nucleus acumbens—and a seahorse-shaped structured called the hippocampus, where you store your memories. Collectively, these are parts of the brain that are part of what is sometimes called the limbic system—the parts of the brain where emotion and memory are deeply intertwined. A memory or experience is not simply a series of events. Memories are wired to emotional triggers that help you make decisions based on a startling number of inputs that would be too hard to think through on a purely cognitive basis. A few of the major parts of the brain involved in gameplaying are illustrated in Figure 5-1.

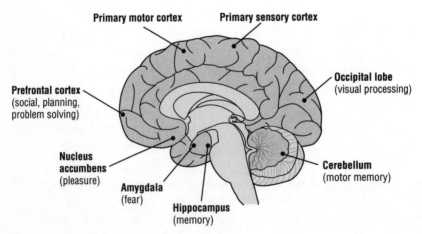

Figure 5-1: Major Neural Structures for Games

The limbic system is closely connected to the prefrontal cortex, the part of the brain where we make plans and solve problems. This may be a large part of why solving problems or thinking about the outcome of games is so pleasurable. Another function of this structure is involved in trying to predict the motivations and beliefs of other people, which suggests that problem solving, emotion, and social behavior are part of one large system. One of the explanations for why the human brain grew so much larger than other mammals is that humans are capable of complex social behaviors that have given rise to city-states, nations, corporations—and the guilds and factions within online games.

Other parts of the brain are involved in playing games as well: Large strcutures, radiating from the occipital lobe (the area at the back of your brain) are involved in receiving and interpreting visual input. The cerebellum, one of the more ancient parts of the brain, helps you learn and coordinate your motor skills—a significant aspect of physical sports or any game in which hand-eye coordination is relevant. Conscious control of muscles is handled by the motor cortex, an area toward the top surfaces of your brain; the sensory cortex, another significant area around the top surfaces of your brain, is involved in receiving and synthesizing sensory stimuli. These systems combine through a complex set of relays and interconnections, all contributing toward the judgments and decisions made during gameplay.

An exploration of the role of different parts of the brain within games could easily fill a book of its own, so neuroanatomy won't be covered. Instead, consider two observations that can help you think about games.

- **Games seem to involve many areas of the brain.** Everything from movement, pleasure, problem solving, social organization, and language—and it is this holistic involvement of so much of the brain that makes games so engaging. Consequently, it is this weaving-together of several facets of gameplay that may yield compelling games.
- **A common denominator between the different parts of the brain involved in fun is emotion.** You imbue stories and memories with emotion; and it is your involvement with symbols, stories, and experiences that make games so fulfilling. As you think about the example of providing stickers as a reward for a reading game—and the comparison to things such as loyalty reward systems—keep in mind that "points" are actually only blunt cognitive instruments for changing or creating compelling experiences. Only when they are combined with emotion do they take on sufficient depth to create long-term memories and transformational experiences.

Sixteen Human Motivations

Marketing 101 teaches you that it's usually a lot better to focus on the benefits of a product over its features. For example, it's more important to understand that a car is designed to save your life in an accident—not simply that it has crumple zones. You may not understand the advantage of crumple zones, but you sure do understand survival. Appealing to a basic human motivation about preserving your life and safety has more impact than any technical description.

Games have the appearance of pure entertainment, but the reason they're captivating is because they act on psychological and physiological motivators. To see how that's the case, consider what it would sound like if you described *FarmVille* only in terms of its features:

- Advancing through successive levels as a farmer
- Interacting with a 2D graphical interface that shows a farm
- Clicking the screen to plant, fertilize, and harvest crops
- Selling the crops at a market
- Accumulating play money to buy decorations for your farm
- Turning your friends into farm "neighbors" to complete advanced tasks

That explanation isn't that compelling. (Many people in the game industry were surprised when a game about operating a farm became so popular.) The narrative structure of the game—running a farm—is easy to understand, which helped make it accessible to a large number of people. Although the features and rules created the framework for a successful game, it is the way *FarmVille* made people feel that catapulted it to success:

- You have the feeling of owning, growing, and nurturing.
- You feel more connected to your friends.
- You gain a feeling of mastery and control over your environment.
- Among friends who are also playing, you become more important because you get to provide them with materials that can make them more successful.
- You feel like you're completing and organizing interesting collections.

In games, the benefit of playing is often the emotional payoff. The point systems and reward mechanisms are just ways to provide the player with feedback that they are advancing toward something with emotional value. As explained in the previous section, the more you can weave emotion into the experience of play, the deeper your connection to the player can become.

Emotion is a complex subject, and psychologists and neuroscientists haven't even agreed upon a consistent definition for it. The English language has at least several hundred emotion words—words as diverse as guilt, joy, pride, lust, anger, and exaltation. Emotions extend beyond the brain, moving you. You tremble with fear; you burn with lust. Much of the potency and experience of emotions comes from their physicality. Emotions play a role in everything you do: They help you form expectations about the future, reward or punish you, shape your behavior, give you the ability to make "gut decisions" and give your stories depth and meaning.

The building blocks of emotions are your motivators, which appear to be inborn behaviors and instincts that help you survive. A challenge with classifying motivators is that there is still so much unknown about the brain, and whether classifications have any specific biological basis. Most of the understanding about motivation and emotion is based on observations of people and animals, rather than any reverse-engineering of the brain.

Historically, many psychologists had a tendency to divide human motivators into dualistic categories: for example, pleasure and pain. Others described it as *intrinsic* (your built-in, hardwired desires) and *extrinsic* motivators (those that come from outside yourself).

Around 2000, Dr. Steven Reiss, a psychologist with a strong interest in human motivation, was frustrated by this narrow, dualistic approach. In response, he developed a testable system of sixteen biologically based human desires that are, as it turns out, more specific and useful for game designers. Given the imperfect knowledge, any list of motivational categories is incomplete; nevertheless, Reiss's categorization, summarized in Table 5-1, benefits from the virtue of simplicity—and you may find that it helps to think about some of the major motivators that can give rise to emotion. Furthermore, these motivations can also help you identify, brainstorm and associate characteristics that may be useful for describing the player personas covered in Chapter 4.

Table 5-1: Reiss's Sixteen Basic Motivators

Motivator	Object of Desire
Power	Influence
Curiosity	Knowledge
Independence	Self-reliance
Acceptance	Be part of a group

continues

Table 5-1: Reiss's Sixteen Basic Motivators *(continued)*

Motivator	Object of Desire
Order	Organization
Saving	Collecting things
Honor	Loyalty to one's parents, community
Idealism	Social justice, equity
Social contact	Companionship
Family	Raising your own children
Status	Social standing
Vengeance	Competition, getting even
Romance	Sex and beauty
Eating	Food
Physical Activity	Exercising the body
Tranquility	Emotional calm

 ARTISAN Here's a simple test you can apply against any game mechanic: Go down the list of the sixteen basic motivators, and check off the ones that are present within your game. Then, go back through the list and identify any of the motivators that should be in your game but are missing. Furthermore, if you pretend that your marketing program, customer service, or any other customer experience is actually a type of game, it can help you think about your business the way a game designer thinks about providing fun. In other words, recruit human biology as one of your allies.

By reviewing the list of motivators, you can gain an appreciation for why social games have become so popular. Early computer games lacked the capability for players to share their experiences with others in a meaningful way. Without the social aspect, these single-person games could not take advantage of some of the more powerful motivators, such as acceptance and status. These two motivators are easier to deliver within a multiplayer game experience. As you learn in the next section, games have the capability to create the illusion of situations relevant to almost any psychological or physiological motivator.

The Power of Belief and Alief

How is it that a game can appeal to motivators such as order, saving, and power? After all, you don't actually collect objects; when you grow crops of wheat in *FarmVille*, earn achievements on Xbox Live, or win a magical sword in *World of Warcraft*, these things exist only as a few electrons. They don't *really* exist. Likewise, all the military might you hoard in *Kingdoms of Camelot* won't influence the real world. Why do you care?

Horror movies provide part of the explanation. The first time I saw *Alien*, I was horrified when the creature burst forth from the stomach of one of the astronauts. It was so disgusting that I had to look away and remind myself that it wasn't real. It seems that there are two parts of our minds at work when we watch a scene like this in a movie: The logical part of our brains that knows we're completely safe, and an older, more primitive part of our brain that reacts as if the situation were real.

Sometimes, the illogical part of your brain takes over. For example, my father-in-law drives his car on dangerous, high-speed freeways in California. However, he doesn't dare drive over bridges even though traffic is slower and conditions are probably safer. This is not a rare condition. Many others suffer a similar fear of driving off the edge of bridges even though they know that the bridges are safe, and they wouldn't normally be concerned about randomly driving off the road.

In 2008, Tamar Szabó Gendler, a Yale professor of philosophy and cognitive science, wrote an influential paper on this subject, dubbing a term she called *alief*. When you have an attitude toward a situation in conflict with the reality you believe to be true, that is alief. Like the example of driving over bridges, Gendler observed how people react to the Grand Canyon Skywalk, a transparent walkway that enables people to go 70 feet beyond the edge of the cliffs. Many people make the 120 mile trek from Las Vegas to visit the Skywalk and then find that they aren't brave enough to walk on it—even though it is clearly well constructed and just as safe as any other solid surface you might walk on. That's alief at work.

In another experiment, researchers gave participants a box of Domino sugar. They were told that the sugar was really just sugar. They then gave them a couple of clear glass containers and another set of containers containing unsweetened Kool-Aid. Participants were then asked to pour the sugar into the two empty containers and then told to label the containers: one as sugar and one as sodium cyanide. Even though the participants knew that it was sugar, and that they had been in full control of the entire situation, many were still unwilling to drink Kool-Aid sweetened by sugar they had just labeled as cyanide. Even as I write this, I'm feeling like I'd act the same way.

Creators of all types of media—theater, literature, movies—have known about alief for a long time, although there wasn't a term for it until recently. Screenwriters, novelists, and game designers also know that alief isn't limited to the emotion of fear. Most of the basic motivators mentioned previously can all be invoked. To do that requires a narrative structure that gives the players' mind a story that helps them understand the game they are playing.

The basic mechanics of *FarmVille* could be presented as a purely mathematical abstraction:

- Start with a two-dimensional grid.
- Exchange a number of resource points to place a timer on one of the squares in the grid.
- Upon expiration of the timer, win a number of victory points.
- Based on another timer that runs in parallel, add back some resource points until it reaches a maximum allowable value.

However, *FarmVille* provides a plausible rationale for why your friends need to help you to achieve the best results. This is what transforms it from a boring mathematical puzzle into a game that utilizes alief: Not only do you want the farm to grow, it also bothers you when the crops start to wither!

It's as if alief is a projection of stories, truths, and perceptions from the emotional parts of your brain—able to override your purely cognitive processes. This phenomena is a reminder to designers of the power of emotion. Alief explains why things that aren't real; for example, the idea of collecting virtual items and badges feels *real enough* to be a strong motivator within games. As you design experiences for customers, ask yourself the following:

- How can I create narratives that ground the customer experience in emotionally charged visuals, words, and ideas? (If you are interested in using stories to help create experiences, you can turn to Chapter 9.)
- How can I use alief to transcend the logical mind and speak directly to older, deeper, and more emotional parts of the brain?
- Even when I can't create experiences that actually use the motivators in Table 5-1, can I make them feel real enough that they'll feel fun to customers?

Social Status as a Reward

Social networking websites were created to provide people with a better way to maintain social contact with their friends and family. Another effect—perhaps unintended—is that social networks have the power to convey social status of their members. The power of these motivators is proven by how popular social networks have become. As of January 2011:

- More than six million people use Facebook.
- More than 100 million people use Orkut, a social network owned by Google that is popular in Brazil and India.
- China has several large homegrown social networks led by RenRen.com, which in aggregate attract more than a hundred million people.

Companionship is fairly straightforward to understand; people use social networks to stay connected with people who might be separated by geography or time. This motivation is satisfied simply by posting messages and photographs on people's feeds or exchanging notes.

Whereas companionship is about maintaining connections to people, social status is deeply rooted in your genetic imperative to find and attract the best mates. The things you believe are important to gaining social status are entirely based on your perceptions of what's important to society. Perhaps the best guide to the contributors to social status goes back to Max Weber, who developed the three-component model of social stratification over a century ago. The three components include the following:

- **Wealth:** The amount of material resources someone has. Money, real estate, and ownership of capital generally increase someone's social status in society.
- **Power:** The ability to influence or control the behaviors of other people. Generally, this comes from positions of authority such as a government, religious group, or corporate office.
- **Prestige:** The degree to which someone is well known for a particular quality.

Each of the components of social status can exist in isolation to each other. For example, a government official in a democracy could have considerable power without significant wealth, or a famous scientist could have a great deal of prestige but lack in wealth and power. The importance of each component is highly dependent on the person's specific role. In addition, different cultures may perceive each element somewhat differently; in China, people may judge prestige to be more important than wealth.

With the exception of gambling, you usually can't acquire "real" power and wealth from social games but because of alief, the illusion of power and wealth is all that many people need. This came as a surprise to many people when *Zynga Poker* proved that people will buy virtual chips that they can never redeem for real money.

Although wealth and power remain virtual, you *can* acquire real prestige because you're playing with real people, and the things you achieve while playing games can become a real subject of interest and discussion within your social sphere.

Games now occupy a unique and powerful role within social networks: They can reward people with real social status. Features such as leaderboards and community spotlights that highlight top members work well because they grant the prestige that leads to this status. Chapter 6 shows you how several social media websites share many properties with games.

42 Things That Customers Think Are Fun

Now that you understand *why* games are fun, you can use the information to help evaluate ideas and determine whether they fit into the games you've imagined. This section deals with *what* specific things people think are fun. As you might imagine, people enjoy doing an infinite number of things but this section discusses 42 of the most important.

The following are three ways you can play with the information in this section:

- Go through the 42 items sequentially, absorbing the ideas and learning from them.
- Identify the category of motivator you want to tap into most, and then go down the columns in Table 5-2 to locate the Fun Things most relevant to that category. (The eating motivation has been excluded from the list; although there are some eating and drinking games, they are not plentiful enough to include in a list focused on the fun factors in social games.)
- Or play the *42 Fun Things Game*.

Rules for the *42 Fun Things Game*

It's fun and helpful to create games to assist with your own creative brainstorming. Here's a simple game you can play with the list of 42 fun things included in this section:

1. **Find a pair of ten-sided dice.** If you're a geek like me, you already have more than you can count. If not, you can get them from any hobby store, or you can download an application for your mobile phone that does the trick. If you search for "dice" on your phone's application store, you can find several free options.

2. **Roll the pair of dice, assigning one die to the first digit and the other die to the second digit.** This gives you a number between 1 and 100 (treat 00 as 100). Refer to the "dice roll" number in Table 5-2 to see which Fun Thing is indicated.

3. **Roll the dice a second time.** Then look up a second entry in Table 5-2.

4. **Now, ask yourself: How can I combine these two Fun Things into a new idea?** If you come up with something that hasn't been done before, you might have a whole new game concept that already has fun built in.

#1: Recognizing Patterns

One thing that all games share is a set of rules that govern how to succeed within the game world. Simple games such as *Tic-Tac-Toe* could be explained by only a couple of simple rules, but more advanced games can challenge the player to observe and learn the winning patterns. This is the essence of what makes games fun because the human brain is an amazingly curious, order-seeking, pattern-recognizing machine that rewards us whenever we figure something out. Some of the major types of patterns follow:

- **Visual:** Such as the game *Bejeweled*, in which players need to move the same-looking gems adjacent to each other
- **Motion:** Such as the movement of the ghosts in *Pac-Man*
- **Strategic:** Such as learning optimal opening moves in chess
- **Mathematical:** Such as learning the ideal rate for gaining experience points in exchange for your time in *Mafia Wars*

Table 5-2: 42 Fun Things

	Motivator	Power	Curiosity	Independence	Acceptance	Order	Saving	Honor	Idealism	Social contact	Family	Status	Vengeance	Romance	Physical Activity	Tranquility
										Social					Physical	
01-03	#1: Recognizing Patterns	X	X			X										
04-06	#2: Collecting	X				X	X					X				
07-09	#3: Finding Unexpected Treasure	X					X					X				
10-12	#4: Achieving a Sense of Completion	X		X		X										X
13-14	#5: Gaining Recognition for Achievements				X					X		X				
15-17	#6: Creating Order Out of Chaos					X										X
18-20	#7: Customizing Virtual Worlds			X						X		X				
21-23	#8: Gathering Knowledge		X							X		X				
24-26	#9 Organizing Groups of People					X				X	X	X		X		
27-29	#10: Noting Insider References				X					X						
30-32	#11: Being the Center of Attention	X										X		X		

Motivator	Power	Curiosity	Independence	Acceptance	Order	Saving	Honor	Idealism	Social contact	Family	Status	Vengeance	Romance	Physical Activity	Tranquility
33-35	#12: Experiencing Beauty and Culture					X								X		X
36-38	#13: Romance							X			X			X		
39-41	#14: Exchanging Gifts				X			X			X			X		
42	#15: Being a Hero	X		X				X	X	X		X	X	X		
43	#16: Being a Villain	X		X									X			
44	#17: Being a Wise Old Man	X		X	X			X			X	X				
45	#18: Being a rebel	X		X						X			X	X		
46	#19: Being the ruler	X				X		X			X	X		X		
47-48	#20: Pretending to Live in a Magical Place		X						X					X		X
49-50	#21: Listening to a Story		X							X						
51-52	#22: Telling Stories	X			X							X				
53-54	#23: Predicting the Future					X										
55-57	#24: Competition	X										X	X		X	
58-59	#25: Psycho-analyzing		X			X										
60-62	#26: Mystery		X											X		
63-65	#27: Mastering a Skill	X		X											X	

continues

Table 5-2: 42 Fun Things (continued)

	Motivator	Power	Curiosity	Independence	Acceptance	Order	Saving	Honor	Idealism	Social contact	Family	Status	Vengeance	Romance	Physical Activity	Tranquillity
66-67	#28: Exacting Justice and Revenge	X											X	X		
68-70	#29: Nurturing			X				X			X	X		X		
71-73	#30: Excitement														X	
74-75	#31: Triumph Over Conflict	X											X			
76-78	#32: Relaxing															X
79-80	#33: Experiencing the Freakish or Bizarre		X													
81-82	#34: Being Silly				X											X
83-84	#35: Laughing														X	X
85-86	#36: Being Scared														X	
87-88	#37: Strengthening a Family Relationship							X		X	X					
89-90	#38: Improving One's Health		X												X	
91-93	#39: Imagining a Connection with the Past					X										
94-96	#40: Exploring a World		X	X												
97-98	#41: Improving Society							X	X			X				
99-00	#42: Enlightenment		X	X												X

#2: Collecting

This chapter began by talking about how everyone loves to collect things. When gained, people hate to give up their possessions, and these can contribute to customer loyalty. However, loss aversion is only one of the reasons why collecting games are so popular. Now that you understand more about neuroesthetics and intrinsic motivators, it's possible to see many other reasons why collecting can be so powerful:

- **Many collections communicate status:** Harder-to-acquire objects can make people more important to their social group, especially when the collection is put on display. The form of the display could be a profile page within a game, their character avatar, or a post on their Facebook news feed.
- **Collections suggest organization:** When the player is provided with a lists of things to collect, all organized into neat categories, the need for order takes over—the set becomes a sort of to-do list that tells what you need to obtain in the game. When you're missing items on the list, it defies your need for orderliness and completion.
- **Being rewarded for collecting:** In some games, collecting items and sets might also unlock other game features or abilities that lead to a sense of increasing power.
- **Collections as wealth:** When people realize that what they collect is scarce, they'll think of it as a form of wealth, especially if the resources can be exchanged for other things they might want. Examples include loyalty reward programs, "gold" within games, or the Godfather Points you accumulate within *Mafia Wars*.
- **Collections as mementos:** Many collectible items act as a type of souvenir to remind people of the things they've done in real life, or in past episodes of the game.

#3: Finding Random Treasures

Finding shells at the beach, opening up a Cracker Jack box to find a surprise, winning a jackpot on a slot machine, or looting an epic item from a boss in *World of Warcraft* are all examples of finding random treasure. Collecting is part of the motivation here, but so is the desire for order. It is fun to recognize the patterns, figure out where and how to obtain the new things, and then repeat the actions required to uncover more treasure. Although the players know that they are going to get some sort of treasure, they don' know exactly what they'll get; but after people gets their first taste, they'll be back for more!

#4: Achieving a Sense of Completion

Completing tasks contribute to our sense of tranquility and order. Effective games are good at giving players a constant sense that they've finished something, and following that up with information on what to do next. This can take several forms:

- **Progress bars:** Tell people how close they are to finishing a set of tasks.
- **To-do lists in various forms:** Disguised as features such as "quest journals" (in MMORPGs) or lists of missions (in *Mafia Wars* and similar games).
- **Achievement systems:** For example, award players with badges for completing certain tasks. As mentioned, these could also double as a sort of collecting game.
- **Levels:** Give people a numeric representation of how advanced they are within a game.

#5: Gaining Recognition for Achievements

Achievement systems can give people a sense of accomplishment, but for them to also act as a means of recognition, the players need features to showcase them, for example:

- News feed posts in which people can brag about what they've done
- In-game activity feeds and broadcast messages
- Community spotlights
- "Titles" that can be attached to the players' name or profile page
- Virtual trophy cases and badge galleries

#6: Creating Order out of Chaos

Sorting, lining things up, and classifying objects are ways that you can obtain a sense of control over your environment. Many games give players satisfying ways to access their inner neat-freak: organizing your possessions into an inventory, ordering farms and city blocks into efficient structures, or clearing a grid of shapes in Tetris.

#7: Customizing Virtual Worlds

People enjoy leaving their mark on the world. In games, this can be achieved by personalizing an avatar and building and decorating virtual homes and items.

Experimental evidence has shown that people place great value on the things they've made. The same appears to be true in games, which may explain the appeal of "crafting systems" that allow players to produce virtual items from the raw materials made available in the game world. For less complex games, a similar satisfaction can be achieved by simply allowing people to name things: their character, their home, their pets, and so on.

This creativity harnesses several motivators including:

- Making someone feel more individualized and therefore more independent.
- Making someone feel more sexually attractive using virtual adornments, which satisfies a need for personal beauty and romance.
- Increasing virtual wealth in games that enable players to sell and exchange their creations. This further feeds a desire for collecting.
- Enhancing the player's sense of power and control via created items. Depending on game mechanics, some player-created items can also contribute to success within the game.

#8: Gathering Knowledge

Studying is not fun; being taught is rarely fun—but learning is fun. Our minds are naturally curious, and that "a-ha" moment experienced upon understanding something new is one of the purest joys of being human. As previously explained, recognizing patterns is part of what makes a game fun but so is acquiring random trivia, knowledge, and information. The trick is to immerse people in an experience that helps them absorb knowledge passively, rather than attempt to force an education on them.

One special type of knowledge is gossip: Not only does it contribute to our natural curiosity, it also helps people make sense of social structures. Gossip that acclaims certain behaviors can reinforce a desire for idealism and family, whereas negative gossip can help someone feel superior to those who have made mistakes. If you look at the comments happening in most news feeds on Facebook, you can notice that much of it is gossip.

#9: Organizing Groups of People

Although achieving a goal is its own reward, the organizing of people to achieve shared goals is also a source of enjoyment. The leader of a group may enjoy the feeling of power and social status. Members of a goal-focused group gain a sense of acceptance and companionship. This is why games include features such as guilds, organized teams, or systems that require you to get your friends to help you complete tasks.

In addition to the motivators that spur players to form groups in games, compelling reasons exist why you might leverage them as a way to help your marketing (see Chapter 8 for more information).

#10: Noting Insider References

Easter eggs are hard-to-find parts within a game, usually discovered only after exhaustive searching. More often than not, you only stumble on them because you heard about them from somewhere else. Likewise, certain names, metaphors, inside jokes, or even the use of certain numbers might suggest references to other content, games, or ideas that the players appreciate. When players detect them, it satisfies a need for order, rewards previous investments in gaining knowledge, and can even provide a sense of acceptance—the feeling of being part of an "in crowd."

#11: Being the Center of Attention

Humans are gluttons for attention. It starts with sibling rivalry when you're a child and hungry for your parents' attention—and it never stops. This is a big part of why people enjoy commenting online. In games, you can create the illusion of being the center of attention by placing the player at the middle of an epic story, or you can set things up so that the game is based on real interactions with other players.

#12: Experiencing Beauty and Culture

Games feature artwork, music, and designs that appeal to your senses. For years, the emphasis has been on immersive, increasingly photorealistic interfaces. However, newer games are exploring new artistic boundaries that sometimes look like modern art, graphic novels, or sophisticated industrial designs. Although some of the newer social network games on Facebook look campy (*FarmVille* comes to mind), it's simply an indication that designers are starting to explore new designs that can appeal to new audiences. Art design will continue to be a key area in which games differentiate themselves, and there's a big opportunity for social network games to distinguish themselves in the future.

#13: Romance

In this chapter's introduction, I explained how in 1991, when the molten surface of the earth was still cooling, and dinosaur-games still wandered the Internet, I met my wife Angela in an online game called *Gemstone*. After a series of steamy electronic encounters, we got married within the game—and later moved in together and got married in real life.

Although this was an unusual story at the time, many people have found love and romance through games since that time. Games provide ample opportunities for flirting, wooing, exchanging gifts, beautifying oneself, or performing acts of chivalry—all of which contribute to feelings of romance. Even when someone isn't interested in a real-life romantic outcome, the experience of romance is something many games can take advantage of. And although more sophistical social games such as MMORPGs have known this for a while, it remains a large area of opportunity for social network games.

#14: Exchanging Gifts

Friends enjoy giving each other gifts, and the act of giving can also create a desire for reciprocity; people often respond by giving back another gift. Facebook includes built-in gift-giving interfaces, but social network games have also come to rely upon them as a game mechanic. Virtual gifts can also increase the stickiness of the game, by bringing people back who might have become less active.

#15-19: Imagining Yourself as a Character

People enjoy imagining themselves as someone different than they are. Role-playing games such as *D&D* are an explicit way this is done, as are online social games such as *Mafia Wars*, *Road to Fame*, or other social games that exist within a narrative structure. However, the idea of pretending to be someone else is what makes a wide range of entertaining experiences possible: Attending costume parties and visiting certain rides at Disneyworld are two examples. Most forms of fiction also depend on this idea; when you identify with a character in a movie or book, often you experience their challenges as if they were you. Depending on the type of character, you might experience many of the sixteen motivators: power, independence, acceptance, honor, idealism, and romance are some of the most frequent.

Chapter 4 presents the idea of the Hero's Journey, explaining that there are a number of recurring themes that occur within fiction. Many of these are roles that players enjoy imaging themselves as. Following are a few of the major ones that you can include in the *42 Fun Things Game:*

- **Being a hero (#15):** A hero is someone who faces great personal risk— and often needs to make terrible sacrifices and decisions—for the good of others. People enjoy playing a hero because it appeals to their desire for power, independence, honor, idealism, vengeance, status, and often romance. MMORPGs such as *World of Warcraft* and social network games such as *Castle Age* focus on placing the player into the role of a hero.
- **Being a villain (#16):** Just as people enjoy the idea of being a hero, many also enjoy playing the role of villain, exploring (and surpassing) the boundaries of what's considered acceptable by society and wielding power over others. It's about the fantasy of having power without the consequences. For many people, it allows them to safely explore their own dark side. In 2010, more than 25 million people per month took part in *Mafia Wars*, in which they indulged in exactly this fantasy.
- **Being a wise old man (#16):** This Jungian archetype could also be female, although fiction has typically made this into a male role: Merlin, Gandalf, Obi-Wan Kenobi, and Mr. Miyagi. People enjoy the role not only because of the power expressed by such an individual, but because it is a high-status role that also may touch upon the motivator of family. (Typically, the mentor fulfills the role of a surrogate parent for the protagonist in a story.)
- **Being a rebel (#17):** Sometimes a person can play a role that flaunts society's rules while remaining basically good. Popular rebels from fiction include Han Solo, Robin Hood, Drizzt Do'Urden, and almost any pirate and many vampires.
- **Being the magician, a keeper of secret knowledge (#18):** People enjoy the thought of being someone who knows things that nobody else does and can do things that nobody else can. In the modern day, this role is publicly played by people like David Blaine or Derren Brown, or even by scientists possessing certain esoteric knowledge
- **Being the ruler, (#19):** A person with considerable power over other people.

Although these are some of the major archetypes that work within games, you may find that the *Mythmaking Game* introduced in Chapter 4 gives you other ideas on ways to help your customer imagine themselves as fun, epic characters.

#20: Pretending to Live in a Magical Place

Just as people enjoy pretending to be other people, many also like to imaging being in worlds different than their own: places governed by different rules and populated by interesting people and in enchanted locales. This is part of the appeal for why people read novels and watch movies, visit Disney's Magic Kingdom, and visit certain retail establishments and restaurants that transport them away from the everyday world.

#21: Listening to a Story

Many theories exist about why stories are interesting to people. They appeal to your curiosity about people, places, and things; depending on the content of the story, they can satisfy your need for romance, tranquility, and other motivators. Stories also take the abstract rules and mechanics of the game and ground them in plots, themes, and characters that are easier to relate to.

#22: Telling Stories

The flipside of listening to stories is that people also enjoy telling a story. If you watch young children playing with toys, you can notice that they're usually telling themselves a story, using the toys as props. Games can provide an environment for players to do the same thing within a more organized format. You can allow players to tell a story using sophisticated techniques that literally allow them to combine parts of the game together into their own unique narrative, or you can provide automated tools such as news feed posts, activity feeds, or other features that enable players to share parts of their in-game experience.

#23: Predicting the Future

People enjoy feeling like they are good at guessing the future. Horse-racing, stock picking, fantasy football, and virtually every strategic game appeal to the idea that people think they know enough about a situation to guess the future. Predicting the future or forecasting new trends makes people feel smart, in-control, and influential.

#24: Competition

To create an environment of competition, people need to win or lose. This can be an overt form of competition, for example, a head-to-head contest between two people; or it can be a softer form of competition, such as competing for rank on a leaderboard.

Competition works because people love the sense of power that comes with winning, and when they lose they seek revenge.

#25: Psychoanalyzing

Because you are reading a book about energizing your business with social games, it is likely that you are curious about human nature. This is a trait that many people share in common—being interested in what motivates other people and animals. This instinct can even extend to inanimate objects. ("Why does my computer hate me?") Guessing, predicting, or understanding the motivations of other people (and people-surrogates) can be a source of fun.

#26: Mystery

J.J. Abrams claimed that mystery is at the center of the enjoyment for all the television shows he has created, which includes well-known dramas including *Alias, Lost,* and *Fringe*. These and other television series rely on your curiosity about why strange things are the way they are. By striking a balance between revealing a little information (to reward people for their effort) while holding back enough (so that the desire for knowledge is never totally satisfied) you can create a compulsive, fun experience.

#27: Mastering a Skill

One way that players obtain a sense of progress is by being told that they're advancing, such as the levels mentioned in #5. Even more important is the feeling that they are getting better at something. This means that the game has to subtly increase the challenge level as the player gets better or else they'll become bored. When players are consistently feeling like they are increasing their mastery without becoming frustrated, it is called flow, which is discussed in detail in Chapter 10.

#28: Exacting Justice and Revenge

People hate injustice, and it provides a sense of idealism, tranquility, and vengeance when wrongs are righted. Many role-playing games are about heroic acts that result in restoring justice to the world. Even in games in which you play a villain, it's possible to experience personal justice. For example, if someone abuses you in *Mafia Wars*, it feels "just" when you get your friends together to beat the virtual snot out of them.

#29: Nurturing

Growing things, such as families, crops on farms, and pets, stems from your motivations for family, saving, and power. It's not surprising that these three things are the basis for three of the most popular Facebook games: *FrontiersVille*, *FarmVille*, and *Pet Society*.

#30: Excitement

In China, a company called Giant Interactive offered players a virtual treasure box that contained special prizes. The feature was so exciting and compelling that the Chinese government banned the company from continuing to offer it, causing its revenue to fall substantially.

What this shows is that excitement can be a part of any game—not simply those that feature immersive 3D environments. Elements such as suspense, horror, competitive action, and anticipation can all help create an addictive, exciting element in any game.

#31: Triumph over Conflict

Think of all the conflicts you were taught about back in high school English class: man versus man, man versus nature, man versus society, and man versus technology. All these narrative structures can provide the player with a sense of victory. The form of the conflict can be based on the story, strategy, or tactical encounter between the player and the game.

#32: Relaxing

Sometimes you just need to get away from it all, and an intense game experience just adds more stress. The great thing about many casual games is you can pop in for a few minutes and take a mental vacation, which can lead to a state of tranquility. Before the era of social games, *Mahjong*, *Solitaire*, *Tetris*, and other simple fare filled this need. Although Facebook is clogged with purportedly social games, many people play them as if they were a new kind of *Solitaire*.

#33: Experiencing the Freakish or Bizarre

In #20 it mentions how people like imagining themselves in magical worlds, but they also like things that are downright weird. In the past, people satisfied their taste in the bizarre by visiting "freak shows" at circuses (which were appalling and exploitive by today's standards). Today, due to the wonders of game technology, people can have a brush with strange beliefs, biology, and cultures from the safety of their computer.

#34: Being Silly

One of the most innovative console games in recent years was *Katamari Damacy*, in which you roll an adhesive ball over increasingly large objects. Starting with small items like paperclips and tea cups, the items gradually grow in size, so that you eventually accumulate cats, cars, dinosaurs, and aircraft carriers. The story behind this is that the King of All Cosmos (who dresses as a freakish half-king, half-clown who might be more at home at a 70s disco) had previously destroyed the stars and planets, and you must collect enough material to re-create them.

Katamari shows you how much people enjoy a completely silly experience. The world is far too serious—and too many games are serious.

#35: Laughing

Even tragedies and horror movies include small elements of laughter to break the tension and ready people for the events to come. People love to laugh—especially with their friends, with whom it provides a sense of companionship—so think of ways you can make laughter part of your experiences.

#36: Being Scared

For most people, it isn't fun to be scared—to fear for your safety. Thanks to the property of alief described earlier, people can enjoy the sensations of being scared without the actual danger.

#37: Strengthening a Family Relationship

One of the great discoveries of games is how they can be a part of modern family life. In *World of Warcraft*, families go online to play with sons and daughters who are deployed in Iraq. In *Rock Band*, parents share songs with their children that had been popular in their own youth. In *FarmVille*, grandmothers and grandchildren help each other raise barns. By encouraging cooperative play and populating a game with accessible content that has broad age appeal, you may make a game that bridges the generation gap.

#38: Improving One's Health

Many people dislike exercise, although most enjoy the feeling of being fit. Games are just starting to explore ways that game mechanics based on recognition, collection, and achievement can be used to help people stick with a fitness program. A case study in this area is explored in Chapter 6.

#39: Imagining a Connection with the Past

> *Nostalgia, it's delicate but potent...the pain from an old wound. It's a twinge in your heart far more powerful than memory alone...it takes us to a place we ache to go again...a place we know we were loved.*
>
> DON DRAPER (JON HAMM), SEASON 1 FINALE OF MAD MEN

The past is like magic; it is mostly hidden, but it connects together all things and all people. Imaging your connection with the past is potent. Your curiosity about the past is so strong that you are probably interested in completely mythical pasts, such as the history of J.R.R. Tolkien's Middle Earth—perhaps because you wish that such pasts were your own.

#40: Exploring a World

People are intensely curious about their environment. In the past, survival depended on how well you knew an area, where the best food could be obtained, and where you could find shelter. Today it's still good to know how to get in and out of places, and understanding your environment gives a sense of power and control. To take advantage of this instinct, give players an opportunity to see around the next corner of whatever virtual landscape makes up your game environment—whether a 3D environment, a set of maps, or an interesting set of cross-linked web pages. Wikipedia is a great example of a place that people love to explore for hours at a time.

#41: Improving Society

In 2008, Pew Research conducted a study that found that 97 percent of teens play games. Rather than despairing over the decline of youth culture, the study also found that some games teach teens about ways to improve the world. For example, teens learned about how public policies could impact cities through *Sim City*.

I'd like to leave the world a better place than when I came into it, and I'd like to believe that others feel the same way. Idealism is one of the sixteen motivators, so it's possible that we can appeal to the desire for great social equity within games. It's helpful to remember that games don't need to always be about blowing things up; they can also reflect many of the other things that people value in life. Chapter 6 will discuss `PracticallyGreen.com`, a website that uses game mechanics to help people become more environmentally-friendly.

#42: Enlightenment

Fictional environments have the power to show the world as it actually is, as it could be, or as it should be. Ayn Rand's novel *Fountainhead* is used as a platform for the philosophy of objectivism, or *rational self-interest*, and the video game *Bioshock* attempts to show flaws in the philosophy. The *Star Wars* universe presents the quasi-religious philosophy of the Force. Because games largely deal with decisions and their consequences, they have an opportunity to bring enlightenment to a player in a way that noninteractive fiction alone might not, which can satisfy a player's motivation for idealism.

Chapter in Review

In this chapter you learned about why things are fun and numerous features that make things fun. At this point, you're ready to dig deeper into existing social games and figure out why they work, or you could even jump ahead and start thinking about how you'd like to design your own games.

This chapter also made use of one of the principles used throughout this book: Almost anything can be turned into a simple game. The chapter attempted to take the idea of brainstorming product features and create a random way to combine fun features in novel ways. The products of this process could be thought of as a form of "unexpected treasure" and your own creativity. For fun, try taking some dice and a list of ideas and work to see if you can get people thinking more creatively over lunch. You might enjoy the results!

Two important themes emphasized in this chapter were the role of rules within games and the role of emotion within games. It isn't just that games are constructed of rules; it's that the recognition, learning, and exploration of rule systems is a big part of why games are fun in the first place. However, to create deep and memorable experiences, these rules must exist within a framework of emotional payoffs.

Choose Your Path

The following list gives areas of the book you might want to visit next.

- If you'd like to dig into a few of the popular social games played today and learn how they apply the various techniques explained in this chapter, move on to Chapter 6.
- If you like the idea of using stories to increase the power of your products, games, and customer experiences, skip ahead to Chapter 9.
- If you'd like to understand more about the important concept of flow, a powerful game design technique merely touched upon in this chapter, check out Chapter 10.
- If you'd like to go online and learn which games other readers think make best use of the fun factors mentioned in this chapter, go to `www.game-on-book.com` and enter **fun** in the secret codes box.

6 Turning Work into Fun

In this chapter, you'll learn:

- About the opportunities and risks of gamification
- How games make tasks and goals into fun experiences
- How to apply the techniques of social games to many nongaming experiences to make them fun and rewarding
- How to critically evaluate the content of games and social media experiences

Throughout this chapter, you see ways in which different social games have used elements of games such as imagination, emotion, clear progress and goal-setting to create compelling, fun experiences for players.

How Games Make Ordinary Tasks Addicting

That sunny dome! those caves of ice!
And all who heard should see them there,
And all should cry, Beware! Beware!
His flashing eyes, his floating hair!
Weave a circle round him thrice,
And close your eyes with holy dread,
For he on honey-dew hath fed,
And drunk the milk of Paradise.

Samuel Coleridge, "Xanadu," lines 47–54

When my wife and I moved into our home, we wanted to make it a special place, and one of the ways we did that was to give it a name: the Pleasure Dome. Those who interpret the name as a tongue-in-cheek nod to a hedonistic lifestyle wouldn't be entirely incorrect, but the more important reference is a favorite poem: Coleridge's "Xanadu," where the milk of paradise is a symbol for the awesome power of the imagination—and how it compels both artists and conquerors to simultaneously share their visions and act upon them.

Imagination compels us because it shows us ways we'd like the world to be, rather than what it is. When I gave my home a special name, it was because I wanted to imagine living in a place where anything is possible, and where great dreams could be dreamt. Just as names and stories can help us cross into the world of imagination, games do the same thing: They weave the player into a narrative that is meaningful— one where they occupy an important role and can impact the outcome.

Many people have recognized the magical quality of games to transport them to their own personal pleasure domes. Compare this to the recent gamification trend mentioned in the introduction—the placement of game mechanics into everyday products and businesses. Gamification has had an unfortunate tendency to suggest that common mechanics of games—badges, levels, and progress meters—are silver-bullets for shaping a wide range of behaviors. Although these are effective feedback mechanisms, what's missing is imagination and emotion, which go hand-in-hand with media, stories, and games.

Now return to the Pleasure Dome to look at how game mechanics can be applied to one form of labor that most people find incredibly boring: housework. The game *Chore Wars*, playable at www.chorewars.com and shown in Figure 6-1, illustrates how things like cleaning the bathroom, making a bed, or preparing dinner can become an adventure when presented in the right context.

You can immediately observe a few key points about *Chore Wars* that bring fun to typically mundane tasks.

- The game doesn't take itself too seriously; it knows that the idea of creating a fantasy adventure around household tasks is inherently silly.
- Different tasks are associated with rewards: experience points, and "treasure," such as various kitchen objects.
- The social aspects of *Chore Wars* enable you to involve other people to help you achieve your goals, providing a means of cooperating as a team. For example, your children can be invited to participate and "level up" their

characters based on doing various forms of household work. The overall flow of *Chore Wars* is characterized by the flowchart in Figure 6-2.

Does *Chore Wars* work? Although it is difficult to know how effective it is at changing long-term behavior, many families and households have found that it has provided an opportunity to come together and solve their housework problems. It's a necessity for games to keep things fresh and new—not simply rely upon the same content forever. In the *Chore Wars* case, the game can inject fun into tasks that would ordinarily be thought of as drudgery.

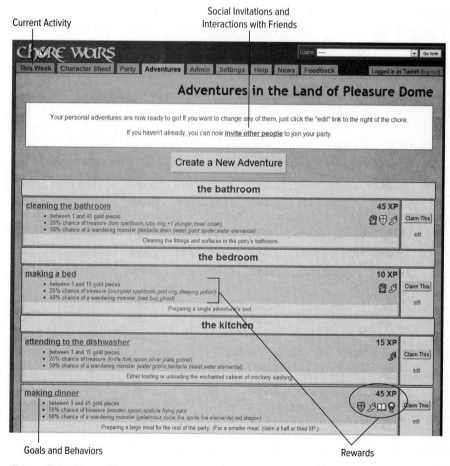

Figure 6-1: *Chore Wars*

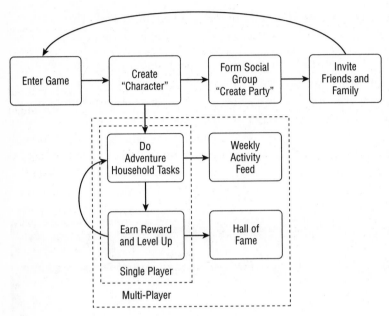

Figure 6-2: Gameplay Flow in *Chore Wars*

We have three children, ages 9, 8, and 7. We have tried every tactic imaginable to encourage our children to complete their chores and help around the house. Chore charts, allowance money, special rewards—everything fizzled after only a few days.

Enter Chore Wars! I sat down with the kids, showed them their characters and the adventures, and they literally jumped up and ran off to complete their chosen tasks. I've never seen my 8-year-old son make his bed! And my youngest actually completed an entire chore in under 20 minutes. (Usually it takes her more than an hour for the simplest job.)

A PARENT AND CUSTOMER OF *CHORE WARS* FROM TEXAS

When to Turn Something into a Game

An important point needs to be made before digging into this chapter: Not everything should be turned into a game. Sometimes the process of gameplay can add new steps, create annoyances, or get in the way of activities that might be easier without them. Following are some questions to help decide whether adding gameplay might be appropriate:

- **Is the activity something that requires the utmost speed because it impacts health or life?** For an extreme example: You wouldn't want to turn using a defibrillator into a game. You just need it to work. On the other hand, a training program that teaches people how to use a defibrillator—well before it becomes an emergency—might benefit from some sort of game-like elements.

- **Is the narrative of the game idea disconnected from the underlying behaviors you want to change?** It's often easier to come up with clever stories than it is to define game mechanics that correlate to them. Ask yourself whether the game elements or narrative get in the way of understanding the system you want to present.

- **Is the activity primarily utilitarian?** For example, if you want to gain access to a certain set of information (such as the status of a package you just ordered from Amazon) you don't want to be annoyed by additional game-like steps. However, game elements might still make sense if they can be incorporated in a way that surrounds and deepens the experience of interacting with the order-status system—without adding extra steps that slow you down.

Understanding the Business Decisions beneath Modern Games

Social games often share several (if not all) of the following elements:

- **Built-in mechanisms:** These facilitate introducing the game to friends, thus providing the game with another potential customer, while simultaneously deepening the player's engagement and commitment to the game.

- **Opportunities and interfaces:** These are for sharing progress with friends.

- **Clear pathways:** These are for understanding what to do next and for feedback mechanisms for communicating how close the player is to the next phase.
- **Elements of customization or creativity:** These enable players to individualize their experiences.
- **Recognition:** The value of fame often trumps fortune.
- **Asynchronous gameplay:** Moves can be placed independently from the order of other players' moves.

All these elements were present in *Chore Wars*: player introductions, shared progress, goal-setting interfaces, customization of your avatar, and an emphasis on granting recognition to players who have done best. Likewise, you can find these aspects present in most successful social game products. Current games have used these elements to create better games.

Glory Days: *Gods of Rock*

My own company, Disruptor Beam, set out to create a game that appeals to a fantasy that many have shared from time to time: becoming a musical superstar. In *Gods of Rock*, you can become a pop, country, hip-hop, or rock star. Figure 6-3 shows a screen shot that illustrates some of the core elements.

Simply clicking on missions or quests was not interesting enough gameplay. We want players to have the ability to contribute to certain game events in ways that are unique to them and touch their creative sides, too. A good example is the Epic Gig wherein players join with friends to perform at Woodstock-like and Lalapalooza-esque events.

When a player creates an Epic Gig, the resulting event announcement is so entertaining that players want to share it on their walls. Because it looks interesting and unique to their audience of friends and family members, those people are more inclined to join in the fun and thus become engaged in the game, too. Boring rote wall posts are out. Customized mini-stories around people's alter egos are in.

When friends arrive, they can contribute to the epic performance with basic moves such as "Rock-out." In the course of becoming a superstar, long-term players have discovered various performance moves, some of them rare, even legendary. Players make great use of these rare moves and dramatically improve applause, thus garnering extra fans and money for everyone participating. In addition, if enough contributors "call in your posse" by posting about the epic gig to their walls, a super-move will be executed to the benefit of all. In Figure 6-3, that is the coveted Mega Mosh Pit.

Figure 6-3: Gameplay in *Gods of Rock*

Carrot on a Stick: *World of Warcraft*

World of Warcraft (WoW) is one of the most successful social games in existence, with more than 12 million subscribers as of October 2010. Although it isn't played on a social network, it features extensive social gameplay—both cooperative and competitive. However, as explained in Chapter 5, social games usually need to begin with a single-player experience because that is what draws people in before they're willing to interact with others. This game makes wonderful use of a single-player experience called a "carrot on a stick." Figure 6-4 illustrates how *WoW* does this by providing clear indications of what you should do next (the exclamation point over the heads of quest-givers) and an organized list of goals that you'll want to complete next.

Character with Quest   Things to do Next

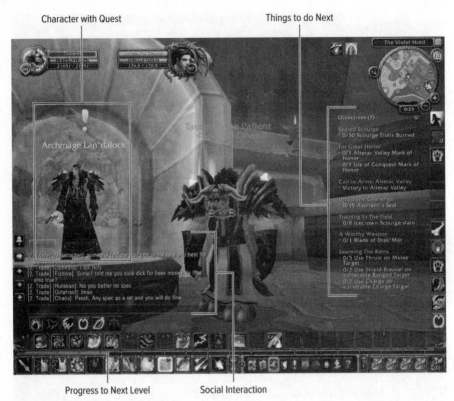

Progress to Next Level   Social Interaction

Figure 6-4: Progress and Goals in *World of Warcraft*

The organization of the *WoW* user interface shows the importance of several social and gameplay dynamics:

- The list of quests shown on the right side lists some of the things you can do next. You're constantly reminded that there's something more you can do—and you have a nearly inexhaustible supply of things to do.
- The character on the left has an exclamation point over his head, which means that he's offering a new quest, which would add to the list of objectives on the right side.
- There is a chat window in the lower-left side that enables you to communicate with other players in the game. This is helpful for contacting other

people who might want to try certain quests that require the cooperation of several partners, and for coordinating activities.

- The bar toward the bottom of the screen grows as you perform different quests, which tells you how close you are to the next level (at which point you can take on harder opponents).

These interface elements are central to the overall gameplay of *WoW*, described in Figure 6-5.

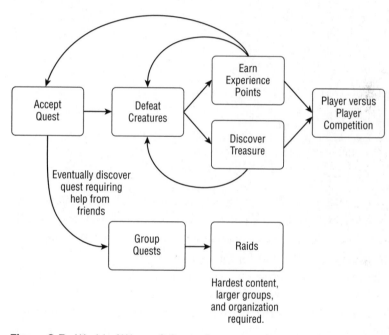

Figure 6-5: *World of Warcraft* Gameplay

There's Always Work to Be Done: *FarmVille*

FarmVille was the most popular game on Facebook in 2011, peaking with more than 80 million players and eventually leveling out to approximately 50 million players by the end of the year. Figure 6-6 describes the flow of gameplay within *FarmVille*.

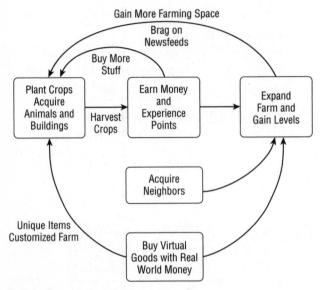

Figure 6-6: *FarmVille* Gameplay

Crops in *FarmVille* are harvested after varying amounts of time, which means that players need to revisit the game regularly. This clever mechanism for constantly reinvolving the player helps keep people actively involved in the game. Whereas *World of Warcraft* focuses the player on moving forward with a carrot-on-a-stick, *FarmVille* game mechanics are more of a carrot *and* stick—because *FarmVille* actually punishes the players who don't participate frequently enough. If you return you'll benefit, earning experience and money. However, if you fail to arrive in time, your crops wither, and you'll be forced to start the growing process over again. As you continue to play the game, you discover ways to increase yields, plant unique crops, or decorate your farm with objects that personalize your experience—unique animals and pets have proven to be especially popular.

Viral player adoption in *FarmVille* is realized by providing ample opportunities for players to brag about their accomplishments through Facebook news feed postings and invitations to become a "neighbor," which is necessary for expanding one's farm (see Figure 6-7).

Level

Reengage over Time

Limited Time Offer

Special Rare Items for Real World Money

Figure 6-7: *FarmVille* Interface

Living the Life You Imagined: *Dungeons & Dragons*

Dungeons & Dragons is one of the most influential games in modern history. One of the first games to introduce concepts such as levels and experience points within a fictional narrative, *D&D* has affected everything from fantasy role-playing games such as *WoW* to more casual social games such as *FarmVille*. The key to understanding *Dungeons & Dragons* is the character sheet, which reveals most of the elements of gameplay relevant to each gaming session.

Players in *D&D* retain a copy of their own character sheet (as shown in the photograph in Figure 6-8), which records the level, progress, powers, and possessions of their character. In many ways, *D&D* was the first significant "virtual goods" game to come into existence because much of the gameplay revolves around the acquisition of rare and magical items that enable the adventurers to perform great deeds. If you look at the basic model of gameplay that exists within *D&D*, it shares striking similarities to the models already discussed in *World of Warcraft* and *FarmVille*. The major elements of *D&D* gameplay are diagrammed in Figure 6-9.

Figure 6-8: *Dungeons & Dragons* Paraphernalia

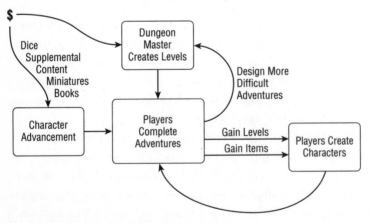

Figure 6-9: *Dungeons & Dragons* Gameplay

What is it that makes *Dungeons & Dragons* so compelling beside the continuous treadmill in which you can acquire treasure and points, which enable you to fight harder monsters (which are guarding more powerful treasure and points, which enables you to fight even harder monsters….)? The answer is the overall narrative: In a good *D&D* campaign, the players navigate a story. There's the story that the Dungeon Master creates (the person who acts as the lead storyteller, dungeon creator, and referee). There is also the story that players create in their minds—the story of how they envision their characters will evolve over time. Without story, *D&D* wouldn't be much fun at all—it would be a constant grind involving probabilities and abstract variables. In this case, it's the story that turns work into fun.

By providing players with the ability to imagine the ways in which they'll develop—and providing a systematic means to enable social groups to tell stories and navigate a set of rules for getting there—*D&D* has had staying power across four decades and inspired generations of game designers and players.

Evolving a Community: *Spore*

The popular PC game *Spore* describes itself as a "massively single player," a game in which many players coexist and share content but don't interact directly with each other. This demonstrates a new means to provide asynchronous gameplay; players can choose when they want to play and gain a sense of being in a universe populated by others without needing to arrange for gaming sessions with each other.

How can a game be social without direct interaction between players? In *Spore*, you encounter aliens created by other players without needing to communicate with them directly (see Figure 6-10). The content of the universe is created by other players who use a sophisticated creature creator capable of creating more than a billion unique aliens.

By associating each unique alien with the name of each player, *Spore* becomes a stage for players to showcase their creativity, and by eliminating the need to arrange times to play with other people, *Spore* created a unique asynchronous gameplay environment that enables you to enter and leave on your own schedule.

Spore would be fun on its own thanks to the stories and creative aspects of the game. This fun is enhanced because players have the knowledge that their creativity is projected to a community of other players. This parallels the functioning of social media: creating, commenting on, and sharing content interests with people when they know their work will be seen by others.

The creature content in *Spore* is all player created.

Figure 6-10: *Spore*'s Massively Single-Player Content

Political Drama: *Kingdoms of Camelot*

At first, *Kingdoms of Camelot* (shown in Figure 6-11) appears to be a game about building a city. However, as you become more immersed, you learn that the game is actually about the alliances and politics within the game. Although many "social games" are critiqued for not being social enough, *Kingdoms* is an exception—a game in which finding a social group and working with others is not only possible, but also necessary for success.

In *Kingdoms*, your alliance can do the following:

- Help protect you from massive assaults from other organized groups of players.
- Coordinate attacks upon your enemies.
- Pool resources and collaborate to build things that would be nearly impossible as an individual player.
- Chat with each other in real-time to coordinate activities.

Figure 6-11: *Kingdoms of Camelot*

Kingdoms presents an interesting combination of synchronous and asynchronous gameplay. Although moves are placed at any time players want, attacks are synchronized to happen at particular times. The ability to sprinkle this sort of scheduled activity into a game that otherwise enables players to enjoy a great deal of control over when and where they play is emerging as a way to enhance both accessibility and engagement.

Many games allow players to form teams and coordinate activities. In social media, "groups" typically allow members to leave messages for others who share a particular affinity. What if groups had ways to collaborate with each other while competing with other groups? Imagine the ways that the typical social media group could be energized if it took some lessons from *Kingdoms*.

Always Time to Play God: *Godfinger*

One of the more enchanting social games of 2010 was ngmoco's *Godfinger*, in which you play the role of a deity. As you grow in level, you gain new abilities—suitably divine powers, such as creating rain, hurling lightning bolts, and creating floods. Your followers collect gold for you by farming the land and produce mana by worshipping you. A scene from *Godfinger* is shown in Figure 6-12.

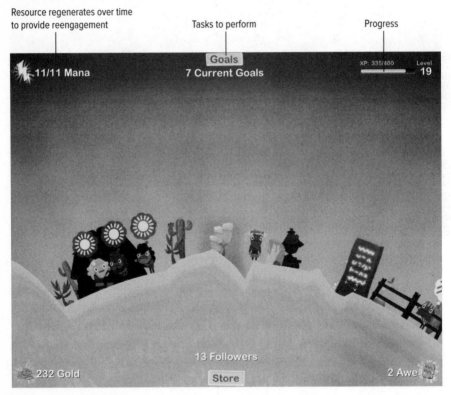

Figure 6-12: *Godfinger*

Godfinger makes innovative use of the tactile nature of the iPad: You can fling your worshippers into the air by touching them and dragging them. You can spin the world around by rotating your finger about its circumference, and you can create rain by dragging your finger from a cloud toward the ground. As you are drawn in by the interface and the acquisition of new powers, the social aspects are revealed:

- **As you level up, the game takes a picture of the way your planet looks.** These pictures can be automatically posted to your Facebook account. Because the look of *Godfinger* is unique, and these screenshots contain unique content, they tend to get a lot more interest from your Facebook friends than the run-of-the-mill news feed posts.
- **If you zoom out from your planet in *Godfinger*, you discover that you occupy a universe.** Like *FarmVille*, the planets around you can be occupied by your friends. You can visit each other's planets and help each other out, and exchange gifts that enable you to advance in the game more quickly.

The convergence of mobile devices and social gaming is a perfect fit for asynchronous gameplay. Because of the iPad's portability, players can check in with their planets more frequently than they might if they were bound to a PC-based web browser.

Godfinger is another example of how a story makes the task of placing objects into scenes more fun. Furthermore, it connects you with your friends, and lets you check-in on progress through your mobile device. Work is more fun when it is done alongside friends, includes simple ways for friends to help each other, and allows some amount of bragging. Here's a little thought experiment: How would your own business be more fun if it acted more like *Godfinger*?

Fame Is Greater Than Fortune: *Zynga Poker*

Online gambling is almost as old as the commercial Internet. However, *Zynga Poker* isn't actually a gambling game because you don't bet with real money. The innovation that drove *Zynga Poker* to more than 35 million players was a twin realization:

- The number of people who play poker as a social activity might be as large— or larger—than people who play it as a serious form of gambling.
- People don't need to win real money to enjoy playing the game. The virtual fame one earns by playing is enough to satisfy millions of people.

These aspects of *Zynga Poker* are revealed in Figure 6-13.

The potential application to business is enormous: Many companies have focused on providing direct financial incentives (discounts, prizes, free service, etc.) when in fact customers might enjoy simply getting recognition. Giving customers a fortune will cost you a fortune—but giving them fame, which might be even more powerful, is often free!

Gifts bought for table members

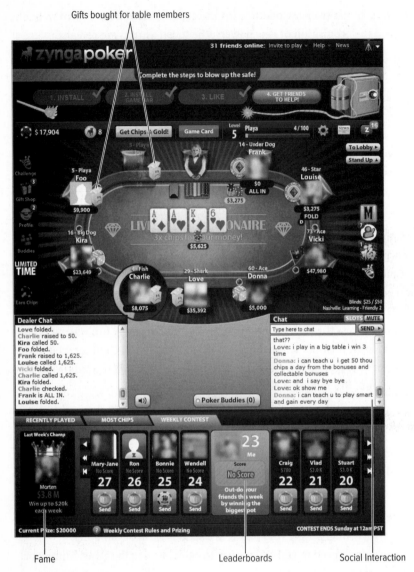

Fame   Leaderboards   Social Interaction

Figure 6-13: *Zynga Poker*

Metagames: Xbox Achievements

On the Xbox 360, players earn badges called *achievements* for completing various challenges within the games they purchase. These points aggregate together into a point system called *gamerscore* that tracks how well each Xbox owner has done overall. To ensure that each game can affect a player's gamerscore by only a fixed maximum amount, each game is allotted up to 1,000 points in a way defined by each developer.

The Xbox achievement system, shown in Figure 6-14, has resulted in surprising dividends for the Xbox Live platform: Players play games solely to win achievements, buy games to win achievements, and join websites such as 360voice.com dedicated to sharing your achievement progress with other players.

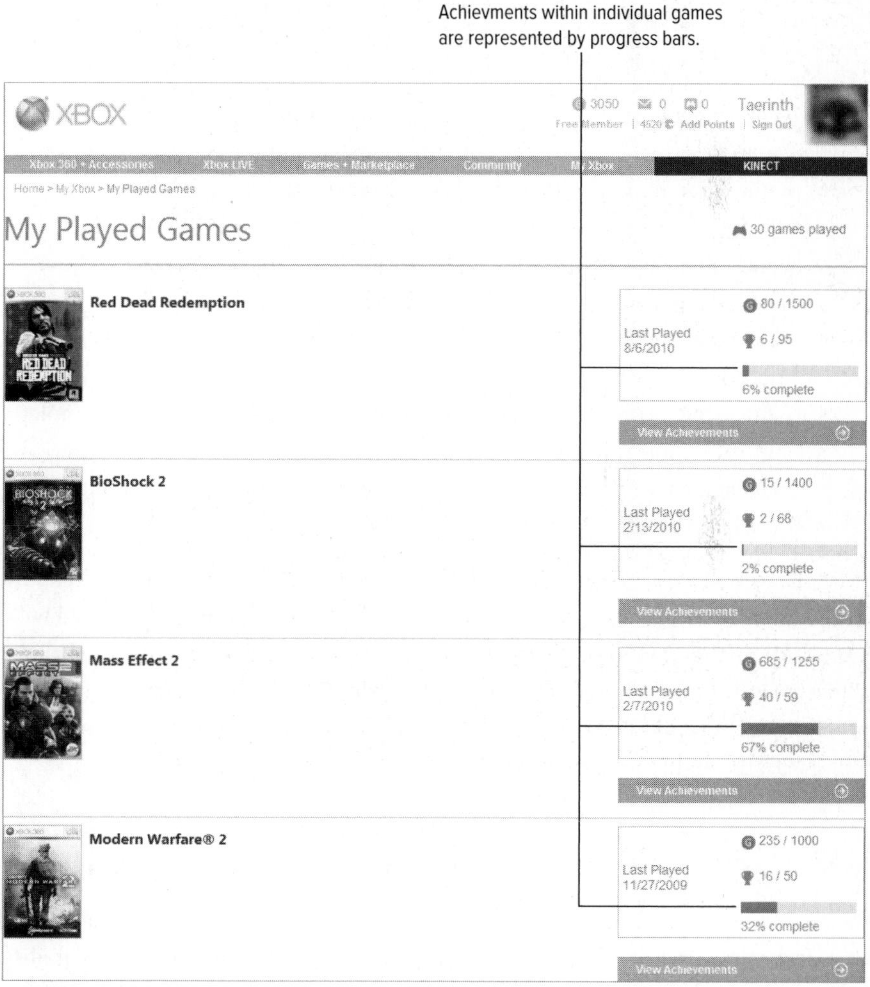

Achievments within individual games are represented by progress bars.

Figure 6-14: Microsoft Xbox Live

Microsoft didn't invent the idea of winning badges for playing games; sites such as Pogo.com had already done so. However, the Xbox proved the worth of badges in a big way. Microsoft has pointed to its achievement system as one of the reasons why people buy an average of 8.9 games per console sale—the highest "attach rate" in the industry.

Following are several reasons why the Xbox Live achievement system worked so well:

- Achievements combine across games into a player's "gamer card" that displays their total score and is sharable on other websites where players hang out.
- Achievements serve as more bragging rights for players; they add interest to games by providing a roadmap for engaging and fun experiences.
- Rather than designing the achievement system on its own, similar to how a casual game's portal might do, Microsoft effectively crowdsourced its achievement system to all the developers of Xbox games, increasing the quality and quantity of achievements overall.
- Achievements provide a standard user interface for players to learn about cool content within games.
- Achievements provide a means to compare your progress toward "completing" each game in your collection.
- Achievements give players a simple way to talk to other players about what they've done within particular games.

Many Xbox Live achievements are for strange and obscure activities that players would never bother with. By creating a system of awards, players are provided with a set of goals they can accomplish and then brag about to their friends. Without achievements, these actions would be work; with achievements, they're fun. Many other products would be far more fun if only they gave customers clear directions along with the ability to share progress.

The Problem with Serious Games

Badges, social status, fame, progress meters—these are all techniques that people outside the game industry have identified as powerful cognitive levers that can modify behavior in the same way that games do. Products created to modify a behavior or teach a skill wherein the entertainment value is secondary (or nonexistent) are called *serious games*. However, they've often seriously fallen short of expectations.

The problem with serious games comes down to a fundamental issue: their seriousness. Games need to be inherently fun. This fun comes about because of the emotional content of the game—something that happens when you connect the gameplay with peoples' passions, interests, and imagination. When these aspects are ignored, serious games are often seriously boring.

There's a need in the world for good educational software, good simulations, and good training systems. Many of these systems could also benefit from some of the basics of game design, such as progress meters to convey how close you are to achieving goals—or social components to celebrate your successes with friends. Nevertheless, most of these products can't actually be called games because they forgot to include the emotional elements that make games so compelling.

If you are thinking about creating a serious game, I applaud your desire to apply innovation to the process of learning. By raising the problems of serious games, it isn't my goal to dissuade you from trying but to help you avoid some of the pitfalls encountered by so many others in the market. The following are examples of activities that would normally be considered challenging and full of hard work:

- Learning a foreign language
- Adopting a more environmentally-friendly lifestyle
- Changing your behavior to use the stairs more often

In the sections that follow, you'll read how tasks such as these can be made more fun by incorporating emotion in the form of games.

Learning Is Fun

One of the reasons why games work so well is that they involve you in a learning process. Learning is extremely fun when it happens naturally, through a process of exploration and discovery. As many people experienced in school, it is far less fun when it's about *being taught* as opposed to *learning*.

Most people hate help systems; when they access them, it is usually out of desperation. How many times have you quit out of the tutorial mode given in the introduction of a piece of software? If you're like many people, you find that they slow you down. You want the software to be so obvious that help isn't necessary.

It isn't necessary to reveal all the details of how something works in advance. You work through a continuing process of action and reaction, learning when you observe how your actions modify the environment. When you interact with a game, you ask yourself questions such as: I wonder what happens if I move my pawn to this position? What happens when I open this chest? What is behind this door? How will my opponents react if I carpet bomb their base?

In essence, when you play a game you conduct a series of experiments. When things turn out well, you're more likely to do it again. That's learning.

Rosetta Stone

Before showing an example within a social game, consider how game mechanics are applied to the problem of language-learning within one of the most popular training products on the market: *Rosetta Stone*. In it, you can find a number of learning techniques that draw upon the successes of games.

In *Rosetta Stone*, you are not presented with the typical elements of language training: vocabulary lists and grammar rules. Instead, *Rosetta Stone* presents photos of everyday people, objects, and situations. These images are accompanied by words that appear on the screen and are also spoken for you. To advance to the next screen, you need to match a spoken word to one of the pictures; to do that, you need to figure out which rule is at work. In Figure 6-15 is one of the first screens you see while learning Spanish in *Rosetta Stone*.

Figure 6-15: *Rosetta Stone*

To proceed, you need to recognize that the difference between the two pictures at the top is that one is a man and one is a woman. When "una mujer" is spoken to you, you can advance to the next scene by correctly associating the image with the woman in the lower right.

Rosetta Stone gets you involved with language by immersing you in the world of a language, which is a world of sounds connected to images. It's the way you learn to speak as children. It's also fun: Each individual page is an accomplishment of its own, providing immediate feedback. Along the bottom of each screen, you can see how far you've progressed and return to learn more when you're ready.

Another aspect of *Rosetta Stone* is that the experience of seeing photographs may create a deeper emotional connection to the participant than text or sound might alone. However, *Rosetta Stone* is not a social game; you interact with it entirely as an individual. How can something such as language training be improved by combining the game-like features here along with the social aspects of gameplay?

Language Learning on *Livemocha*

Livemocha, shown in Figure 6-16, is a social application for language learning. Like *Rosetta Stone*, it also offers an image-enriched learning process. It has less pattern recognition and rule-discovery but instead features game mechanics and social interaction between teachers and learners.

On *Livemocha*, you gain points for participating in learning programs. However, you can also find other people to role-play with and can locate mentors who can earn points for their quality as an instructor. In the coming years, the combination of deep game mechanics from systems such as *Rosetta Stone* coupled with the more socially oriented learning in *Livemocha* have the potential to transform the way people educate themselves.

Language learning is one case benefitting from social game mechanics, but there are other cases equally promising. How about games that help you learn to become healthier?

Using Games to Improve Health

Something that must be admitted about games—at least the kind you play from a seated position—is that they don't do much to enhance physical health. Their sedentary nature leads us to burn less calories and neglect physical fitness. But could the tricks of the gaming trade help facilitate positive changes in someone's health?

Points for learning

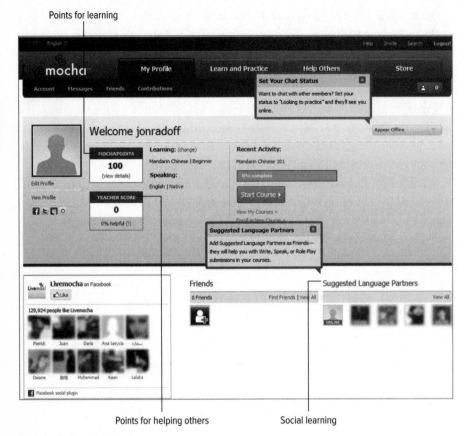

Points for helping others   Social learning

Figure 6-16: *LiveMocha*

MeYou Health is a Boston-area startup "dedicated to engaging, educating, and empowering people to achieve and maintain a healthy life." MeYou Health's parent company, Healthways, is a company that generates revenue by helping to decrease the costs of health care—largely through improvements in fitness and wellness. By investing in the creation of games, it hopes to help change people's behavior in ways that can help them lead healthier lives, while also decreasing the costs for insurers.

Health care is a challenging market for games because the adjustments people need to make to become healthier aren't fun. It requires long-term dedication, and the changes are often painful. However, MeYou Health found that with its game *Monumental* (shown in Figure 6-17), people take some positive steps toward health improvement by uniting a sense of accomplishment with a fun experience, clear progress feedback, and the ability to brag about your accomplishments socially.

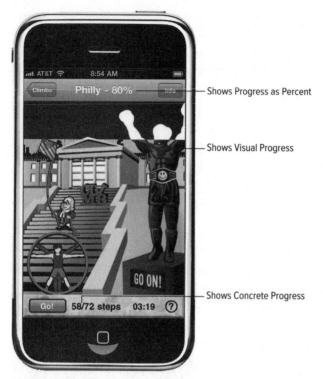

Figure 6-17: *Monumental*

The premise of *Monumental* is simple: to get people to think about climbing stairs. You are presented with a series of challenges based on real-world locations, starting with the 72 steps of the Philadelphia Museum of Art. It's enough steps to make you feel as if you've accomplished something, but not so many that you'll feel overwhelmed. Because the game runs on the iPhone, it can track your actual climbing progress using its built in motion-sensing technology. As you make the climb, this progress is reported several ways:

- A visual progress meter reveals a graphic image of the location you are virtually climbing, revealing a bit at a time.
- The percentage you complete.
- The actual number of steps you made versus the number of steps in the location where you're performing your simulated climb.
- An overview of multiple locations, each of which become colored-in as you make progress on them.

After the Museum of Art, you can make more challenging climbs up locations such as the Statue of Liberty and Big Ben. To make the accomplishments more fun, you can share your climbs with friends on Facebook after you complete them.

What works well in *Monumental* is that the designers realized that progress meters alone wouldn't make the experience fun. By tying your progress to real-world locations, you become more than a stair-climber; you're a character in a narrative, and you relate to the experience through iconic locations that most people are familiar with. By crafting your progress as a story rather than a set of chores, you form a deeper connection with the changes you need to make to improve your health.

Using Games to Improve the World

Just as games can help you improve yourself through learning or health, another class of social games have set out to make the world a better place to live in. A good example of this is `PracticallyGreen.com`, shown in Figure 6-18 that tries to teach people how to live more environmentally friendly lives.

Most people who come to PracticallyGreen initially experience it as a quiz—not unlike Chapter 1. This helps visitors learn about their impact on the environment in a more personalized, fun way. From there, you're assigned a level: You might start out as Barely Green or Lightly Green, but you have the opportunity to level-up all the way to "Superbly Green." By associating points and achievements with the common actions you can do to lead a more green lifestyle, PracticallyGreen provides visitors with a clear pathway for becoming more green.

Quiz helps immerse
you in green knowledge.

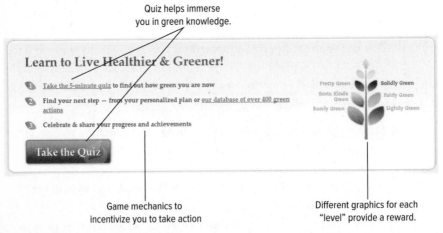

Game mechanics to
incentivize you to take action

Different graphics for each
"level" provide a reward.

Figure 6-18: PracticallyGreen.com

You can celebrate your progress toward Superbly Green by sharing your achievements with friends: Here, it goes beyond bragging. The emotional payoff is not only pride but it's also the opportunity to project yourself as an advocate for a greener world, mentoring others along the way.

Social Media as a Game

As explained in Chapter 5, social status is a reward that most of us find compelling. When we're recognized by our friends and peers, we get a warm feeling inside—whether it's because we enjoy admiration, acknowledgment, or validation. This reward is a large part of why social media is inherently viral and engaging for so many people. Social media also enables us to express ourselves creatively and feel connected to other people—deep emotional needs that haven't been satisfied by traditional media. Much of these elements have drawn heavily from games, with varying degrees of success.

How LinkedIn Turned Business Networking into a Game

When I first came upon LinkedIn (shown in Figure 6-19), I was in work mode. That is, not looking for any kind of game experience, just looking to touch base with people on a professional level. Perhaps because I had my work hat on, I felt compelled to finish up the to-do list. I dutifully filled out my profile and work history until my progress bar filled to a respectable level. Then I realized some people were apparently better connected than I. That couldn't stand! I invited everyone in my contact list and then some—even people I barely knew but who had a juicy network of their own. It was as if someone designed a game just for business people like me to win at. So I did.

Figure 6-19: LinkedIn as a Game

How YouTube Creates the Dream of Celebrity

According to Alexa, YouTube has grown to become the fourth largest website in the United States—right behind Google, Facebook, and Yahoo. The reasons are many: The technology works great, it's easy to embed videos in web-based content, and there's a thriving community—all of which work together to create a hard-to-beat game mechanic.

For content contributors, YouTube (shown in Figure 6-20) is a game about celebrity. The number of views each video receives is the basis of competition. Every time people upload a video, they're hoping to see that number shoot for the stars. However, YouTube isn't just a game for content contributors: The "sharing" game on YouTube is also carefully crafted so that people are rewarded for feeling that they are good at finding new content before it has risen to fame.

The game of being first to show your friends something

Number of views
Lure of fame

Figure 6-20: YouTube as a Game

How eBay Leverages Reputation and Reciprocity

The game of eBay, shown in Figure 6-21, involves two powerful human motives: honor and reciprocity. Because your transaction history is public, eBay helps ensure the honesty of participants. Your history becomes a score that people can use to compare different sellers—and even includes a badge (eBay's different-colored stars) that you earn for reaching higher tiers of trust.

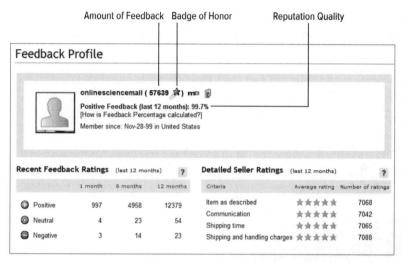

Figure 6-21: eBay as a Game

Not only does social media often act like a game, but it also really *is* a game. Reputation, fame, progress, achievement—these are the emotionally-charged elements of these websites that make them so compelling. Without gameplay, they'd just be applications for uploading video, maintaining a rolodex, or conducting auction transactions. Game mechanics such as progress bars, collections, and social spotlights have transformed them into deeper, more engaging experiences.

How Location Makes Work Fun

Mobile devices give you another way to access games during times you might otherwise be waiting around. In this sense, they're a great fit for asynchronous gaming; you can pick up a mobile device while riding the train or sitting in the doctor's office and instantly fill a few moments with gameplay. However, a new aspect is emerging: combining the location-aware features of mobile devices to craft entirely new types of games.

How *Foursquare* Harnesses Competition and Collection

Foursquare, shown in Figure 6-22, is a mobile application that enables you to "check-in" wherever you are: a restaurant, a school, your home—anything. The more frequently you check-in, the more points you acquire. Foursquare provides added incentives by offering more than 200 different badges for completing a number of activities:

- Checking in to increasing numbers of venues (10, 25, and 50 different places)
- Returning to the same place several times
- Checking in multiple days in a row
- Checking in to certain types of locations (movie theatres, pizza places, schools, conventions)
- Visiting specific locations related to brands and television shows (such as the Gossip Girl badge, which can be obtained by visiting places where the television show was recorded)

Figure 6-22: *Foursquare*

Foursquare, in essence, can turn running errands into a fun-filled activity. Another aspect of *Foursquare* is a simple form of competition: You can become the "mayor" of a location by checking in more times than anyone else. This leads to a habitual behavior to either defend your mayor-ship (by always remembering to check-in) or to compete (you might catch up to someone else).

Although there's a certain fun in completing collections and unlocking badges, it is the actual act of visiting and discovering the uniqueness of a location that is the real experience of *Foursquare*. While you are at a location, you can see the comments left by other people, which can give you ideas about what to do there. These comments serve the same function for real locations that commenting serves on blogs, Facebook pages, and forums.

Foursquare seems to have recognized that there's a bit of "check-in fatigue" and that people will eventually become bored with seeking points for the sake of points—already, new features are being introduced that enable participants to learn what other people have done at locations and assemble lists of activities they'd like to try. Although *Foursquare* is superficially a game about point acquisition, I believe its success will increase as it becomes more about experiences.

SCVNGR and Creativity, Movement

Whereas *Foursquare* provides a set of badges defined by the company, *SCVNGR* approaches it from a different direction: Focus on the activities people like to do at locations, and then crowdsource the ability for people to add new "challenges" they can complete while they're there. Just as Microsoft's Xbox Live service enabled game developers to create their own achievements, *SCVNGR* enables location-owners to create activities that lead people toward interesting experiences (Figure 6-23).

Whereas *Foursquare* describes itself as an application for discovering new things, *SCVNGR* is clear that it is a game. Its model is more like an adventure than a "discovery tool"—just as one travels from place to place in *World of Warcraft*, *SCVNGR* has you perform treks between places where you can conduct challenges, which are like simple quests you can complete after you're there. By completing treks and challenges, you can receive rewards from the businesses.

SCVNGR represents a new and emerging trend in location-based gaming: transcending point systems to offer experiences based on story, exploration, and challenge. Figure 6-24 diagrams the gameplay within *SCVNGR*.

Figure 6-23: *SCVNGR*

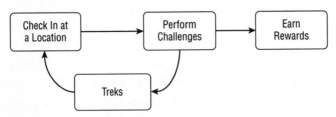

Figure 6-24: *SCVNGR* Gameplay

As you travel through the hustle and bustle of daily life, location-based games give you the sense that there are others on the same journey—and reconnect you with your communities in new and fun ways. Let's face it: Most of what you endure to travel from place to place simply isn't fun, and entering a new place is often intimidating. Games are transforming these experiences by making them about goals, stories and achievements.

Chapter in Review

In this chapter you learned some of the central elements of social games: Asynchronous gameplay, connectedness to friends, social recognition, and clear communication of goals can be established through tools such as stories, achievements, and effective user interfaces. Games have the uncanny ability to take seemingly mundane tasks—like moving from place to place, completing a job or collecting an item—into something fun. Much of what you do in everyday life can become more fun—and therefore more likely for you to repeat it in the future—when you restructure the task into a game.

Already, games are transforming a range of applications beyond entertainment: health, learning, and social media are a few that were discussed. In the following chapters, you learn how to design your own social game experiences that use some of the approaches you observed here.

Choose Your Path

The following list gives areas of the book you might want to visit next.

- If you're ready to start to understand the structure and mechanics of social games, you can jump forward to Part II, beginning with Chapter 7.
- If you'd like to go online and learn about new websites that are adapting game mechanics to new applications, visit www.game-on-book.com, and enter **websites** in the secret code box.

Designing Social Games

7 Anatomy of a Social Game

n this Chapter, you'll learn:

- How social games work with Facebook
- The features that make a game social
- The three life-cycle phases that social game players experience
- How social games spread through social channels

The social games industry has confused the subject of what social games consist of by associating them with the place they are distributed: social networks. Think about social games more broadly by thinking of them simply as games where players interact with each other. Over the next few years, social games will be increasingly defined not by where they are distributed, but *how* they are played. When discussing what goes into a social game, you'll see examples that exist both on and off social networks because this can enable you to gain a more holistic understanding of how social games work.

In many of the games played on social networks, social interactions are limited to viral marketing: The game provides mechanisms that make it so that customers share their experiences with their friends. Similarly, social media has attempted to use the close ties between friends to spread interest in non-gaming applications and businesses. Games have taken this further by providing social incentives in the form of badges, bragging rights, and leaderboards.

However, the most persuasive social games and applications go beyond recognition systems such as badges—and make social interactions the actual substance of gameplay. This isn't limited to big-budget, immersive social games such as *World of Warcraft*, in which people need to cooperate within real-time teams to triumph over the harder challenges within the game. Increasing numbers of social network games feature compelling interactions that go beyond marketing transactions. For example:

- *Gods of Rock* features the ability to asynchronously participate in team challenges, in which each of your friends can contribute special moves and actions within "epic gigs" that help you win as a team.
- *Zynga Poker* features the ability to engage in friendly banter with others sitting around a virtual poker table and offer them gifts that reflect your feelings about them during the course of play.
- *Kingdoms of Camelot* requires you to form alliances of players who work together to challenge other players and conquer the world.
- *Starcraft 2*, a hardcore title targeted at PC gamers, runs separately from Facebook but uses knowledge of your friend list on Facebook to help you find friends who are already playing *Starcraft 2*.

Outside of games, one can find similar mechanics at work both on and off social networks:

- The social application Causes has raised over $30 million (as of January 2011) for non-profit organizations by allowing people to promote donations to the charities they like. Causes helps people "donate their birthday" to a charity, which utilizes the high level of communication that frequently surrounds a birthday on Facebook into an opportunity to make charitable donations—which not only helps the charity, but makes the birthday-person the center of a positive social activity.
- Amazon.com members compete to provide the most helpful product reviews. These rewards can translate into fame as well as fortune: reviewers can earn a spot on certain leaderboards, but can eventually qualify for Amazon Vine, where they'll receive free copies of products that have been submitted by vendors willing to pay a fee for added exposure. Here, the social transaction isn't simply the posting of large numbers of reviews—it is the helpfulness rating that other members have assigned the reviews.

 ARTISAN The first games on Facebook focused on using social interactions to create viral marketing programs for themselves. Next, games began to use social interactions within their gameplay. Can you imagine ways that social interaction might create entirely new types of gameplay that are impossible without social connectedness?

Understanding Where Social Games Live

Social games, even those that exist off of Facebook, increasingly take advantage of the *social graph* that is part of Facebook. The social graph is a map of all the information about users and friend lists that exist on Facebook, mapping them with each other. The data within this social graph resides inside Facebook's servers and is made available via an application programming interface called the Graph API. Any application can use the Graph API to retrieve information including the following:

- Information about users, such as their names and affiliations
- Friend lists
- The content "liked" by users of Facebook
- Pages within Facebook
- Events scheduled by users of Facebook
- Groups that users are a part of
- Applications installed by users
- Photos uploaded by Facebook users

Various privacy settings are available to members of Facebook to control how this information is available to applications. When you first install an application, only certain data is available via the Graph API. To gain access to a user's private data, the application needs to ask for permission.

When applications exist inside the Facebook user interface, they are referred to as *canvas applications*. Although canvas applications on Facebook often appear to be tightly integrated with the Facebook user experience, they don't actually run on Facebook equipment. All social applications run from servers operated independently. Canvas applications can deliver their content in either of two ways:

- Facebook Markup Language (FBML) can generate pages that use a special version of HTML. This includes tags for generating certain interfaces that share the look-and-feel of Facebook. FBML applications generate pages inspected by Facebook servers and then are re-served to users after being translated into HTML readable by the user's web browser.
- Applications can be served in an *iframe*, which is a standard web technology for delivering part of a page from a separate website. In this mode, FBML is not needed because application servers communicate directly with your web browser; Facebook merely provides part of the page that passes directly through to a remote server.

SOCIAL NETWORK GAMES OFF FACEBOOK

Although most of the revenue being generated by social games is happening on Facebook, it's not the only place to distribute social games. In fact, distributing a social game outside of Facebook has one major advantage: lack of competition. While everyone is carving up a piece of the Facebook market, you ought to consider some of the other options available:

- **Twitter**, one of the most popular social networks on the Internet, focuses on exchanging short messages between members. Twitter features looser ties between members—because you "follow" who you are interested in (a one-way connection) as opposed to the bidirectional friendships formed on Facebook. However, games haven't been too successful on Twitter because people are less tolerant of seeing game-related messages—and members are more willing to stop following as soon as they feel they're getting spammed with information they don't care about. However, it may be that games will take a much different form on Twitter—and the features that work on Facebook simply don't make sense on Twitter.
- **MySpace** has experienced enormous difficulties in its competition with Facebook, resulting in its popularity ranking plummeting since 2009. But it's still one of the most popular sites on the Internet, and a number of games have thrived there—and face less competition. Myspace may also be more willing to help promote developers who want to take a risk there.

Some social networks are very popular outside of the United States, and although the revenue per user is often less—so is the cost of acquiring new customers.

- **Orkut** (owned by Google) is particularly popular in Brazil.
- **VZ-Networks** is a popular and growing social network for the German-language audience.
- **RenRen** (人人网, meaning the *everyone network* in Chinese) is a popular network used by students and others in mainland China.

Applications may also exist within the Facebook ecosystem without being displayed within a Facebook canvas page. This is the case with a game such as *Starcraft 2*, which uses Facebook information but operates within an entirely separate program.

Such applications also have access to the Graph API (or in some cases, older versions of the Facebook API), which they can use to retrieve information about users.

Figure 7-1 shows the Facebook application ecosystem.

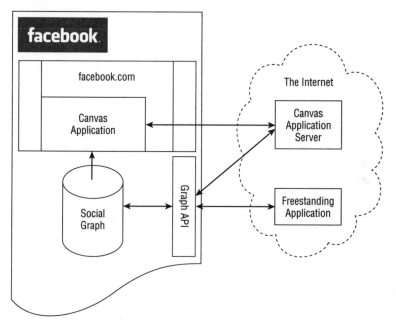

Figure 7-1: Facebook Ecosystem

Three Phases of the Player Life Cycle

It is helpful to think about the player's life cycle as part of a funnel. Every interaction with the player is either an opportunity to move them to the next phase—or lose them as customers. Figure 7-2 details the three major phases in the life of every player.

1. Players *discover* the game through advertising or through communications from other social players. These communications are usually in the form of news feed messages, status updates, or direct messaging.

2. Players *engage* with the game as they find an experience they enjoy doing. They repeat the activity to advance through the game. After the player runs out of immediate things to do, they stop for a bit but are reintroduced to the game through timed events, notifications from friends who are playing, or other reengagement mechanisms.

3. Players perform an *economic exchange* to accelerate events, unlock special content, or customize their experience.

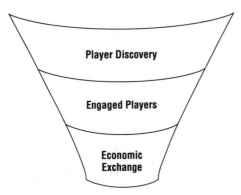

Figure 7-2: Player Life Cycle in Social Games

Along the way, players perform actions that introduce other players to the game (which is essentially a specialized type of economic exchange) and continue to reengage with new content.

The following sections in this chapter dig into each of the stages of the player life cycle and further elaboration on them is available throughout the remainder of Part II.

Player Discovery on Facebook

You might think of gaining players as "customer acquisition." From your customer's standpoint, however, they aren't being acquired; they're discovering you. How they discover you and what they do after they arrive at your landing page is the first step toward creating a long-term relationship with them. Start by digging into the ways that players discover games within Facebook and what happens from there.

Finding Customers with Social Communication Channels

Most people discover a particular social game by one of two ways: Either they see an advertisement for it, or they see content about the game through social communication channels. The latter include all the features built into social networks that enable members to spread contents among each other.

Discovery Stories

The primary automated way that players can learn about a new social game on Facebook is through a *discovery story*, which is a message Facebook automatically posts to your news feed when several of your friends start playing the same game and surpass certain engagement metrics. You don't have any direct control over whether a discovery story appears in someone's news feed; however, you can include it in several ways:

- By creating an engaging experience so that players spend a larger-than-average amount of time in it
- By encouraging players to "like" the game
- By encouraging players who play games to interact more frequently with their friends

It is likely that discovery stories appear in news feeds based on the same algorithms used in Facebook's EdgeRank calculation, which is discussed later in this chapter in the section "Social Reengagement."

Invitations and Requests

Games and applications on Facebook can send you specific messages that occur outside the news feed system. These are called "requests" because you are expected to individually respond to or dismiss each item, as shown in Figure 7-3.

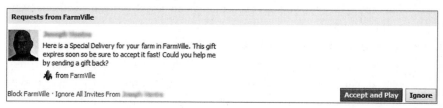

Figure 7-3: Facebook Request

At one time, Facebook requests were a lot more important. However, Facebook has made changes that have buried requests in areas of the interface that are less frequently visited by members. Although requests can be helpful for introducing newer Facebook members to a game, they tend to be ignored by most active Facebook users. For this reason, most games have shifted their emphasis toward using the news feed.

Chat

Facebook applications can detect which of your friends are currently logged in. By encouraging you to use the chat system to talk to your online friends, you might ask them to join a game that you are in. In addition, games and applications can integrate with Facebook's XMPP server directly, which means that if members have given permission to your application, you can send specific messages to other chat users.

Pitfalls of Using Social Channels

Although social communication channels can be a potent way to get your product in front of a lot of customers, they can just as easily backfire. Games need to focus on creating messages with good content with a low enough frequency that they won't annoy people. The following list gives some tips to avoid common mistakes that games have made when using social channels:

- **Avoid making players feel out of control of their feed**: Social applications can request permission to post messages directly to a person's news feed, and many players grant the permission, but if you post messages without telling the players, you can expect them to remove permission or even discontinue use of the application.
- **Don't create excessive spam**: If you post every tiny detail of how players use the application, you can expect people to block your game without even looking at it.
- **Keep the content relevant to someone's friends**: People might appreciate a wall post that enables them to receive a gift, look at some interesting content, or participate in some sort of event. If the content seems to exist purely to advertise the existence of the game, people won't care about it.
- **Lack of a call to action**: If it is just noise, but nothing that a person can react to, people won't care about it.

Things to Do When a Player Discovers You

When a player clicks a link to your game, time is of the essence. Each second and each click is critical because each is an opportunity for the player to abandon and do something else.

The first thing someone sees when first connecting to a game on Facebook is a request to grant the game some permissions, as shown in Figure 7-4.

Figure 7-4: Application Permission

At this point, the player might abandon if any of the following occur:

- **Excessive permissions:** The game asks for permission to something that the person doesn't want to share. Some people might not pay close attention to this, but if you are overly demanding in what you want the player to provide (asking for things such as email access, and so on) some people won't be willing to proceed. Remember that they barely know you at this point; it's a lot to ask them to trust you with information they might regard as private!

- **Boring description:** Decisions to install a social game are often made on the basis of how the game is described; think of this as your first opportunity to make a brand impression on the player. Generate excitement and give them some positive expectations.

- **Boring logo and visuals:** The logo shown for the game turns them off, or the visuals look amateurish.

- **Complicated interface:** If there's too much too digest on first sight, they'll go back to something else.

- **Fears about excessive wall posts:** If the player thinks your game will post messages without asking for permission, they'll do something else.

- **Lack of positive feedback and reviews:** Social applications can be reviewed on Facebook, and many players see a positive review as a reason to trust a game. You'll find it helpful to ask the players who are enjoying your game to share a positive review of it.

- **Lack of immediate gratification:** That's right, games are supposed to be fun! Don't throw tons of requests, forms to fill out, or other demands that get in the way of enjoying the game.

After they decide to install the application, the clock keeps ticking on their willingness to proceed. The first screen they see needs to be intriguing, informative, and fun. If it looks boring or complex, or if they can't figure what the game is going to be about, you can expect them to turn their attention elsewhere. Following are some things to think about during these first few seconds and minutes:

- The player should form a concrete goal about what they'll be doing in the game within the first few moments.
- Initial interactions should enable the player to quickly get involved in the action. Lengthy, noninteractive tutorials or videos will likely lead to abandonment. When you hear people asking for videos and help systems, it usually points to a deeper problem—that the game is too confusing. Use this as a suggestion to revisit the larger issues in the game, not necessarily as a need to present more tutorial content.
- Set a goal to involve the player in the actual action of the game within the first click or two upon entering.
- Telling the player about items they can purchase with real money—or suggesting that they need them to succeed—might alienate someone prematurely. Many people are willing to purchase virtual items, but they don't want to be hit over the head with it when they're still trying to figure out what the game is all about.

Engaging and Reengaging Players

Naturally, the most important mechanism you'll have for engagement is to make the game fun. Furthermore, good games are excellent at communicating what the player can do next. Bad games make it confusing, obscure, or hard to learn. The most important aspect of your game for fostering engagement is to constantly tell the player about what they can do next. As soon as there is nothing more to do and no indication that there will be more in the future, you'll lose the player—possibly permanently.

For social games, the art of engagement is largely about the *re*engagement. This is central to making games sticky. For that, several methods are widely used by social games:

- time-based limitations

- leaderboards
- social reengagement, using both game mechanics as well as social channels to keep players coming back over time

Time-Based Limitations

Sometimes, it's clear what players can do next, but the players aren't allowed to perform their moves right away. This helps make sure that the player doesn't exhaust their interest in the game within a single sitting and sets the stage for their later return.

Many social games limit the amount of content and gameplay that a person can consume within a particular period of time. One technique is to create a resource such as "energy" that is depleted as the players perform actions. Eventually, energy drains to zero, and the players need to wait for a period of time before they can continue; this is the approach used in games such as *Gods of Rock* and *Mafia Wars*.

Another technique used by social games is to enable players to place moves that require time to resolve. When you plant a crop in *FarmVille* or build a building in *Kingdoms of Camelot*, you need to wait for some period of time before you can enjoy the benefits of your move. Many players will take note of the amount of time required and return to the game just in time to continue, and others will keep a tab on their browser open at all times just so they can watch the clock, as shown in Figure 7-5.

Strawberries
Sell for: 35 Coins
Harvest in: 4 Hours
XP Gained: 1

★ ★ ★

10 BUY

Figure 7-5: Item Harvested in Future in *FarmVille*

Rewards can also be doled out to players who return to the game on a regular basis. In this case, the players aren't placing a move that consumes a resource or completes after a period of time; they are simply limited with the frequency with which it can be performed. Timers that limit frequencies of repeatable actions are often called *cooldowns*. You can see the case of a cooldown in the Facebook game *Vampire Wars* in Figure 7-6.

Figure 7-6: *Akem's Gamble*

In immersive games outside of Facebook, time-based mechanisms are also common. For example, *World of Warcraft* makes use of them in several ways:

- Many special powers have cooldowns that limit the frequency with which they can be used. In some cases, this is a tactical limitation so that a player can't overuse a powerful attack; in other cases, timers are longer and require a player to wait before they can use the more interesting capabilities.

- Players can create their own items (called "crafting") but certain rare items can be made only once in a while. Players need to come back to the game regularly to maximize the frequency with which they can make these items.
- Players can consume only certain content with a certain frequency. For example, players may enter dungeons in "heroic mode" and fight harder versions of the bosses there for better-than-usual rewards once every 24 hours. Bigger events, called raids, can have players waiting for a week before they can repeat the same content.
- When players aren't playing, their characters are "resting," which means they'll regain experience points at an accelerated rate for a period of time. The longer it's been since you've last played, the more rest you can enjoy upon return.

In the real world, retail stores have realized that cooldowns and time-limited offers can be good ways to get customers to return regularly:

- Limiting special offers to one per customer per visit
- Using punch cards that track how many times you visit a store and giving you a special discount upon a certain number of visits
- Announcing sales for a future date

Leaderboards

Leaderboards have several roles within a game. By showing how you compare to other players, they can appeal to competitive motivations. However, when displayed externally, they can also incite players to reenter the game. Furthermore, players have a tendency to slip in rank while not playing, which means that they'll be making a mental note to return to the game to maintain their position.

Social Reengagement

Just as social communication channels can get someone involved in a game for the first time, they can be even more effective for leading someone back into a game experience. After someone is committed to playing a game, they'll become more interested in things that can help them unlock new content or advance within the game environment:

- Gifts can be offered by players of a game that can enable players to perform new actions in the game or advance their character more rapidly.

- Players can announce events and invite their friends to participate.
- Friends can ask each other for help to accomplish harder tasks within the game.
- Special opportunities can be presented to players that are available only for a limited time.

In addition, the social channels available on social networks can be used to spur reengagement. On Facebook, this mostly includes using news feeds as well as direct wall posts.

News Feed

When your friends post messages to their news feeds, their messages are automatically aggregated into the news feed that you view on Facebook. This includes messages that they manually post and messages automatically streamed into their feeds from the games and applications that they use. Figure 7-7 shows an example of such a news feed item from a game.

Figure 7-7: Facebook News Feed Item

As of September 2010, Facebook began restricting the display of wall messages generated by games so that only other players of the game can see them. This was in response to a large number of complaints they had received from people who felt that game posts were overwhelming people who didn't care about games. Originally, wall posts helped games spread awareness to brand-new players; however, those days are over. Instead, wall posts are mostly helpful for reengaging people who are already players.

Facebook automatically sorts your news feed to favor posts from friends with whom you have the highest level of interaction. Each post to a wall is assigned what Facebook calls an *EdgeRank*, a particular score for each news feed item based on how much you seem to interact with the specific individuals in your friends list. If Facebook didn't do this, you might be overwhelmed by the quantity of messages being posted—especially if you have a large friend list. Figure 7-8 shows the winnowing down of a news feed.

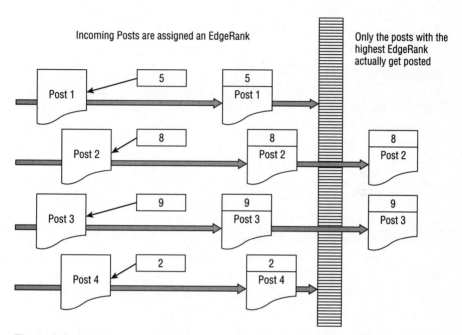

Figure 7-8: Facebook EdgeRank

Every time you interact with someone on Facebook, you create what Facebook calls an *Edge*, which is a record of your interaction. The value of an individual Edge is the product of the following:

- **An affinity score that attempts to determine how close you are to individuals in your own social graph:** Facebook hasn't described exactly how the affinity score is determined, but it appears to be based on things, such as how frequently you respond to their news feed posts, visit their profile, or exchange private messages.
- **A weight for the particular interaction:** Things such as commenting on a news feed post, "liking" their content, or tagging content each have different values associated with them. It isn't clear which of these have the greatest impact, although liking appears to have a significant role.
- **A time decay factor:** More recent Edges imply a more important connection with someone than Edges that happened a long time in the past.

All the Edge scores are added up for each individual friend on your social graph, and these scores determine which items end up in your news feed.

Your friends can post messages directly to your news feed, which they might do if they want to get your attention. This is common for things, such as offering a specific virtual gift that you might receive from one of your friends.

EDGERANK AND PAGERANK

Facebook's EdgeRank algorithm shares a lot in common with Google's PageRank algorithm, although the similarities are not in the mathematics. When Google first started, it used an algorithm developed by Google co-founder Larry Page called PageRank, which was a means to score the importance of web pages by looking at the number of incoming links to each page. PageRank was used (and today is still used, although to a more limited extent) to decide which items should appear first in search results. EdgeRank's goal is similar: to show you the most relevant content. In Facebook this is based on the strength of your relationships with people in your friend list. Google's PageRank algorithm led to an industry called *Search Engine Optimization (SEO)*, which is the art and science of using Google's search index to help a user find your web pages. Developers use news feed optimization techniques that manipulate Facebook's EdgeRank. This begs the question, if search engine optimizers focus on *link building*, will the future of news feed optimization be dominated by "like building?" Just as Google's search engine keeps changing formulas, you can expect Facebook to keep changing theirs to make them difficult to exploit.

Direct News Feed Posts

In addition to the aggregate news feed, your friends can also post directly to your news feed. To do this, they need to take the time to choose you as the specific recipient of a message. Consequently, you have a much higher chance to see the message. Other people visiting your profile page on Facebook may also see the messages that others have left for you.

Economic Exchange

Although the original way that social games were played involved making an economic exchange in advance of playing (you'd pay for your chess board and then start playing with your friends), most successful online social games are sustainable businesses because they create opportunities for economic exchange over the lifetime of the product. In most social games on Facebook, this means selling the players a virtual item that customizes, accelerates, or unlocks contents. Other ways to create transactions include the following:

- Delivering advertising impressions to a targeted audience
- Generating leads for other products or websites where economic transactions can occur
- Involving the player in a wider network of games, products, and interactions that collectively can generate revenue from the customer
- Learning information about a customer that has an identifiable value

Unlike many web-based products, games create sufficient incentive for players to part with money or perform actions so that they can continue to enjoy themselves. What this means is that web-based games can become sustainable; the value they create over time can be used to reinvest in player acquisition or improvements in the game that can lead to deeper engagement. Chapter 8 will discuss the various models and metrics used for generating revenue in a social game.

Figure 7-9 summarizes the overall flow of value creation discussed throughout this chapter.

 OTAKU Economic exchanges in online games are not limited to microtransactions. *Entropia Online* was entered into the *Guinness Book of World Records* in 2008 for the $100,000 sale of an asteroid used as a virtual space resort. This was later exceeded in 2010 with the sale of the Crystal Palace Space Station (again, at *Entropia Online*) at a price of $330,000.

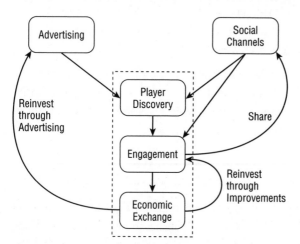

Figure 7-9: Value Creation in Social Games

Adapting Social Games to Business

This chapter discusses the anatomy of a social game. But how can you adapt these structures to a non-gaming business? The following are some ways you can challenge yourself:

- **Create social rewards and perks.** Most businesses are focused on providing direct value—in the form of their products and services—to a particular set of customers. How can you also make your customers into heroes? Amazon makes its top reviewers into heroes, lavishing social status (and sometimes actual gifts) upon them. Can you do the same?

- **Create social communities.** Social media has opened up new ways for you to interact with your customers; many companies are already doing this. But how can you allow your customers to interact with each other? Once customers start helping and supporting each other—and advocating your brand—you've gone from simply having social media to having a community that adds powerful barriers to competitors.

- **Games are concerned with discovery, engagement, and economic exchange.** These stages of customer acquisition are similar in almost any business, but what if you rethought each of these stages in your business—making each an opportunity for presenting the player with a game? Even a grocery store could be a game; people play the coupon-clipping game, the find-the-shortest-route-through-the-store game, the discover new goodies game, and the learning-new-facts-about-food game. Imagine how you can break down all the processes in your business and make them into fun experiences.

- **Utilize social channels.** If your customers are playing your games and interacting with each other, use features like sharing, the Facebook wall and social status, to create opportunities for reengagement.

In the remaining chapters in Part II of this book, you'll read more about how games do all of the above. As you read on, jot down notes to yourself about ways that you could adapt the techniques of social games to whatever you need to accomplish in business.

Chapter in Review

In this chapter you learned how the customer life cycle for a social game involves three phases: player discovery, during which players learn about the existence of the game; engagement, during which players enjoy the game and increase their involvement with it; and economic exchange, which is the point where players are willing to take actions (including spending money) to improve or continue their gameplay experience.

Social communication channels are critical to help players discover a game and also to reengage them with a game they're already playing. On Facebook, this means using features such as the news feed effectively, which is governed by the EdgeRank algorithm, a means to channel content to users based on the friends they interact with most.

As you continue to read Part II, you can expand on all the concepts introduced in this section.

Choose Your Path

The following list gives areas of the book you might want to visit next.

- If you want to learn more about the business models introduced in this chapter, the next chapter covers the various forms of economic exchange in greater detail, including ways to model growth, revenue, and customer acquisition.
- If you want to review the types of fun that are important to design social game experiences, turn back to Chapter 5.
- If you'd prefer to read more about how you can start designing your own social game, flip forward to Chapter 11.
- If you want to stay current on the latest techniques for using the social communication channels mentioned in this chapter, go online to www.game-on-book.com and enter **channels** in the secret code box.

8 Understanding Social Game Business Models

In this chapter, you'll learn:

- Why attention is the ultimate currency in social games
- Approaches used by social games to monetize players
- Techniques for acquiring players
- Metrics for measuring player acquisition, attention, and revenue
- How to create a spreadsheet that captures your game's business model
- Different modes of testing you can use to design, develop, and operate your game

This chapter shows you how social games can earn a profit by managing customer acquisition costs and maximizing revenue. A few simple tools can help you think about your own products, whether they are games or aspire to be game-like. The central idea of this chapter is that *attention* is the ultimate currency that exists within games, and the business goal of a successful game is to convert that attention into dollars.

This chapter also further discusses the pairing of emotions and numbers that is prevalent throughout this book. Emotions are associated with the right brain—subjective, intuitive, and random—whereas numbers are part of the left-brain modes of linear reasoning and objective analysis. Still, each is essential to game design, especially social media games.

Emotions drive the game experience, explaining why people play a game and think it's so fun. Without emotion, there is no game, but it is through coldness of numbers that you can detect whether you're eliciting the emotions you hoped for because emotion is how you create attention—and as you'll read, attention is the key to creating a successful social game.

Converting Attention to Dollars

The business models for almost every type of media involve converting the attention of an audience into dollars. If millions of people watch a television show, the advertisements are a way to convert that attention into the dollars collected from sponsors. Subscription fees, such as those charged by HBO, are another way of monetizing attention; if people are watching and enjoying the premium shows, they'll keep paying for the subscription fee. The only difference between this and advertising is who writes the checks.

Although attention is essential to games just as it is to all forms of media, some important differences exist with games:

- **Most media has a finite length of consumption.** For example, a song or movie has a particular length, and then it is finished, unless you repeat the same thing again. On the contrary, each game experience is different, and few games impose a maximum amount of time on your engagement.

- **Games demand attention because of their interactive nature.** They can't be watched or listened to in the background. You can get up from the television and visit the refrigerator while continuing to hear a show in the background, but a game demands that you pause. Of course, television can be paused as well, but it doesn't insist on it in the same way that games do.

- **Because games are usually nonlinear experiences, they create a greater sense of curiosity.** Players are paying attention and interested in exploring new aspects of the game: With other types of media, consumers only need to passively receive information, whereas in games, the level of attention required to explore is a deeper level of interaction than what happens when watching, listening, or even reading.

- **Social games engage you along with your friends in a shared activity.** You can watch a television show or talk about it with your friends afterward, but games cause you to have numerous interactions with each other during the course of play.

Casual versus Hardcore Games

In the past several years, a tension has existed between two artificially defined categories of games: casual and hardcore.

- **Casual games:** These are typically defined as accessible, frequently playable via a web browser, and enjoyed for brief bursts of time. They take little experience with previous games to enjoy and have attracted audiences of players who have lacked prior exposure to games. A game such as *Bejewelled* is the quintessential casual game.

- **Hardcore:** Games such as *World of Warcraft* and *Call of Duty* appeal to people who own consoles, require significant time commitments, and are typically purchased only by experienced gamers.

On the one hand, games such as *Bejewelled* show a great deal about what you can accomplish by making a game highly accessible. However, I think all designers should aspire to create "hardcore" games in the sense that you should want players who are going to be heavily immersed, deeply engaged, and returning frequently. Although *Bejewelled* might be a "casual" game, the way many people play it is hardcore: For instance, Mike Leyd, a steel contractor, spent more than 2,200 hours on *Bejewelled 2* to achieve its highest known score in 2010.

Some people think of social games as the latest category of casual games, as if they're trivial experiences that have viral marketing and friend-lists built in. I look at them differently: Social gameplay is a way to take almost any game experience and create a deeper level of engagement—in other words, they help you create more attention.

Just as *Bejewelled 2* is a great example of a simple, accessible game with hardcore players, it isn't hard to find console-based games that have made their way into the hands of more casual audiences. The music-gaming phenomena that peaked in 2009 serves as a good example: Games such as *Rock Band* and *Guitar Hero* are played in places (at nightclubs, parties, and events) and by people who normally wouldn't pick up a "hardcore" console game.

The *Bejewelled* franchise has sold more than 50 million copies, which is more than any of the top hardcore games—a testament to the deep engagement that the game delivers. Many factors contributed to the success this series has enjoyed, but it wouldn't have ever gotten close to these numbers without its deeply engaging play experience. Although the sales of games in the series have generated substantial revenue, the publisher of the game (Popcap) has realized that there were additional revenue opportunities within the social gaming sphere, where it's possible to introduce more players to the game for free—and extract revenue by offering various boosts players can use to increase their score. This is an example of using virtual goods as a way to capture additional revenue from the attention directed at the game.

Social Play as an Attention Generator

Chapter 5 explains how our brains are hardwired for social interaction, which helps explain the power of games to engage the highest-order processes of our minds. This is a large part of the attention-generating power of social games. Another reason why social gameplay generates attention is that it provides additional opportunities for people to play together: Single-player computer games and other solitary activities (such as reading) can be enjoyed only at times someone is willing to enter a state of isolation. On the other hand, social games are an activity that can provide the entertainment and interaction wherever people appear together—whether at a party, a sporting event, or on Facebook.

The music gaming genre offers a good example of how important social gameplay is for generating attention. In 2007, *Guitar Hero III* and *Rock Band* were published within months of each other. Although *Guitar Hero III* sold more units, players of *Rock Band* make more frequent purchases of downloadable content—new songs you can download and play with your friends. In March 2008, while both games were still relatively new, *Guitar Hero 3* owners purchased new songs at the rate of one every 15 days, but *Rock Band* players were buying faster, at the rate of one song every 10.7 days (although it also leveled off later in the game's life, as you might expect).

A number of possible explanations exist for why *Rock Band* might have done better. Maybe people simply liked the music choices in *Rock Band* more than those offered in *Guitar Hero*, and maybe Harmonix (the publisher of *Rock Band*) was simply better at promoting this aspect of the game. Harmonix also released new songs more often.

Now for a different theory: At the time *Guitar Hero III* was published, it was still mostly a single-player experience. On the other hand, *Rock Band* had just introduced the idea of having other band positions such as a singer and drummer, meaning that people tended to play as a group rather than as individuals. The increased social play led to much greater attention, and these higher levels of attention resulted in greater DLC (downloadable content) sales.

At the time these two games released, I was busy at a previous company—GamerDNA—creating technology for tracking the games people played. This gave me some insight into how often people were playing each game. Figures 8-1 and 8-2 show how many people tracked by GamerDNA were playing *Guitar Hero 3* and *Rock Band* respectively.

Although the number of players GamerDNA tracked was in a similar range, it isn't the absolute number of players that is revealing about these two games: It is the shape of the curves. There's a distinct falloff with *Guitar Hero III* players, whereas *Rock Band* grew somewhat.

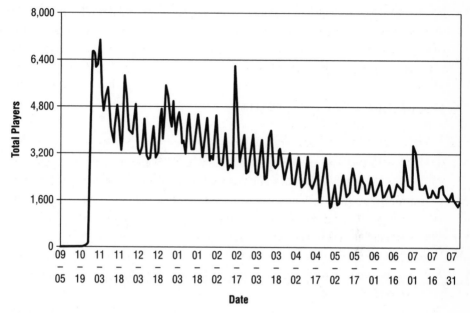

Figure 8-1: *Guitar Hero 3* Players/Day

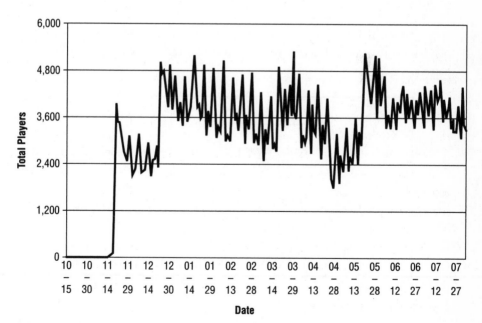

Figure 8-2: *Rock Band* Players/Day

One significant variation in gameplay helps explain the profound difference in attention that each game received: the social gameplay within *Rock Band*. I hope that this, along with the correlation to DLC sales, helps convince you that attention is one of the best ways to measure the success of a game.

Social Game Business Model

The payoff from attention is twofold.

- The players who are the most engaged with the game are the ones most likely to get their friends to play as well, especially in social games that allow for friend-to-friend interaction. This means that even the nonpaying players can generate substantial value by introducing people to the game who may end up engaging in economic exchanges.
- The people who spend the most attention on a game are also the most likely to spend the most money—or engage in other exchanges important to your product.

Chapter 7 describes the anatomy of a social game in terms of a funnel with three distinct stages: player discovery, engagement, and economic exchange (see Figure 8-3). In a business model, the output of the economic exchanges can fuel ongoing player acquisition, with the remainder providing your business profit. Meanwhile, engaged players are also spreading the word about your game, which leads to even more players.

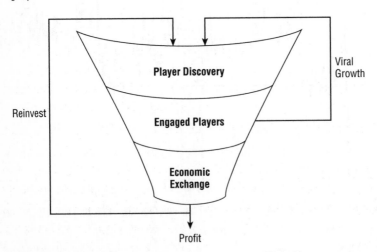

Figure 8-3: Business Model Funnel

Revenue Models

Before explaining the mechanics of how attention can convert into dollars, consider the various methods companies use to conduct their transactions with customers. Today, the dominant model is virtual goods: selling bite-size content to the player for small fees (often called *microtransactions*). Virtual goods are discussed after first discussing some of the other models that have been used for social games because it will put the advantages and disadvantages of virtual goods into perspective.

Subscriptions

The model favored by most of the big-budget online social games that predate Facebook was monthly subscriptions. The advantage of this method is the predictability of the revenue stream—as long as you understand the churn rate (the percentage of players who cancel each month) you can have a fairly good understanding of near-term revenue. This is the model that continues to be used by *World of Warcraft*.

Subscription fees haven't caught on within social media games for a few reasons:

- **Subscription Fatigue.** People simply don't like having to remember all the fees they are responsible for each month.
- **Do or Die.** After a trial period runs out, the customer is forced to subscribe or quit, causing you to permanently lose the opportunity to sell them something.
- **Competition.** There are too many alternatives that don't have a subscription fee. Also, people compare the monthly subscription fees to everything else they pay a subscription for, ranging from magazines to cable channels to commercial massively multiplayer online games. Although social games can deliver significant entertainment value, their relatively low production values might lead people to conclude that a subscription fee isn't worth it.

As production values for social network games continue to increase, you're likely to see the emergence of some successful subscription-based models. In the meantime, some companies offer a hybrid model: For example, Challenge Games (which has since been acquired by Zynga) created a model where players can play for free, purchase virtual goods, or buy a subscription that provides access to special periodic content at a discount.

Software Purchase

Purchasing individual games is virtually unheard of for online social games; although, it remains a part of how larger commercial games are sold within the retail channel. Competitive pressure is likely to keep this model out of the social media universe for quite some time.

In the mobile gaming market, the *freemium* model is popular, in which people try a game for free and pay a fee to upgrade to a full-featured version of the game. In some ways, this is a virtual goods model in disguise. Instead of buying individual goods through microtransactions, you're buying a whole package of goods through a single transaction.

Advertising

One of the oldest models for deriving revenue from attention is advertising: The customer pays with their eyeballs instead of with their wallet—and someone else pays for their time. Several forms of advertising are relevant to online games: traditional banner advertising, incentive-based offers, and product placements.

Traditional Banner Advertising

You've seen web-based advertising. These are banners that appear on the top, bottom, or side of a website. Some games feature these as well because they can supplement income from other sources. Be cautious here because traditional advertising could actually decrease total revenue by decreasing the attention within your game. Here's why:

- **Real Estate:** Traditional ads take up valuable real estate within your game, which could be filled with more calls-to-action, features, or content pertaining to your game. If you run within a Facebook canvas page, also remember that you have relatively limited space because much of the page is already taken over by other things (including advertisements).
- **Interrupted play:** When players do click on ads, they've stepped away from your application and might not return. There might be better ways to derive revenue from the player that you can't take advantage of now.
- **Annoyance factor:** Players might find ads annoying or distracting. When players see advertising inside a game, it may drive them into other games with less advertising.

To decide whether traditional advertising banners make sense, you need to determine how much the ads are worth to you. Ads within social games are typically priced using one of three mechanisms:

- **Cost per Thousand Impressions (CPM):** In this pricing scheme, an advertiser pays for ads based on the number of times someone views the ads. Because of the high volumes involved, payments are typically made only for every thousand ad impressions delivered.
- **Cost per Click (CPC):** Advertisers pay for a click someone makes on the ad.
- **Cost per Action (CPA):** Advertisers pay when your player takes some action that creates value for them, such as buying a product or requesting more information.

CPM ads typically provide the most risk to the advertiser (because it's harder for them to pay based on return on investment) whereas CPC and CPA shift more of the risk to the publisher (who won't get paid for situations such as players learning about something interesting through the ad and then making a separate visit and purchasing on their own later). Most brand-oriented advertisers agree to pay on a CPM basis, but the more transactional advertisers tend to demand CPC or CPA pricing.

Whichever way you go, the challenge with advertising models is that they require substantial numbers of unique visitors—what advertisers call *reach*—to amount to any meaningful number. In 2010, the top CPM rate from the top brand advertisers was only a few dollars. New games would be lucky to command as much as $1 CPM; at that rate, you'd need to display an advertisement a million times to earn only $1,000. When you consider that most advertisers limit how many times you are allowed to show the same ad to the same person (called a *frequency cap*) that means you need a huge number of people playing.

If you feel you have the reach to make traditional advertising worthwhile, you need to decide how to actually sell the ads. Direct sales of advertising is usually the hardest and most expensive way to go—the median salary for an advertising sales executive in 2010 was approximately $70,000, not including commissions. Capable digital advertising executives can earn well into six figures. These costs mean that in-house sales of advertising are limited to only the largest online businesses.

An alternative to hiring your own ad sales force is that you can join an *ad network*, which is a company in the business of aggregating many publishers together and hiring a sales force that can sell advertising for all of them. The advantage with this approach is that you can significantly save on the costs of doing it yourself; although, you now split your revenue with another company (often up to 50 percent) and it probably won't get the rates you might have gotten on your own. Different ad networks have widely varying models: Google AdSense is probably the best known ad network, and just about anyone can join; it pays exclusively on a CPC basis and typically delivers text-based ads. Other ad networks specialize in different types of content, including games—and may pay using CPC, CPM, CPA, or a combination of multiple methods. In Appendix B, you can find several traditional ad networks that specialize in the games market.

Offer-Based Advertising

Another form of advertising that has grown popular with the operators of online games is the offer-based model. In this situation, players are paid by an advertiser with virtual currency, and the creator of the game is paid with cash equivalent to the value of the currency paid to the player. This is a new take on CPA advertising, with two distinct advantages: The players initiate their interaction with the advertiser on the basis that they can gain a benefit within the game, which increases the likelihood that they can complete the action. Because they've been paid with virtual currency, they'll have a greater chance to return to the game to enjoy their reward. Thus, offer-based advertising closes the loop between the game and the advertiser in a way that traditional CPA ads can't. This is a case of the endowment effect mentioned in Chapter 5.

Players are typically presented with a list of offers along with the virtual-currency payoffs for completing individual offers. These aggregated lists of offers are referred to as *offer walls*. Figure 8-4 shows an offer wall from one of the leading offer networks, TrialPay, as it appears within a social game.

Offer walls typically include the following:

- Products that people can purchase or apply for, such as coffee, credit cards, insurance, magazine subscriptions, or other products that people frequently buy online
- Market research surveys that people can complete
- Other social games and applications to install

Offer walls have gotten a lot of criticism in the past, and for good reason. In the early days of offer walls, some of the offer networks did a poor job of screening their advertisers. Some promised payouts of virtual currency without requiring a purchase but then tricked people into signing up for subscription-based mobile phone services—or forced them into endless sequences of web pages that attempted to trap people until they gave in. Some of these tricks had more in common with the practices within the web-porn industry than the game industry.

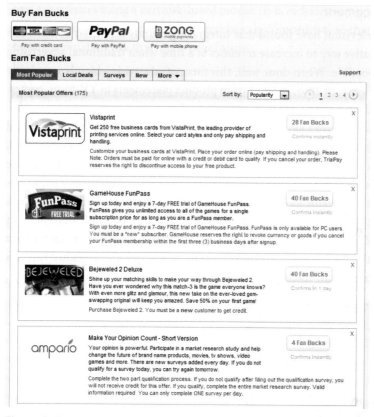

Figure 8-4: TrialPay Offer Wall

Unsurprisingly, a rebellion occurred against some of these early offer networks. One of the earliest, Offerpal Media, ended up replacing its CEO and ultimately changed its name to Tapjoy amid the controversy. (Although the company and its original CEO have been adamant that they never scammed anyone.) The market for offer networks has been cleaned up significantly since then and is a lot safer to work with than they once were.

Most of the offer networks provide the ability for people to pay for virtual currency with credit cards and with offers. By combining the offer wall feature with a payment solution, they can serve as a single vendor for the monetization needs for many games. In addition to Trialpay and Tapjoy, other major vendors include Peanut Labs and Super Rewards. You can find contact information for these companies in Appendix B.

- **Branding:** As previously described, virtual goods can also be branded for advertisers, who can pay for the virtual goods for players as a form of advertising.
- **What the people want:** Virtual goods are what players have come to expect. They don't want to pay for subscriptions.

Virtual goods take advantage of many techniques that have been used in retail: sales, limited-time offer, and collections. Some even share properties with real-world consumable products such as razor blades, where the same product is sold to the same customer over and over again. Chapter 12 tackles designing games for virtual goods.

THE STARBUCKS PHENOMENA

Tim Harford provided an analysis of Starbuck's business model in the *Undercover Economist*, revealing that there's a negligible difference in the cost to Starbucks between the various beverages it sells. The major costs of operating an individual Starbucks location is real estate and labor; the actual material cost between the cheapest and most expensive drinks is only a few cents. Nevertheless, numerous people (including this author!) are apparently willing to pay at least a couple of dollars more for their fancy drinks.

In other words, customers are willing to opt-in to paying extra. If Starbucks offered only one product—say, a cup of coffee of exactly one size—this wouldn't work. If it raised the price, some customers wouldn't go there at all. If it lowered the price, it would have more customers, but some customers would pay a lot less than they'd otherwise be willing to—depriving Starbucks of potential per-unit profits. By offering a large number of products, Starbucks can enable some customers to pay more, even though the increased cost to its business is minor. This practice is what economists call price discrimination.

Social games have the same opportunity to offer a wide range of products to customers, enabling some to opt-in by paying more and others by paying less (or nothing). The Starbucks model, which is compelling in a situation where the cost of goods sold varies by only a few pennies, becomes overwhelmingly advantageous in a situation where the marginal cost is nearly zero. After all, a new virtual good costs only a few electrons to produce a copy.

Business Metrics for Social Games

Although television networks still struggle with Nielsen as the best estimate of audience size and magazines depend on circulation numbers and pass-along, few forms of media can match the precision with which social applications can measure every aspect of who, how, and why people use them. This is because games and social applications require constant input from the user, processed on servers that you control.

Now take a closer look at the metrics you should be paying attention to as you build your application.

 ARTISAN As you read about the different metrics you can use for measuring a social game, you might be inclined to think that they detract from the art of game design—indeed, there's more to making a game than looking at usage statistics. Furthermore, short-term metrics often don't reveal the whole story of how players will stick with a game over the long term. That's where the magic of branding, story, and emotion can payoff big, and those facets might take longer for you to figure out. My advice: Use metrics as a powerful tool to help you decide what's working in your game, but don't be afraid to question them either.

Metrics for Attention

In the early days of social games—at least the variety running on social networks—the conventional wisdom was to initially focus on player discovery (through viral user acquisition) ahead of everything else. However, things have changed a great deal. Many of the social channels are far less effective than they once were, and there's increasingly good content to compete with. Therefore, you need to focus on what matters: attention. Attention is the outcome of your hard work, good entertainment, and fun. No amount of viral propagation can matter unless people stick with your product.

First focus on attention; second, focus on attention; and third, focus on attention. Make it fun! Know your audience! As you master that, everything else is easier. With that in mind, now take a look at the numbers that help you measure the attention your game receives.

Total Installed Users

Total installed users are all the people who have ever installed an application, minus anyone who has removed the application. For a standalone website, this would be equivalent to the total number of unique visitors that have ever viewed the site. (Although websites don't have the concept of an installation.)

For social applications, total installed users are easy to track. On Facebook, anyone listed as a developer for an application can access this information by going to `www.facebook.com/insights/` and clicking the name of the application to view. You see a graph similar to Figure 8-6.

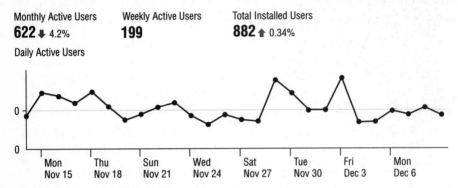

Monthly Active Users	Weekly Active Users	Total Installed Users
622 ↓ 4.2%	**199**	**882** ↑ 0.34%

Figure 8-6: Facebook Insights

The total number of installed users displays in the upper-right portion of the Users graph.

Monthly Active Users

The next metric that's somewhat less coarse than total installed users is *monthly active users*, usually abbreviated as *MAU* and pronounced as "Mao" (just like the founder of the People's Republic of China). This is simply the number of people who have accessed an application within the last month. It includes everyone, even people who try an application and leave within the first few seconds. For that reason, it isn't a particularly helpful measurement; although large absolute numbers of MAU certainly indicate the larger applications online, particularly when the MAU numbers sustain or grow over time.

After you have several months of data, you might find it helpful to compare MAU data to look at overall trends. You can also compare MAU to total installed users to understand who is sticking over the long term. However, there are lots of ways that MAU can be juiced without having a big impact on the real attention your application receives. For example, an expensive advertising campaign could result in a huge MAU without actually producing any meaningful attention. For that reason, focus on some of the other metrics more than MAU. Nevertheless, you need to understand MAU if you're going to make sense of some of the other presented metrics.

On Facebook, the MAU information is contained in the same chart shown previously in Figure 8-6. If you don't run within Facebook, you'll want your engineers to create a field in your application database to track the last time someone accessed your application. By querying on the number of people who have connected within the last month, you can get your own version of MAU.

Daily Active Users

The focus of Facebook's Insights report is *daily active users*. By looking at this regularly, you can gain a more accurate picture of how popular your application is. Changes to advertising, competition, and user patterns will be reflected rapidly within this number, abbreviated as *DAU* and pronounced like Dow. Like the Dow, it provides a daily snapshot of how business is faring. It's also pronounced the same as dao, the Chinese word for "the way" (道), which might help you remember that this is the way to understanding attention.

DAU to MAU Ratio

DAU and MAU become most useful when you compare them to each other. If you divide DAU by MAU, you have a measure of how often your monthly users are returning to the application each day. In general, applications with the highest level of engagement—which means they're generating the most attention over time—are those with the highest ratio.

Beware of the law of small numbers: When an application is still new, the DAU to MAU ratio might not be helpful. A new application with only a few thousand users might have a fantastic ratio because the first customers are extremely dedicated, perhaps representing a cross-section of fans for your previous work. Likewise, don't be discouraged in the early days of an application if the ratio is awful because new applications often have a number of serious flaws to overcome.

DAU/MAU can be useful as you start growing and can also help you assess the impact of new features. The subject of using DAU/MAU is revisited after you understand how to use daily cohorts of new players to split-test new features (see Chapter 13).

If you are on Facebook, calculating your DAU/MAU is as simple as dividing the numbers you see on the Insights report. If you need to track this information for activity outside of Facebook, you need to have your player database track the last time someone interacted (just as explained with MAU) and perform the calculations based on the data you observe.

Conversion Rates

Some number of your players won't do much after installing the game; therefore, you need to understand the rate at which players return. This is the *conversion rate*, the percentage of people who become converts to your special blend of magic. You might have other conversion rates pertaining to engagement as well, such as the following:

- What percentage of your players are still players after one day? (Think of this as a conversion to a "returning player.")
- What percentage of players still return after a week?
- What percentage of players convert to deeper parts of the funnel, including players who spend money?

Customer Lifetime

How long do players stick? This is an important number to understand, because it can help you forecast their revenue potential.

You have to decide what you feel a meaningful return frequency is. If there's a period of inactivity that correlates to a sharp decline in whether customers will ever make purchases again, a good way to track things is to mark customers as inactive after that much time elapses without purchases. Understanding the size of your active customer base is important to make sense of many other variables.

Tracking customer lifetime usually takes a bit of database magic, because you can't derive it directly from MAU, DAU, or any other high-level metric. One way you can approach this is to have your application developers flag individual players as active customers or not based on the criteria you've established. For example, if players stop accessing or monetizing for a period of time and you've determined that it means they're no longer a customer, an automatic process on your database could flag them as inactive. Likewise, players who returned to the game could be automatically flagged as active again. Having these hooks in your system is essential to manage the game over time.

Session Frequency

If DAU is more useful than MAU, why not look at how many times a day people return? Popular games are often used several times per day, and because attention is so important, you need to set a goal for yourself to get players to return often.

Facebook doesn't track these statistics, so even Facebook applications need to find a way to accumulate this information. The best way is to add information to your database's application to track how many times people visit your game and bump it each time they start a new session. If you do this, you can divide the number of sessions people have by the length of time they've been active players.

Time per Session

In the world of website development, there's a common metric referred to as *time on site*. This is the amount of time a person stays on a particular website. For games and social applications, the more appropriate term is simply *time per session.*

This metric helps you understand how deeply someone is engaging: Are they visiting several times a day for only a few seconds, or are they visiting once per day for a long session of 10 minutes or more? Longer periods of time tell you that you're garnering more attention.

This metric begs the question of how much time per session is considered good. For those who are coming to the world of games from the world of website development, a few minutes might seem to be a good number. When I operated GamerDNA, we managed a network of websites that received up to 10 million unique visitors per month, with session lengths averaging about 4 minutes. Although session lengths above the range might be considered good for websites, they aren't particularly high for games, given their potential for engagement. You should look for at least 10 minutes or more for a successful game experience.

This can be a somewhat tricky number to track on your own. You can do it with a bit of database creativity, but you might simply find it easier to use a website tracking tool designed for this purpose. Google Analytics, which you can access via `http://google.com/analytics` can track this information via its *Avg. Time on Site* report. Although Google Analytics is mostly used by websites, it works perfectly fine as part of any social application, including those that operate exclusively within Facebook. Google Labs has also made available an Adobe Flash component that makes it possible for a Flash-based game to use many of the same tracking techniques.

Determinants of Attention

All of the statistics on how long and how frequently people are spending attention is interesting to know—but they're only useful if you understand the factors that contribute to moving them upwards.

Are your players skimming along the surface of your game, or are they delving deep into your experience? You need to identify the points at which players give up, slow down, or abandon. This could be because there aren't enough features along the way, that they've run out of interesting content, or that the game's complexity has outpaced the players' willingness to understand it.

Table 8-1: Attention Determinants

Metric	Description
Level progress	Games that contain levels have the advantage of a simple linear scale for tracking how far someone has gotten into a game. By measuring how long someone has been stuck at a given level, you can identify cases in which people are getting bored or giving up.
Achievement popularity	You can use games with badges or achievements as a means to see which parts of the game players play the most. Track the number of people who have initiated progress against each achievement, and compare this to the number who have completed it. Rarely completed achievements might be too hard or uninteresting to players.
Collection completion	Many games depend on players collecting a set of virtual goods. Track each collection type, and measure which collections have measurable progress and which have been completed. This can tell you a great deal about opportunities for other collections or issues that prevent people from completing their collections.
Goal-based completion	Achievements and collections are two types of goals; whenever you can identify the underlying set of goals for a game system, you should consider measuring it. For example, in a game such as *World of Warcraft*, each individual quest is measured to see how many people begin versus finish. This reveals information about quests that are buggy, too hard, or placed in unlikely locations.
Customization choices	What choices do players make as they experience the game? For example, in *Mafia Wars*, you should know whether players invest the points they gain leveling up in energy, stamina, attack, or defense because it reveals what elements people value most: Energy suggests that they are more interested in leveling through jobs; stamina implies interests in player-versus-player aspects. When particular players signal a preference for a type of play, you can correlate this with the types of goals they've completed to see whether you're delivering on the implicit promise of delivering fun based on their strategic choices.

Metric	Description
Competitiveness	In games with competitive player-versus-player inter-action, you can track wins and losses for players and compare them to the customization choices and tactical options they've chosen. This can uncover problems in game balance long before players begin complaining about them.
Latency	This is the most technical of the metrics mentioned here, but it's an important one. Research, including data from Amazon.com, has shown that even slight increases in page-load times for web applications can lead to notice-able drops in revenue.

Levels can be a helpful tool for measuring depth of engagement. Players enjoy levels because it gives them a linear sense of progress; likewise, you might like levels because they can show you where players are bored.

Figure 8-7 shows the actual data for *Zoo Kingdom*, a game about running zoos, which features levels. The data reveals the magnitude of attrition at each level of the game.

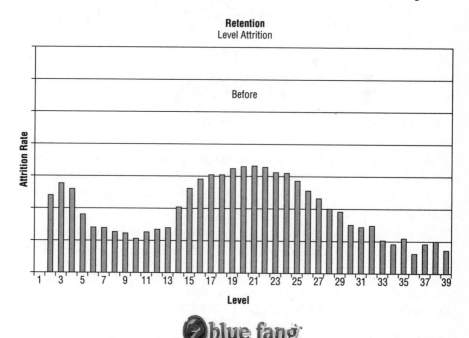

Figure 8-7: *Zoo Kingdom,* Level Attrition Before Changes

Here, you can see that *Zoo Kingdom* was experiencing a big problem with attrition during the middle levels. Blue Fang (the publishers of *Zoo Kingdom*) realized it needed to add some features to make the mid-game more engaging. Figure 8-8 reveals what happened after a set of changes were implemented in the game.

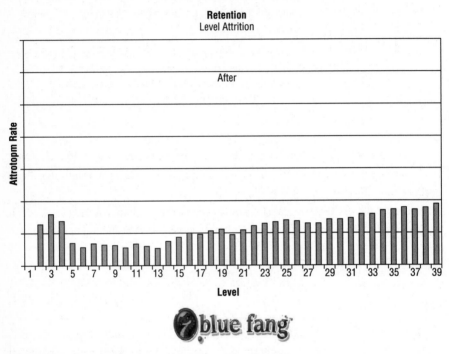

Figure 8-8: *Zoo Kingdom*, Level Attrition after Changes

The point of looking at your depth of engagement is that it reveals not only the actual amount of attention being received, but also the quality of the attention and the points of abandonment. You can use this information to guide improvements to the game.

You can track and compare gameplay-oriented metrics in a number of ways to help you decide whether you are making the right changes to your game (refer to Chapter 13).

Economic Exchange Metrics

Because this book is intended to help everyone think about ways to leverage social gaming techniques within their company, the concept of income for a game into economic exchanges is generalized. Potential economic exchanges include the following:

- **Direct revenue:** This is directly delivered to a game, using any of the usual business models previously described.
- **New leads:** Other transactions might have a dollar value to you, such as a new lead for your business or gaining a Facebook fan. In this case, if you normally pay a certain amount for a lead, then the economic exchange is equal to this value.
- **Feeders:** Certain social games could be a "feeder" into other types of social games or online experiences, which more directly monetize your player. For example, some companies have created simple games that have spread virally with the purpose to use them to introduce people to other games or products they might be interested in.

The key to success with any social game is turning it into a regular generator of profitable economic exchanges so that you can reinvest the profit toward attention-increasing improvements in the game or use the profit to acquire more customers.

In the following models, assume that your revenue comes directly from players in the form of things such as virtual goods purchases. However, you can easily replace revenue with whatever value is appropriate for your business to associate with a new player.

Purchase Conversion

Just as you want to track conversion rates to determine how many people become engaged players, you want to know the rate at which people are entering into economic exchanges. This is fertile ground for split-testing to determine specific offers and incentives that work within your game. Slight differences in the conversion rate can make a big difference in whether your game is profitable.

THE ADVENT OF FACEBOOK CREDITS

In 2010, Facebook introduced its Credit system. Members buy credits with their credit cards and use the credits within online games to make purchases. This is introducing a great deal of change within the social gaming market.

Facebook collects 30 percent of any in-game purchase as a transaction fee, which is substantially higher than the rates charged by other transaction vendors such as Trialpay. However, many social game developers are finding that Facebook credits have decreased friction, increasing the total number of purchases that players are making. In other words, Facebook Credits have increased purchase conversion for many companies.

ARPU

ARPU, pronounced "are-poo," stands for *Average Revenue per User*. In certain industries, such as telecommunications, this has been further depersonalized to stand for Average Revenue per Unit. Sadly, all of us have felt like little more than "units" when dealing with certain large companies. Earlier this book stressed thinking of people as customers or players—not users. However, ARPU is a term so embedded within the industry that I'll make an exception here.

The concept of ARPU is simple: Divide your total revenue by your total active players. This is usually expressed within a period of time. For example, the ARPU for a month would be the total revenue for the month divided by the MAU during that month.

Lifetime Value

Lifetime value (LTV) is the total revenue you can expect to receive from customers until the day they quit. This is one of the hardest numbers to model accurately in the early days of any business because you don't yet know the answers to certain key questions:

- **Does ARPU change for players over the course of time?** For some products, ARPU could drop significantly for players, even if they remain active—and even if ARPU across all players is relatively constant. You need to look at how ARPU changes for individual cohorts over time.

- **How long does a player remain a customer?** This isn't known at the outset of a new game. Some games might figure this out quickly (some games have a lifetime measured in days or weeks) but hopefully you'll encounter the high-class problem of not quite knowing because your players stick around for so long. Games such as *World of Warcraft* have had some players for years, so isn't there an opportunity for that to happen in social network games as well?

- **How can competitive pressure change your market over time?** This is always impossible to predict.

Although LTV is difficult, it's something you need to create assumptions for early: Only by knowing your LTV can you know what a reasonable *Customer Acquisition Cost (CAC)* is for your game.

Virtual Economy Metrics

Games with virtual economies have a special set of metrics that ought to be considered. You can consider them to be a second-order determinant to engagement: Virtual economy metrics might not have an impact immediately, but they'll eventually have a profound impact on whether players continue to engage with a game. The major virtual economy metrics are included in Table 8-2.

Table 8-2: Important Virtual Economy Metrics

Metric	Description
Money supply	How much currency is added per day to the economy? When possible, you can also correlate the increase in money supply to player levels, which can reveal discontinuities in how much players can earn.
Money sinks	How much currency is subtracted per day from the economy? To be accurate, you also need to consider money that has been temporarily removed because a player has become inactive. As with the money supply, you can analyze the money sinks for players across particular levels to identify places where money sinks have become inadequate or excessive.
Average net worth per player	This is an indication of player wealth in the economy. Comparing net worth to player level is a good way to see whether players are increasing in wealth as they advance through the game in the way you expect.
Velocity of money	How many times does the same virtual currency change hands between players? This can give an indication of how active the virtual economy is.
Most popular virtual goods	A ranked listing of the most popular virtual goods tells you which items have the most perceived value. You might want to make more items of this type or add content to the game that makes more use of them.
Most common purchase contexts	What was the last place a player visited before performing a purchase? This can provide insight to the most compelling content of all—the stuff people are willing to pay for.
Price sensitivity	You need to identify the price points for virtual products, particularly those based on real money. Experimenting with prices for different virtual goods and then comparing prices versus unit sales and total revenue can help you decide how to price virtual goods.

Player Discovery Metrics

Player discovery includes all the methods you use to get players into your game. These can generally be divided into two categories: the players you pay for and the players you get "for free" through viral player acquisition. Most social games depend on a combination of both.

Customer Acquisition Cost

The most basic way to look at user acquisition is to divide the total cost of your paid acquisition programs by the number of players you gained during the same period of time. Many businesses, including those outside social games, call this the CAC. For example, if you spend $1000 on advertising and gain 1,000 players during the time the ads run, your CAC is $1 per player.

One of your goals is to find ways to decrease your CAC. To do this, you have a number of options:

- **Optimize your advertising spend**: Most companies that advertise on Facebook find that they need to try many versions of advertising copy and images, and target different groups of players. Your goal is to find the customers who deliver not only the greatest CAC, but the highest profit per player. You can optimize your ads by split-testing many versions and identifying which work best. To do this successfully, you need to tag individual ads with a code that you store within your player database, enabling you to see which players came from certain sources. If you find optimizing ads on your own too daunting, third-party companies such as AdParlor and Nanigans can help you out for a percentage of your advertising budget.

- **Work with third-party portals and distributors**: Some companies will promote your product to a large number of potential customers in exchange for a cut of the profits (often as much as 50 percent). For example, 6waves and Viximo operate networks of games in front of millions of players per month. Here, your CAC would be equal to the revenue you give up in exchange for distribution; for example, if your ARPU is $1 and your distributor wants 50 percent, your effective CAC is $0.50.

- **Pay-per-install networks**: Often networks such as Trialpay are most useful to you as a means to monetize your game, but they can also help deliver installs. This is equivalent to advertising, except that you pay on a CPA basis rather than CPM or CPC. Make sure you carefully measure the revenue and engagement of the players you gain via these channels to ensure that they aren't simply disengaging immediately after completing an install.

- **Implement a cross-installation toolbar**: Applifier is a company that makes it possible for you to add a toolbar to your games that advertise other games people can play. Each time someone clicks on another game, you earn a credit, and you consume a credit when someone clicks back into your game. It's a way to swap traffic with other games and can lead to an increase in your total customers. This won't cost you anything; although, you run the risk that someone will end up within a competitor's product. To gain the most value from Applifier and similar toolbars, you need to have a respectable amount of traffic to begin with because you won't gain more players than the number who click outward.

- **Out-of-band marketing**: Use PR, special programs, and real-world events to deliver users to the game. In general, these need to have significant pull to have an impact. For products with a connection to major brands, celebrities, or other media channels, it's something to explore.

- **Maximize viral effects**: Use social channels to gain players for free by using your players to spread the game to other people.

CAC gets a bit more complicated when you take viral effects into account. Because players will do some of your recruitment for you for free, it's reasonable for you to amortize your CAC across all these additional players.

 SNEEZERS AND IDEAVIRUSES

For years, marketers have known that happy customers can be your best advocates; it's the essence of what's called "word of mouth." More recently, the idea of viral marketing has emerged, which is when your customers actively recruit new customers for you

Seth Godin, author of several books about successfully marketing a business, suggests a pair of metaphors that can help you remember how viral marketing works. Idea—which can include everything from scientific ideas to religion to consumer preferences—as a type of virus that's capable of being spread to others, you have an IdeaVirus. An idea that just sits in your head is just an idea; but one that spreads is an IdeaVirus.

A number of people can have a cold, but not everyone sneezes. The sneezers are responsible for spreading the cold to everyone else. Sneezers are the people who spread an IdeaVirus to someone else.

(continues)

(continued)

The essence of viral marketing is to create an IdeaViruses that your sneezers can spread to each other. The fact that I'm mentioning the IdeaVirus in this book is an example of an IdeaVirus, and I'm an ideal sneezer because I can share the idea with many other people thanks to the power of the press. If you remember it, the IdeaVirus has taken hold in you. If you tell a friend about it, you'll become a sneezer as well.

Social media is a perfect environment for sneezers to spread IdeaViruses, because friends are in constant communication with each other. Games are particularly virulent IdeaViruses, because people have so much fun with them that they genuinely want their friends to share the enjoyment. However, making a game into an IdeaVirus requires more than Facebook wall posts and invite-a-friend features: You have to design an emotionally-engaging experience and use social interactions in new and interesting ways.

Borrowing from Epidemiology: K-Factor

Your effective CAC could be substantially less when you account for the "free" players you might gain through viral effects. It is becoming more challenging to gain players virally, but the best games still accomplish this by creating deeply engaging experiences that players spend large amounts of attention on.

Scientists that study epidemics use a term called K-factor to characterize the rate at which a disease spreads from one person to another. A disease with a K-factor of 1.0 means that exactly one other person is infected for each person that contracts the disease. A K-factor of less than 1.0 indicates a disease that spreads to smaller and smaller groups of people—eventually burning out. And a K-factor of more than 1.0 means that each person gaining the disease will pass it along to more than one other person, which will lead to exponential growth. (Think of any of those maps you've seen in an apocalyptic epidemic movie in which a red wave starts in a small town and covers the Earth within days.)

Just as people talk about social applications as *viral*, it's also possible to apply these epidemiological terms to their marketing. Games that have a K-factor of more than 1.0 can enjoy incredible growth, whereas games with a K-factor of less than 1.0 will be more dependent on outside factors (such as advertising) to propel their growth. To illustrate how dramatic the impact of a K-factor can be, look at Figure 8-9. This shows the growth of a typical social game that spends a reasonable amount on advertising to gain customers each month, and has a K-factor of 0.9.

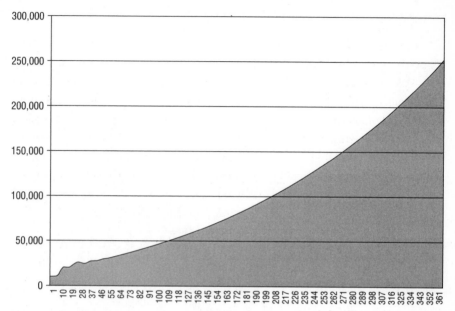

Figure 8-9: K-Factor of 0.9

In this case, the game reaches about a quarter of a million players in a year. Leaving all the other variables equal, but changing only the K-factor, this number jumps to more than 3 million players in the same period of time, as illustrated in Figure 8-10.

Forecasting the growth of a game requires many other variables, which is consolidated toward the end of this chapter where you see how to create a financial model from all these business metrics. However, this simple demonstration of a K-factor should show you how important it can be.

At one time, games could launch on Facebook and expect K-factors of more than 1.0, but those days are long gone—exceeding 1.0 happens only for a few hit products. However, many products can become profitable without a K-factor in excess of 1.0 because even a slight K-factor can have a dramatic impact on your bottom line. Imagine you operate a game with a K-factor of 0, a CAC of $1, and an ARPU of $0.90. In this situation, the product is losing money, but if features can be introduced that increase the K-factor a slight amount, the situation could reverse: A K-factor of 0.25 would mean it takes four new players (at a cost of $1 each) before you'd get the free, viral customer—but now you have five customers, generating a total of $5 in revenue. This subtle lift in the K-factor caused the product to go from a loss to a 20% gross margin. Often, it is this type of difference that pushes many products into profitable territory.

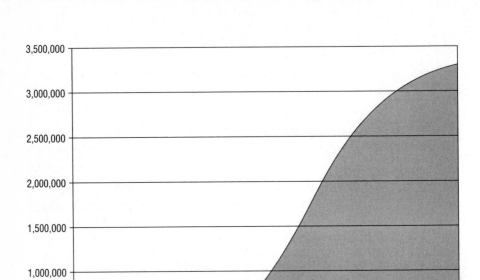

Figure 8-10: K-Factor of 1.1

To track the K-factor, you need a method for tracking how many players are recruited to your game based on the actions of your players. Unfortunately, this isn't a perfect science because some people learn about your game through channels (such as actual word-of-mouth) that are impossible to track. Your goal should be to get the most accurate number you can, without worrying about whether it is perfect.

Most games have tackled the challenge of calculating the K-factor by tagging every message that enters a social channel with information that indicates which player originated it so that a database field can be updated with that player's record whenever someone follows the link and becomes a new player. All your player records can then be averaged to determine what your K-factor is over time. (This is similar to how I suggested tracking advertising costs to determine the CAC for different advertising campaigns, except you're now treating each player as a type of advertisement.) If this sounds challenging—and it can be—you can use third-party software such as Kontagent to help with user tracking or build your game on top of a platform such as Disruptor Beam's Thorium platform, which builds this logic into its player models. Information on obtaining these technologies is included in Appendix B.

Incubation Time

A K-factor doesn't tell the entire story of going viral because it neglects to include the amount of time that it takes for a game to spread to another person. I've chosen to call this the *incubation time* in another nod to epidemiology. This is critical because it addresses the real rate of growth you can expect: a K-factor of 2.0 sounds fantastic, but what if it takes a year to get there? In many situations, a K-factor of 0.5 might be better if it happens within a week.

In the explanation of K-factor, you saw how a change from 0.9 to 1.1 can result in a huge impact. Incubation time can have a similar impact. Figure 8-11 shows that the growth curve for a game takes 10 days to spread to reach a mean K-factor of 1.0.

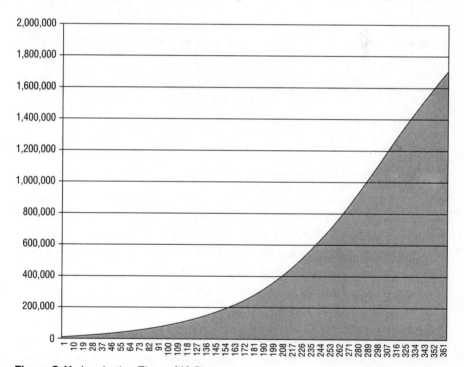

Figure 8-11: Incubation Time of 10 Days

Compare that to the game in Figure 8-12, which has an identical K-factor of 1.0 but a mean incubation time of 15. The first game approached 1.8 million players in a year, but the second game reached only a half million players in the same amount of time. This shows that viral growth depends just as much on the speed of viral spread as on the ultimate number of people it is spread to.

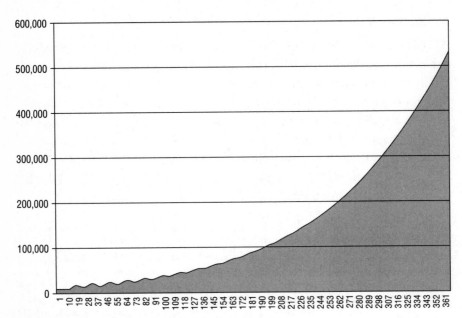

Figure 8-12: Incubation Time of 15 Days

Forecasting Growth

To understand the potential revenue and profit for a social game, you need to build a financial model that uses many of the business metrics presented in this chapter. Two approaches are described: first, a simplified model that uses the metrics but cuts a few corners in favor of helping you produce a reasonable model quickly; and second, a more advanced model that uses probability and cohort analysis to create a more accurate picture of the growth of a social game.

Simple Model

You can construct a simple financial model for a social game in a spreadsheet containing a column for each month, a set of rows for key business assumptions, and additional rows for calculating the various figures that will fluctuate over time.

Key Assumptions to Include

Set up a section in a spreadsheet to capture some of the variables that won't change over time. Place these at the top or on a different tab. For now, keep the organization simple because you're likely to change this spreadsheet a great deal. Some of the basic assumptions you can include are outlined in Table 8-3.

Table 8-3: Financial Model Assumptions

Assumption	Description
Seed population	The initial group of players for your game will be different from the ones you'll gain later through advertising. Some people might have a close connection to a few hundred (or even thousands) of individuals who can quickly be brought into a new game without spending money on marketing. Other games might spend more than usual to get the first set of customers. The main point is that your starting set of customers probably looks a lot different from the people who will follow, so you want to split these individuals into a separate group and associate them with your startup costs, excluding them from your model for marketing expenses in the first month.
Mean K-factor	If you don't have any experience knowing how viral your game is, it's best to err on the low side. Something less than 0.3 is reasonably conservative; few games consistently exceed 1.0. As previously explained, incubation time is as important as the K-factor, but this is difficult to model in a simplified model, so in this model you can pretend that any viral effects for your game occur entirely in the first month.
Mean customer lifetime	Because the simplified model is based on a monthly period, you need to measure customer lifetime in terms of months. In practice, this is unrealistic for many games, but it'll do for this back-of-the-envelope model.
DAU/MAU ratio	The higher the ratio, the more revenue you can expect. By the end of 2010, the DAU/MAU ratio for *FarmVille* was 0.28, which is quite good for such a large game.
ARPU per day	Companies such as Viximo, that have studied average revenue for different games across different networks, have found that DAU is most closely associated with ARPU, which is consistent with the claim that attention is the key to revenue. According to Viximo, it observed ARPU of $0.02–$0.03 for the average Facebook game for each DAU. In other words, 1,000 users active in a day can generate about $20–$30 per day. Of course, these are just averages and many games do far worse—and some do extraordinarily well.
CAC	Different games have dramatically different costs for customer acquisition. It can be as low as $0.10 or up to several dollars and depends on many factors, such as how well you can optimize and the overall competition you face.

Monthly Variables

With your basic assumptions established in your database, you can now create rows for the values that change each month. This includes both automatically calculated values and numbers you might want to modify. For a simplified model, these should include the variables in Table 8-4:

Table 8-4: Monthly Financial Model Variables

Variable	Description
Base advertising spend	This is the amount you spend each month to acquire new players, exclusive of incoming revenue.
Percentage of monthly revenue reallocated to customer acquisition	Many social games spend about half their revenue continuing to acquire customers, especially in the early stages of a game's life. Using customer revenue to spur further growth is one of the most effective ways you can use to grow your product.
Players gained from marketing spend	This is your total spending (using both of the previous marketing spends) divided by your CAC.
Players gain from viral growth	Determine this by looking at how many players you gained in the previous month and multiplying by your K-factor. Because this is a simplified model, you can assume that any viral growth occurs only in the first month, so make sure that you multiply only against the new customers (and not the total player population) or you'll see unreasonably high growth.
Players lost	Based on the mean lifetime of your customers, subtract the customers who you don't expect to keep for more than the current month.
Total players	Add together the total customers at the end of the previous month with the gains from marketing and viral growth; then subtract the players lost.
Revenue	Multiply ARPU per day by the number of days in the month and the total players you have for that month.

Advanced Model

The outlined, simplified financial model is helpful to get a general idea of the revenue and growth a social game can experience, but it has some shortcomings:

- **There isn't enough time resolution.** A month is a long time in the social game business—even a week is fairly long. There are good reasons why you need to look at your growth curves on a day-by-day basis.
- **New customers acquired through viral growth don't come in big chunks.** They appear probabilistically over a period of time.
- **Players don't actually stop playing after a fixed period of time.** This is also spread out over a period of time, organized by probability.

Cohort Analysis

As time passes, players will behave differently, and new features that a brand-new player finds enticing might not interest someone who has been around for a while. You need a tool to understand new customers as they arrive and to compare them against other groups of players.

Many companies employ a *cohort analysis* technique. The idea is that you bracket new customers into groups based on when they arrived in the game. For example, you could have a monthly cohort based on all the players who arrive each month. You'll learn new things over time as you inspect how new versus old players respond to changes in gameplay, pricing, and social channels.

Your advanced financial model should organize players into daily cohorts so that you can track players who join the game every day and track their entire lifetime at a resolution of a day.

Additional Assumptions

Your advanced model can now have new features that take advantage of your daily time resolution. Furthermore, you want to add a few other variables to the model to refine your understanding of growth:

- **Mean customer lifetime:** Track this in days instead of months.
- **Diminishing returns:** A K-factor is likely to erode over time; including some degradation of a K-factor as your player population grows can help you model your growth more realistically as you address an increasingly large market.

- **Mean incubation time**: Rather than treating the K-factor as something contained within the first month, you can now treat viral customer growth as something that occurs over a course of days, enabling you to model the accelerated growth that can occur when players rapidly introduce the game to their friends. This can give you a stronger sense of the real impact of viral marketing.

Using Probability

Because your resolution is now measured in days, you can see how frequently your players quit the game or get their friends to join. In the real world, this doesn't happen in chunks. It tends to happen along a *normal distribution*, which is a curve (often called a *bell curve*) that describes how seemingly random numbers are distributed over certain ranges. For example, the height of people in the United States is approximately 5 foot 10 inches (1.52 meters) on average, which means that most people are close to that height, with a decreasing frequency as you get further from the mean.

How does this apply to your business modeling? If you determine that the mean time for someone to remain a customer is 10 days, it means that most people quit after 10 days—but some people are still around for much longer, and some quit right away. The same principle applies to the amount of time required for a player to virally recruit someone each day.

The way you can think of this is that every day there's a certain chance that a player will recruit another player or quit. Figure 8-13 shows a graph illustrating the probability that a player will either quit or recruit a friend based on a mean incubation time of 20 days and a mean player lifetime of 45 days.

In this example, it shows that half the players have already quit before day 45, but others keep playing for a while. A similar shape is observed for the way in which players are recruited to the game.

Normal distributions also depend on a *standard deviations* input. It is beyond the scope of this discussion to provide a mathematical explanation of this concept, but the main point to understand is that more standard deviations spread the curve over a broader period of time. Figure 8-13 uses a standard deviation of 4.00 for the viral spread and 6.00 for the curve used for player lifetime. To illustrate the impact of changing standard deviation values, Figure 8-14 shows what happens if you decrease these values to 2.00 for viral spread and increase player lifetime to a standard deviation of 10.00.

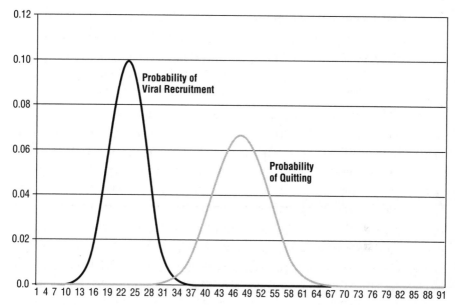

Figure 8-13: Virality and Retention Probabilities

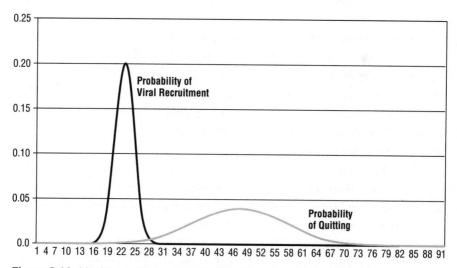

Figure 8-14: Virality and Retention, Modified Standard Deviation

Putting the Models Together

To combine cohorts and probabilities, it means you end up with a big spreadsheet: a column for each day you need to model. Furthermore, each cohort needs its own row to keep track of all the player gains and losses that occur within each individual cohort.

To start, I put together a spreadsheet that you can download online, which includes the probability calculations, daily cohorts, and all the metrics suggested that you use for assumptions. You can get this from `http://game-on-book.com/model.xls`.

A/B Split Testing

You can determine whether your game can be improved by performing scientific experiments between two sets of features. Think of each feature of the game as a competition between two alternative versions; then compare the quantitative outcome for each, using any of the metrics previously discussed.

A WORD OF CAUTION ABOUT QUANTITATIVE TESTING

Social game companies have enjoyed enormous success with quantitative testing. However, keep in mind that it's actually just another set of data you can use to improve the product. There's not much information about the long-term impact of using a numbers-intensive continuous improvement process to turn product engagement. A number of people, including myself, suspect that quantitative metrics are much more effective in optimizing short-term results (such as the rate players monetize in the first few days of playing) at the expense of long-term engagement. Use quantitative data to help guide your development, but use caution before letting this data control your destiny.

Here's why an exclusive focus on short-term metrics can be harmful: By pestering players enough and browbeating them into making certain purchases in the game, how much are you burning them out? Are you sacrificing a long-term customer relationship just to make an immediate sale? Yes, short-term metrics are important because you'll never turn someone into a long-term customer if they don't stick around at all—but be careful that you don't eke out a few extra percentage points on some short-term metric that might actually be subtracting from LTV.

In addition to testing individual features, you can test collections of features by comparing two versions of the entire product against each other. An easy method for conducting this test is to assign players into two separate groups. Then, tie the display of product features to the group a user is associated with. You can then compare the engagement metrics of each group to see whether you've made improvements. Although it is harder to pinpoint the exact features that made a difference, this can be a helpful way for determining whether significant changes in interdependent feature sets might contribute positively or negatively.

Qualitative Testing

There are cases where numbers won't tell the entire story of a product. That's where qualitative testing comes in.

Qualitative testing is all the feedback you get about your game that might not be easily reduced to specific numbers: opinions, reactions, and preferences. Nevertheless, you can create systems for visualizing and interpreting all the qualitative data you receive. You can do this by classifying each response into categories (for example, interface concerns, story confusion, and game balance issues) and flagging each according to a severity scale. Traditional issue-tracking software such as Hansoft or Atlassian's JIRA can be helpful for this purpose. The key is to capture the information in a form that enables it to become actionable for your development team.

The following sections show some of the principal ways that companies collect qualitative information about games before, during, and after launch.

Focus Groups

Focus groups are a select number of people from your target market from which you attempt to gain insights into motivations, purchasing habits, and other preferences. A focus group can help you understand why your game might succeed or fail with a particular market. To form a focus group and use it to gather important information, follow these steps:

1. Identify a group of people who are in your target market. You can use some of the same techniques suggested in Chapter 4 for identifying candidate customers for your personas (although it is best to populate focus groups with people who haven't yet been exposed to your product).

2. During a focus group session, individuals will be shown the product at whatever stage it is ready at. This could be:
   - A presentation deck or video explaining the concept of the game
   - Screen shots or scenes from within the game
   - A fully functional demo of the game
   - An interactive demo of the game where focus group members can try it for themselves
3. After presenting your product, you'll need to have a set of questions to ask the group. You can use similar questions you might have developed when creating personas (as discussed in Chapter 4)

Focus groups can sometimes create interesting results when participants are allowed to interact with each other, because their interactions can lead to conversations and observations you might not have thought of. Sometimes, focus groups might even help you decide whether to proceed with a product effort. However, focus groups have a number of risks you need to be aware of and which are presented in Table 8-5.

Table 8-5: Risks of Focus Groups

Risk	Description
False positives	People are naturally imaginative, so early stage products can sometimes elicit favorable responses because people will imagine features that haven't been built yet. The actual way you might create the product could be completely different from what people have in mind. Furthermore, people may have a tendency to want to please the interviewers by giving more positive reactions than they really think.
Interviewer bias	Focus group facilitators and interviewers need to be careful with the questions they ask because it is easy to introduce bias simply by the way questions are worded.
Explaining too much	Games need to "speak for themselves"; when a focus group presenter tells the focus group members too much about a game, you'll fail to learn about the things that were not obvious enough.
Difficulty in organizing a group:	It's often hard to get a large enough group together that adequately represents your target market.

Risk	Description
Groupthink	Participants can influence each other's thinking. Although the group interactions can lead to new insights, you have to be careful that strong personalities can often dominate a group, and might not reflect the entire market.
Unfamiliar environments	If the focus group sessions are held in an unfamiliar setting such as a conference room or testing lab, you might get different reactions than if the product is experienced naturally; imagine how different the use of a social game product is when people access it a few minutes at a time between bursts of hectic home or office interactions.
High expense	If you hire an outside firm to assist you in putting together a focus group, you can expect to spend thousands of dollars—often $10,000 or more. If you do it on your own, you'll find they're quite expensive in terms of your own time.
Slow speed	The time to organize a focus group might be better spent building game prototypes, conducting one-on-one interviews, and testing ideas quantitatively with your target market.

For these reasons, you should be skeptical of the benefit of most focus groups and prefer many of the other methods explained in this section. However, many companies have had success with focus groups, and your mileage may vary. If you use them, use their feedback as one set of the data—not a complete replacement for quantitative methods, rapid improvement through iterations, and your own intuition.

One-on-One Interviews

Chapter 5 discusses the importance of conducting interviews with customers as a means to create customer personas. The same people can be used for soliciting feedback about the product during the course of development. These interviews have the same risks of interviewer-bias or explaining too much but have the benefit of enabling you to include follow-up questions in which you can learn a lot more.

When you continue to conduct interviews through the course of product development, you may have an opportunity to talk to people who had been exposed to prior information about your game. These people might have opinions based on comparisons to prior knowledge; they can see how the product has changed over time. This can be extremely helpful, but you also need to talk to people who have never heard about the product before because that's the only way to know whether the product makes sense to a total newcomer.

During these interviews, you'll find it helpful to ask questions that allow you to identify common themes. The content of these questions are similar to what you might ask a focus group; while they don't have the freeform interaction that can some-times be helpful in a group setting, surveys don't suffer from the risk of groupthink either. In addition, if you have a pool of people you can ask questions from, you can quickly gather some reactions on new features before committing to development.

Surveys

When one-on-one interviews aren't possible, you can still collect a great deal of infor-mation from your players if you prepare questionnaires and surveys. The best surveys contain some of the questions you might ask in a focus group or in a one-on-one set-ting, but lend themselves to fixed-set, multiple-choice answers; you'll maximize the number of completed surveys you receive by keeping them as simple as possible.

One of the potential advantages of surveys is that you can gather data from a much larger set of potential customers. In addition, you can conduct a survey without consuming as much of your own time, because the process can be automated. In general, you don't need an enormous number of survey responses to obtain helpful data. Unless you are seeing a diverse set of answers with strange outliers, then 100 or so ought to be plenty.

A cheap way to conduct an online survey is to buy Facebook advertising that targets your likely customers, and direct potential customers to off-site survey tools such as SurveyMonkey.com. Another tool you can use is FeedbackArmy.com, which enables you to get narrative responses to various elements of your product design for a low, fixed fee.

Straw Man Versions

When you have a new idea for a product, but you don't have the entire product yet, you can create the first few splash screens that look-and-feel like the real thing. Advertise the product on Facebook in a similar way to how you expect to present the product after release; although, you should make it clear that the game isn't ready yet.

After an initial set of interactions, you can invite players to participate in a beta program or ask them to complete a survey. For people who aren't interested, you can inform them that the product is still under development and thank them for taking a look. The reactions to the advertising and first screens of the game might tell you whether it is worth investing in further.

An advantage of creation straw man versions of a potential product is that it can often be done for a tiny percentage of the cost of creating a complete product. You can even create multiple versions of the same product, or test competing ideas—helping you to identify the best products that should proceed to further development.

Chapter in Review

In this chapter you learned how attention is the key to generating revenue: Socially engaging features have resulted in players returning more frequently to games and have led to increases in revenue in products as diverse as *Rock Band* and Facebook games. This is further supported by data that indicates that DAU is a strong indicator for revenue.

Several models for revenue were discussed, along with an explanation of why virtual goods have become so popular: They enable customers to opt-in to spend at their appropriate level, generally in proportion to the amount of attention they spend on the game.

You also learned how customer acquisition costs (CAC) can be optimized through a combination of advertising optimization and online distribution—and further enhanced by viral growth, which may be measured by a K-factor, the rate at which players spread a game to their friends.

Some of the determinants of attention and revenue were discussed, including the things to look for in how people play and make purchases in your game.

Choose Your Path

The following list gives areas of the book you might want to visit next.

- If you want to learn techniques for organizing your ideas about the experiences which will lead to garnering high attention, continue on to Chapter 9 to learn about storytelling techniques.

- You may want to use this opportunity to review the business metrics you can use to manage the operations of a social game, which was covered in Chapter 7.
- If you are convinced of how important attention is going to be for your success, then jump to Chapter 10 to learn about many of the techniques and examples that can help you keep players coming back.
- If you want to discuss the metrics for managing a social game, go online to game-on-book.com and enter **metrics** in the secret code box.

9 Using Storytelling to Understand Your Design Objectives

n this Chapter, you'll learn:

- How to create player narratives that capture the essence of the fun in your game
- How to use the tools of myths to enhance your games and keep players coming back for more
- How to extract lists of goals and features from abstract ideas
- Suggestions for brainstorming and refining your stories

An ancient tale tells us that the king of Persia, betrayed by his first wife, set out to take revenge against all women by marrying a virgin each night and beheading her in the morning. A brave woman named Scheherazade, appalled by the slaughter, offered herself as a bride to the king, hoping she might end these deaths or die herself in the effort.

Scheherazade had learned countless stories of people and old rulers, and had studied art and poetry. Her plan was simple: to begin telling the king a story each night—but finish only the following day. This way, she avoided the king's fury for a thousand and one nights, during which time she bore the king three children. Transformed by hearing all the tales, the king spared her life and made her his queen (see Figure 9-1).

The legend of Scheherazade is first and foremost a tale about a woman's courage in the face of brutality—but it also is an endorsement of the power of stories. As a social media game designer, your challenge is not unlike Scheherazade's: You must engage players in a way that keeps them coming back day after day, never fully satisfied, hungering for the next revelation. Customers, like the king in this tale, can dispense with you at a moment's notice as soon as they grow bored.

Figure 9-1: Scheherazade

This chapter persuades you of the importance of stories. This isn't simply for those of you who want to create games about stories—role-playing games, and the like—it is for anyone who wants to use the enduring power of story to improve the way you communicate.

Stories are like emotional alchemy: They have a wonderfully transformative power that can change people's minds and convey meaning that might be lost through more analytical explanations. As such, they're a tool you can use for designing customer experiences—a tool that may be adapted not only to games, but also to anything in life and business. Think of stories as the first step that an idea can take in its metamorphosis into something concrete.

Games are always an embodiment of story, even if it is simply the story of how someone interacts. Even the most abstract games—those without any apparent characters, plot, or theme—can have a story told about the players of the game. Telling stories about your players can help you grab people's attention, add clarity to your own ideas, and provide a format for defining user experiences, interfaces, and game mechanics. You begin by focusing on the timeless elements of storytelling, and toward the last part of this chapter, you return to the subject of how to use stories as a way to provide structure to your game design.

One Thousand and One Designs

It seems our brains crave certain patterns: the hero who sacrifices, takes great risks, and overcomes challenges to make the world a better place; the tragedy that shows us the flaws within people and their terrible repercussions; or comedy, which looks at many of the same flaws but leads you only to laugh. Although the form of storytelling has changed through ages—arguably becoming more sophisticated, deeper, and more nuanced over the course of millennia—the underlying patterns that worked within the tales of Homer are just as alive today.

The player-centered design process introduced in Chapter 2 helps you identify the fun of a game. A good way to test ideas and create structure for actual game systems (what the process refers to as "crafting experiences") is to develop stories about them. What are some of the enduring characteristics of storytelling, and how can you use them to develop ideas for your game or business?

Stories Have a Beginning, Middle, and End

Almost any story has a clear beginning, middle, and end. Aristotle wrote about this as the basic requirement for a story in *Poetics*. Subsequent critics have used the idea of these three stages to develop the three-act structure of drama:

- **The Set up:** You're introduced to the characters, the world, and the conflict. In movies, this is usually the first quarter of film. At the end of the first act, something happens (a *plot point*) that propels the characters into a series of actions from which there's no turning back.
- **Complications:** During the second act, people are presented with a series of complications; they want something, but it won't be easy to get there. Most of the substance of any story occurs during this stage; screenwriters spend about half their overall script on it. The action picks up, until a final series of events (another plot point) occurs at which time they'll be forced to make a critical decision.
- **Climax:** At the start of the third act is the climax, where the characters confront each other and either succeed or fail in their goals. Characters are transformed by their decisions. Action falls off, and you learn what the impact of their actions is on the rest of the world.

The Monomyth

Chapter 4 introduced the concept of the *Hero's Journey*, which is a mythical structure found throughout storytelling. This structure is as old as the *Epic of Gilgamesh* and pervades modern-day cinema and popular fiction. Because of how consistent it is Joseph Campbell called it the *monomyth*. Campbell's monomyth contains three overall stages that contain 17 different elements; these three stages map nicely to the three-act structure just outlined.

There's plenty of criticism you can apply to Campbell's structure. For one, it's certainly possible to think of some good stories that depart from it. Also, a focus on the patterns tends to distract you from the nuances and differences between interesting stories. It's also valid to say that this formulaic approach to storytelling has made Hollywood films a lot more predictable. Nevertheless, you can find it helpful to understand the patterns that have worked well for many stories and many games so that when you choose to depart from the tried-and-true patterns, you'll do so with knowledge of what you're doing differently.

Another thing to realize about the monomyth is that this is powerful mojo. Some people don't want to learn about it because they're afraid it will taint the way they think about stories—Neil Gaiman, creator of *Sandman* and *Coraline*, has been quoted as saying that he read half of Campbell's book and then put it down because he didn't want it to affect his work. After you learn about the monomyth, you'll start to see it everywhere you look. Maybe our brains are hard-wired for it?

Now that you've read caveats about the monomyth, I'll summarize Campbell's original formulation before moving on to a simplified version—one that works well for analyzing game stories.

Departure

In this first act, the setting, characters, and conflict are introduced. You meet a potential hero and confront him with a challenge.

- **The call to adventure**: Something changes that tells the hero that there's an adventure beyond the safety of home.
- **Refusal of the call**: Initially, the hero resists the call.
- **Supernatural aid**: A protector or mentor with special powers assists the heroes, helping them to overcome their resistance and prepare them for the next steps.
- **The crossing of the first threshold**: The hero leaves home behind and crosses over into the world of adventure.
- **The belly of the whale**: The hero is isolated from the original home—there's no turning back now! This is the start of the transformation into a true hero.

Initiation

As the story enters the second act, the conflict has been established and the action rises as the hero confronts a number of increasingly hazardous challenges:

- **The road of trials**: The hero encounters various obstacles and temptations, failing some but succeeding in others. The purpose is to prepare them for their confrontation to come.
- **The meeting with the goddess**: This hero encounters a supernatural, all-loving being or has a similar, metaphorical experience, such as finding true love.
- **Woman as temptress**: The hero must resist temptations that might cause him or her to abandon the adventure.
- **Atonement with the father**: A climactic encounter with a powerful being or adversary, which in many myths is represented as a father figure.
- **Apotheosis**: The hero has a new self-awareness, perhaps divinely inspired.
- **The ultimate boon**: The hero is given a reward for his or her efforts.

Return

The hero has already had a victory but now must struggle with how the victory has changed him or her—and return with the reward, so that it might benefit others. The stages here include the following:

- **Refusal of the return**: The hero is enjoying his or her just rewards and doesn't want to return home.
- **The magic flight**: The hero encounters new dangers, which force him or her to flee with the reward, beginning a journey back home.
- **Rescue from without**: The hero is assisted by allies who aid in his or her return.
- **The crossing of the return threshold**: The hero returns home, but now must share the rewards and wisdom with others.
- **Master of two worlds**: Changed by the events of the adventure, the hero may be uncomfortable in his or her home, needing to readjust to a previous life, while remaining ready to return to the world of adventure if needed again.
- **Freedom to live**: The hero can now simply live in the moment.

The Hero's Journey for Games

The monomyth has been adapted to several forms of writing. For example, Chris Vogler refactored Campbell's original formulation into a pattern for screenwriters in *The Writer's Journey: Mythic Structure for Writers*, reducing it to 12 stages. I'm going to reduce it a bit further, taking it down to the five that are most relevant to games.

You'll get the most out of these stages if you think of them as a set of metaphors. Remember that the players are the center of their own personal drama: Games create an environment that enables them to pursue their own hero's journey. To help spur your thinking, consider some questions within each section so that you can compare these patterns to ways in which you might think about your game.

Call to Adventure

Heroes rarely begin their journey by knowing that they are going to pursue an adventure. They begin life in a world in which they know what to expect: They know when their crops will mature, when the moisture vaporators will need maintenance, and how to get along with their families, but then something changes. Perhaps it is a famine, an affair, a galactic war, or simply a realization that they could have a better life. At first, the potential heroes might resist the call—after all, there's risk involved in doing anything outside their normal world.

Sometimes the heroes are forced to action due to events beyond their control. In other cases, they are spurred to adventure by another character—often a mentor or protector—who provides them with tools they'll need to succeed. In *Star Wars*, Obi-Wan gives a light saber to Luke, just as the Greek gods armed Perseus with a magical sword to confront Medusa. At this stage, the character is starting the transformation from a normal person into a hero.

This book argues that people love experiences—and that some of the strongest experiences are those that offer the potential for personal transformation. Perhaps this is because the call to adventure is something everyone secretly longs for?

In a social media game, the call to adventure happens when the players (or potential players) catch a glimpse of a world that's beyond their own. Here are some questions you can ask about your call to adventure:

- How will players catch a glimpse of the world beyond my call to adventure?
- How can I provide the player with assistance in taking up the call—with either artificial characters built into the game, or through the assistance of other players who could take on the role of mentor or protector?

- When the players embrace the call to adventure, do I present them with a clear sense that they are now leaving their world behind and entering something new?
- Will the players sense that they've begun a process of transformation?

An adventure is anything that the player has dreamt of. This could be entirely fantastic, such as taking on the role of an epic hero in *World of Warcraft*, or more true-to-life, as with the creation of a restaurant in *Café World*. There's an implicit promise in each of these different games: Perform the right actions, and you'll become someone important.

Many website designers talk about a *call to action* in their sites, which refers to buttons and interfaces which you'd like visitors to click. These usually aren't calls to adventure. A call to action can become an adventure when the potential for personal transformation is offered. This promise is present in social websites like Twitter and Facebook—as well as online businesses such as Amazon. In each of these sites, visitors can see the attention and admiration that others receive (for example, the fame received by top book reviewers on Amazon). Visitors start their adventure by emulating the behavior of other "heroes" on the site.

Challenges

At this stage of the journey, the heroes are not yet ready for the climactic confrontation. The heroes need to be strengthened through various obstacles. These may be overt, such as enemies who will work against them to prevent their success, or they may be internal, such as the desire to leave behind the path of heroism to seek a normal life again. Sometimes temptation might present itself in the form of love interests or material rewards that might cause them to lose interest.

This will be where the players of a game spend most of their time. Following are some questions to ask:

- Do my challenges strengthen the players' interest and provoke them to continue their adventure?
- How can I keep the challenges fresh and interesting so that the players stay focused on their longer-term reward?
- The players will be tempted to try other games, so how do I keep them in mine?

Rebirth

Having braved many challenges and resisted many temptations, the hero must make a sacrifice. Sometimes this is a literal death and rebirth, such as the Egyptian god

Osiris's murder and resurrection as lord of the afterlife. More often, this death and rebirth is more figurative: Luke Skywalker's rebirth as a Jedi, or Bruce Wayne's rebirth as the Batman following the murder of his parents. It might even be more subtle, such as when one of the characters in a romantic comedy realizes what an ass he's been and changes for the better—like Jack Nicholson's character in *As Good as It Gets*, or Hugh Grant's character in *About a Boy*. In the story of Scheherazade, her rebirth occurs as she becomes the mother of the brutal king's children, an act that changes her from an idealistic girl into an even more powerful heroine, able to alter the flow of history by becoming mother to the kingdom's heirs.

At this stage, the heroes are deeply transformed by the events. They have sacrificed something essential—an element of their personality, a way of life, or their life itself—but gained something that sets them apart from the rest of us. Because of this rebirth, the heroes are prepared to take on their ultimate challenge.

The multibillion dollar self-help industry relies upon this directly, and personal transformation is at the heart of many other experiences people pursue, whether it is education, entertainment, or simply the accumulation of unique memories.

In a game, a metaphorical rebirth can occur by allowing the player to enter into a whole new stage of gameplay. In *World of Warcraft*, a certain type of rebirth occurs whenever a player completes a new level, giving them new opportunities to experience the world anew. An even larger rebirth occurs when a player finishes leveling their character and becomes a "raider," encountering the final dungeons within the game. In other games, the rebirth might happen when someone goes from simply playing, to becoming a mentor to other players. Following are some questions to ask:

- Is my game an endless treadmill of challenges, or do I provide an opportunity for players to be "reborn" and experience a whole new stage of play?
- How do I make it clear to the player that there's an opportunity for rebirth within the game?
- How do I make sure the players realize—through fanfare, story, and visuals—that they've entered a new phase in their play?
- Will players realize that there's no opportunity to rebirth and they'll be doing the same thing forever?

The Boon

Now that the heroes have been transformed by their experience, they are prepared to confront their adversary: They defeat Darth Vader, find the Holy Grail, marry the princess—or they fail, and both the character and you learn something from it.

Scholars of mythical structure have called this "the boon," and it's the point at which the heroes achieve the goal of their quest and is rewarded for it.

Often, the reward might be fleeting: There is some risk that heroes might squander their rewards or keep it to themselves. There might be some final temptation or a previously unforeseen evil to overcome.

In many games, this is the beginning of the end of the game. However, it's where social games tend to be different because they are usually intended to go on and on forever—for clear financial reasons. On the one hand, I think it's possible you'll see some online games with a distinct ending, and this might change the way people play many online games. For those that want to make a persistent game, you can ask a few questions:

- Is there an ultimate boon, and if so, what can I offer the player to stay involved afterward? If they don't, would that be okay?
- If there isn't an ultimate boon, how can I keep the player interested for the long term?
- Is there another game or experience I can channel them toward when they've obtained the boon?
- Is there an ultimate boon that's so hard to achieve that my players will simply resent it?

One of the ways to address some of these concerns is by thinking about a social game as a type of *frame story*. The legend of Scheherazade is one such example: She maintains the action for a thousand and one nights because each night contains a tale-within-a-tale.

In an epic fantasy game such as *World of Warcraft*, many of the plots and campaigns contain their own hero's journey. In this sense, it is Azeroth—the world in which *WoW* takes place—which is the frame story for the many adventures you'll have there. However, these frames are not limited to role-playing environments. If you think about it metaphorically, the achievement system that has become popular on Xbox Live is an example of a frame story: It's about how the players can become Xbox gods, competing in different games, each with their own story.

To make long-play social games, you need to learn to be a bit like Scheherazade. Not only is it a good structure for thinking about gameplay, but Scheherazade shows you how to keep people coming back, night after night. Likewise, think about applying this principle throughout life and business; what are the tantalizing boons you can offer a customer around each corner?

The Return

For the boon to become truly valuable, the heroes must return home, bringing the rewards with them to benefit other people: their family, their kingdom, or the galaxy. For some, this might be among the most dangerous parts of the journey: a magical flight, car chases, escape from a burning building, or an escape from the Death Star before it is destroyed by Rebel forces.

Upon their return, the heroes can share their boon—whether material or simply wisdom—with those around them. At last, they can live happily ever after.

If you think of the social network as the "normal world" and the game as the magic world, the return is something that social game players will make frequently. (Or so you hope!) The essence of the return stage within the hero's journey is the idea of sharing. In that spirit, following are some questions to ask:

- When the players return, what memories do I give them?
- What will the players share with their friends and family about their experience?
- How can I give the players the tools to make their return a good one?
- Do I provide the players with any artifacts that they can take with them?
- What mementos can I give the players so that they'll continue their hero's journey again in the future?

Many games make the return a simulated experience—one that exists only in a pretend story, where the player is told that they've returned with the secret elixir to cure the ills of their land. However, there's no reason that the return can't be a "real" part of the experience; using online sharing features, players can tell their friends all about what they've done and what they've learned.

Furthermore, the return isn't limited only to games. This is another area where game-like features can be added to any social media or business experience. The "share" buttons that appear throughout many websites are really an opportunity to turn visitors into returning heroes. To make share features more compelling, help the visitor see how sharing something will make them respected amongst their peers.

The Craft of Storytelling

What is it about Scheherazade's craft that enables you to hold an audience's attention? Begin your exploration by covering some of the elements of good stories and comparing them to games and other areas of business.

Starting with a Powerful Hook

Novice storytellers often start at the wrong place in a story: too early, before any of the interesting action has emerged, or too late, when things are happening to characters before you've had a chance to empathize with them.

Similarly, if you've ever had to endure boring PowerPoint presentations, you might recall how presenters spent too much time on background. Wouldn't it be better if they thought of their presentations as a story, leaping right into the action with something that hooked your attention?

Business presentations—and business in general—would become a lot more interesting if people cared a lot more about creating interesting hooks. The hook for a business product is whatever is remarkable about it. This is what marketing guru Seth Godin calls the purple cow, the part of a business that is so remarkable that it stands out from the rest. If you have something remarkable, don't waste time getting to it: Shout it from the bulwarks! If you don't have something that meets this criteria, work at it until you do. This is your story's hook.

Like a good story or a good business presentation, games start with a great hook that spurs the player to take up the call to adventure. This could be an entrancing universe, a unique game mechanic, visuals—anything that's emotionally engaging. If you're going to think of your business as a game, a great place to begin is deciding what your hook is and using it whenever you're interacting with a customer for the first time.

Show, Don't Tell

Why is it so many actors win awards for dramatic rolls? It's because they know how to show emotion, rather than tell it.

Say you want to convey sadness. Your hero Axxor has lost something and is emotional. Here are two ways you could convey that sentiment:

- **Telling:** *Axxor the hero is sad at the burning of his hometown by barbarians and swears revenge.*
- **Showing:** *With a shaky voice and moist eyes, Axxor, trembling, looks to the west and swears that no tear will fall upon his homeland until revenge is exacted.*

A mistake made by novice storytellers (and experienced ones who should know better) is to waste precious time by delivering exposition about a story's lore, history, or background. After readers become interested with a story, they might be interested in these facts, but in the beginning, they don't care.

Like most people, when reading a story, I want vivid imagery and characters that perform actions. I'd rather learn the internal state of a person's mind through their behaviors and physical response to emotion—not simply by telling me that they're happy or sad. I'm often interested in the history and background of a world, but I want to experience that information as it emerges from the fabric of the story, not through a series of encyclopedic diatribes.

Our brains have evolved to be extraordinarily good at picking up on motives, emotions, and social structures. Let people use this part of their minds; trust people to understand your emotional content without hitting them over the head with it.

Much can be learned about this art of storycraft within business. Why tell me about how a product works if you can simply show me it working?

One parallel within games are the tutorial system often used. Any time a game needs a lot of explanation about how to play it—rather than simply immersing someone in the action—it's wasting a lot of precious time telling instead of showing. It's often okay to incorporate tutorial content that appears as people play, but advance reading and explanation will just make players anxious to start playing—or worse, make them bored to abandonment. Introductory content should involve players in the call to adventure, not block them from it.

Using Compelling, Active Language

Life is concerned with verbs. Verbs imply movement. Without movement, everything as you know it would cease to have meaning; it would herald the heat death of the universe.

Compare this to the operation of your brain: You can have any number of thoughts in your head, but these thoughts impact only the world when you decide to move your muscles and take action. Your brain processes information, but its orders are carried out through verbs.

Verbs drive most good stories, representing action and reaction, motion and emotion. However, the shape and form of a story also depends on the nouns that interact with each other. Of lesser importance are the adjectives and adverbs, which can be important in the right cases but more often act as crutches for imprecise verbs and nouns.

When crafting a game experience, you need to be concerned with verbs that define how the player interacts with the game. As you develop the story of a game, it's helpful to keep a list of the verbs you imagine the player acting out and being acted upon. Likewise, if you want a business to benefit from the type of action that moves a game forward, you need to focus on the things that are actionable by your customers and employees. Verbs should work for you. Decide what actions you want people to take and give them the opportunity to do it—and ask yourself whether the processes and interfaces you create add to the likelihood of verbs being expressed.

Subtle differences in verbs can also change how you think about an experience. Consider the following sentences:

- Your hero must **fight** the evil villain.
- Your hero must **destroy** the evil villain.
- Your hero must **defeat** the evil villain.
- Your hero must **stop** the evil villain.
- Your hero must **kill** the evil villain.

Precise language is important. Killing and defeating are not the same. Consider how language is used in a business context as well; do customers "buy" a product or "invest" in it? Do you "sell" to them or emphasize "owning?" As you develop the stories that describe your products, be careful that you think about your verbs and the full meaning they convey.

Making Use of Interesting Characters

We don't read and write poetry because it's cute. We read and write poetry because we are members of the human race. And the human race is filled with passion. And medicine, law, business, engineering, these are noble pursuits and necessary to sustain life. But poetry, beauty, romance, love, these are what we stay alive for.

JOHN KEATING, DEAD POETS SOCIETY

People are interested in a wide variety of different things: science, religion, the cosmos, music, and games. There are as many unique interests as there are people on the Earth. However, one thing that almost everyone shares an interest in is other people. It is the people—the characters—within stories that make them interesting to read.

A unique element of games is that they enable the player to take on the role of a character. However, there's no reason this thinking needs to be limited to the domain of games. Chapter 4 suggests that you create player personas to describe your customers; any of these can serve as characters in the stories you'll tell. What sort of characters are they on the hero's journey within your game? Healer? Artist? Mentor? These mythical archetypes can help you create clarity around the hopes and dreams of your players.

As mentioned in Chapter 4's *Mythmaking Game*, personification can also be a helpful tool. Your customers are types of characters, with their own heroic ambitions, but good games are also characters, with their own unique brands and personalities. One can find interesting characters among many unusual places:

- In the movie *Avatar*, the moon Pandora was a type of character, with its own objectives and attributes.
- The clock in the show *24* is a character, appearing consistently as part of the brand but also representing the tyrannical reality of time, demanding actions by the other characters.
- Brands can contain characters: Think of the Energizer Bunny and how Mickey Mouse has become synonymous with Disney.
- The voiceover in *Bejeweled* is a type of character, offering parent-like encouragement.

Have a Fascinating World That People Crave to Explore

Stories take you to places that you wouldn't normally experience. Fantasy epics and role-playing games enable you to voyage into worlds of magic and wonder. Medical shows make you feel as if you can experience the life-and-death drama of hospitals. *Mafia Wars, Vampire Wars*, and even *FarmVille* take you to places many of you could never or would never go.

Disney has created an empire around the idea that people want to explore new worlds. Not only have its many films taken place in extraordinary places, but its theme parks enables people to physically enter into imagined locations. The imagineers who are responsible for Disney World and its other parks have also worked on museums, shopping, and pro sports teams.

You don't need to be a game or a theme park to allow people to enter worlds. Apple and Starbucks are two incredibly successful companies that have made their fortunes by selling not only products that people want, but also experiences they crave. Near my home in Massachusetts, there's a furniture retailer called Jordan's that features amusement-park attractions and IMAX movies; emblazoned on a plaque within the store is a sign saying that "Every Business Is Show Business."

When you enter a Jordan's, an Apple Store, or a Starbucks, you're also entering a world. What type of world does your company offer? How can you craft an experience out of an event, turn a passing thought into a memory?

Surprise and Delight

Even when they use timeless character archetypes, great stories are unpredictable. When you turn back the pages to reread, or rewind the video, the outcome of such stories makes sense, and you wonder why you didn't see it coming.

Surprise-and-delight moments aren't limited only to the climax of a movie, as they are in something like *Sixth Sense* (which I won't spoil here, for the few who haven't seen it yet). You could say that the chief goal of a great story is to not be boring. To do that, stories need to introduce the unexpected and unusual.

Games provide surprise and delight by introducing new ways to interact with the game, strange plot twists, and novel content. Like games, almost any product can do the same. When these moments over-deliver on a customer's expectations, they serve to reinforce the customer's joy and satisfaction.

Mystery

―――――

Mystery, obviously, is everywhere. Is there a God? Mystery. What about life after death? Mystery. Excuse me, what material is the ShamWow made of? Mystery. Stonehenge? Big Foot? Loch Ness? Mystery mystery mystery. McDonald's Special Sauce? I don't care how many bottles of Thousand Island Dressing you show me, it's Special Sauce. Mystery.

J.J. ABRAMS, "J.J. ABRAMS ON THE MAGIC OF MYSTERY"

―――――

The unknown is a powerful lure. It drives you to explore the universe, the inner world of the mind, and the motives of other people. Mystery is fuel that enabled Scheherazade to engage the king's interest for more than a thousand nights.

Mystery is like voltage in a story: It's the driving force that keeps you moving. Without it, you lose interest. If you know everything, why would you care to keep exploring? Even on subsequent viewings of a movie or rereading a book, you're often curious about elements of the story that you missed or forgot from the first experience.

Games invoke mystery in a number of ways: by offering new content that you don't expect or can't predict; plot twists in the story; or new ways to interact with the game that change the way you play. Mystery is a powerful tool that you can use to help describe the stories about your players.

Player Narratives

Games such as *World of Warcraft*, *Mafia Wars*, and *Gods of Rock* are about stories. You play a character in a fictional world and pretend to interact with other people who are also playing characters. For these games, storytelling is central to the gameplay. However, not all games are about a story. In these cases, it is the story about the player that you'll want to focus on.

For example, *Bejeweled Blitz* doesn't have any detectable story. However, this doesn't mean you can't tell a story that's centered around the player's experience:

Jane glimpsed a strange world encircling the border of Facebook; a realm of blue diamonds floating through the sky amid a backdrop of imposing mountains. She had heard of this Bejeweled realm but had resisted the draw. However, a friend had posted of his experiences there, and Jane decided to take a look.

Upon her arrival in Bejeweled, Jane learns about the magic of this realm: By assembling three gems of the same color in a row, she can earn points. Suddenly, the clock starts ticking, and Jane begins placing moves. After assembling a few gems into position, they explode, and a deep resonating voice of the game's Overlord says, "Good," approving of her move. Emboldened, Jane suddenly spots a place where she can switch one gem to obtain four in a row in one direction and three in another.

"Awesome!" booms the voice of the Bejeweled overlord, as the gems shatter.

Soon after, Jane sees and hears, "Time's up" but realizes she's done well. Maybe she's a natural?

Minutes become hours—and Jane begins exploring deeper. She learns of special power-ups that she can acquire to increase her score even higher. The voice

*of the Bejeweled Overlord, like an encouraging parent, is always there to inspire
her to do better.*

*"New high score," says the voice of the Overlord, following a particularly
strong game. Jane has outscored many of her friends.*

*Flushed with pride, Jane posts her score on her Facebook wall, believing that
her friends will be awed by her rapid success. Soon after, her friends are asking
for advice on the best power-ups to use within the game.*

This sort of story is a player narrative. The purpose is to use this as a brainstorming and vision-creation tool to get you thinking about the source of fun in the game,
the peak aspects of the experience, and some of the elements that might become
important to your brand.

Mythical Structure in Player Narratives

The *Hero's Journey for Games* structure explained earlier can help you define those
emotional, enduring elements of story that can resonate with your player. Use it as
a metaphor for the features and experiences of your game and as a way to identify
areas for further development.

Here's how you might break down the preceding above story into the *Hero's Journey
for Games* described earlier:

- **The call to adventure**: Jane is exposed to a world of glittering gems through
  her friends. It looks interesting, but she's initially more comfortable staying within the safety of her Facebook profile page. However, her friends
  are given artifacts from their play that they share with her, intriguing her
  enough to join them there.
- **Challenges**: This is the first several games that Jane plays, in which she dis-
  covers some of the special features of the game.
- **Rebirth**: Jane understands enough of the game that she's now a *"Bejeweled
  player."* As such, she's comfortable about making choices to acquire some of
  the in-game boosts that a beginning player might not be ready for yet.
- **The boon**: Jane wins a "new high score" and is blessed by the Bejeweled
  Overlord. The true reward is the social status this conveys to Jane among her
  peers.
- **The return**: Jane returns to her Facebook wall, sharing her success as a player.
  Because she's becoming an expert in the eyes of her friends, she often comments on her friends' replays, offering advice on ways they might improve.

You can see from this brief example that it is always possible to write a story about an experience, even if the experience is not fundamentally about navigating fiction. Stories of this type can help you understand your customer, develop scenarios that help you identify the potential for surprise-and-delight moments, and create characters within the drama of your experiences.

Extracting Experiences from Stories

Website and software developers often refer to *user experience* and *user interface* as if they're interchangeable terms. They are not.

- **The player (user) experience** is the set of memories that the player takes away from a game, and the ways the game might transform them.
- **The play (user) interface** is the assembly of buttons, gadgets, procedures, and incantations a player needs to learn to interact with a game.

By creating stories about your game, you can identify the key experiences. My story of Jane in *Bejeweled Blitz* identified several important parts of the experience:

- **Branding:** A distinct set of visuals that players can recognize as being part of the *Bejeweled* game
- **The Game:** The basic game mechanics involve organizing three games in a row, but there will be more advanced mechanics as players learn the game
- **A Mentor:** A character that rewards the players with encouragement as they do the right things
- **Special power-ups:** These provide more advanced players with a way to enjoy a deeper version of the game with greater rewards
- **Sharing:** A way for players to share their in-game experiences and high-scores with other people

You need to think of story development as another iterative element of the player-centered design process covered in Chapter 10, "Using Storytelling to Understand Your Design." As J.R.R. Tolkien wrote in the foreword to the *Lord of the Rings*, "this tale grew in telling." As you explore various elements of your design, you'll find yourself revising, rewriting, and returning. By having a story as the heart of your game experience, you'll have something to return to, rather than a random walk through features and interfaces.

Just as previously done, you need to extract a list of experiences from your stories after they've been developed. When you iterate your stories, compare the story to this list. This can become the heart of your product—the player experience. From here, you can move to the next stage: Create a list of requirements from these experiences.

Creating User Stories

In agile software development, there's a concept called *user stories*, which describe the behaviors that a user wants to perform. The purpose of user stories is to create a list of the requirements. The player experiences that you discovered while developing a player narrative provide an overall vision for how people will interact with the game; the user stories are about breaking it down into separate components that can be discussed as individual features and goals.

Player narratives and experiences are a certain type of story, but they're too broad to turn directly into a set of development tasks. You need to break it down into requirements expressed in terms of the player's role, goals, and reasons. The typical format, as used in agile development, is to complete the following sentence: "As a *someone*, I want to do *something* so that I can *achieve some goal*."

Epics: Tell about the Big Picture

The broadest user stories might extract an overall goal without implying a specific feature. This type of story is called an epic and can be used to enumerate the big-picture aspects of a game. For example, following are a couple epics you could extract from the player narrative about *Bejeweled Blitz*:

- As a prospective player, I want to know what's great and unique about the game so that I can decide to try it.
- As a player, I want to share my successes with friends so that I can enjoy the warm feeling of increased social status that comes from being perceived as a winner.
- As a first-time player, I want to have experiences that get me involved with the key aspects of the game so that I don't need to ask others how to play.

These epics organize some of the high-level goals for the game, but they still aren't actionable enough. If you handed one of these to two different developers and asked them to come back with a solution, there's no telling what they might make. This is where you'll break the user stories down into smaller pieces with more specific requirements.

Making User Stories Smaller

It's time to go from big picture to story detail—from the story outline to the actual actions that complete a story. For example, the goals expressed for first-time players could include the following user stories, which contain some of the ideas included in the original player narrative:

- As a first-time player, I want to know the easiest way to try to play the game so that I can quickly see if I like it.
- As a first-time player, I want to understand that the game involves placing three gems in a row so that I'm not confused about what to do.
- As a first-player, I want to be encouraged to keep playing through the words of an encouraging mentor so that I'll feel like playing more.

Although the language is more formal—as is appropriate for software development—the echo of the hero's journey is still present. Among this formal list, you can find the call to adventure, the boon, and the other elements of the story. You can also see that it focuses on the verbs that someone wants to perform and the motivation behind it.

INVEST in Good Stories

Good user stories make the job of creating actual products a lot easier. Bill Wake, a teacher and agile consultant, created the INVEST acronym for remembering the best traits of a good story:

- Independent
- Negotiable
- Valuable
- Estimable
- Small
- Testable

Independent

The ultimate purpose of user stories is to provide you with a list of goals and behaviors that can become tasks assigned to the developers on a team. Thus, the best stories are independent of each other. For example, "As a player, I'd like to view a leaderboard so that I can compare my score to my friends" is a good story because the desire for a leaderboard can likely be created as a task separate from most other features.

As previously explained, games do tend to be more hierarchical than many other types of software development. A change to one game system can have implications throughout the game. Aspire to create independent features, but don't be shackled to it.

Negotiable

User stories focus on objectives, not the explicit form of a feature, so they might lose some of the detail that was expressed in the original player story. For example, the list of user stories previously listed mention that it is important to provide the player with encouraging words, but it doesn't explain the exact form for this. If this is central to the brand, it isn't absolutely forbidden to include such details in the user story, but it might also be helpful to see if refining the essential essence of the idea can spur even more creative discussion around it, rather than enforcing a particular design too early. By engaging the developer of a feature in a negotiation with the creator of a story, you have the best chance to create the best solutions.

Valuable

Will the player care about the feature? Or does it simply gratify the egos of designers or engineers? Is it technically cool but irrelevant to the people who will pay for it? The answers to these questions can tell you if they're valuable.

Estimable

One of the advantages of going through the story-creation process is to remove uncertainty from development. Stories create focus and understanding of what needs to get done. Someone on the team needs to look at a story to determine how large the task is. If it can't be determined, it usually means that the story is either too vague or needs to be broken down into smaller tasks.

Testable

It should be fairly obvious how to test something based on the user story. A good criteria for whether it's testable is to imagine yourself giving the story directly to players and observing whether they could try it themselves. By making stories testable, what you're actually doing is weeding out vague and imprecise stories.

Iterating Stories and Player Narratives

It's also helpful if you think of user stories as part of a holistic process: It isn't that user stories are the final output of the story-creation phase of your design, thrown over the wall to implementers who haven't seen the process unfold. It's a unique element of games that the user interface, the game design, and the player story are so intimately linked that everyone on your team should be a part of the story creation process. That's one of the advantages to having a cross-functional, self-organizing team of the type discussed in Chapter 10.

As you create epics from your player narratives, you'll encounter ideas that aren't fully explored. You might also think of some epics that weren't part of your original narrative and use the narrative as a way to expand upon an idea further.

As you start to create real user stories—ideas with a specific form, which meet the INVEST model—you'll be ready to move forward to the next phase. For games, following are two main branches to pursue next:

- The user interface that might help inform the feasibility of a particular user story, or even uncover new ways to improve the player narrative
- The game mechanics that address the specific rules, systems, and ways that someone will play the game

Visualizing Stories with Story Cards

As you assemble your list of stories, it's helpful to place them on index cards or large post-it notes. The benefit is that you can pass them around the room, place them on walls, and add notes to them. For teams that don't have a physical meeting place, as happens with many virtual development teams today, you can use wikis and software-based collaboration tools to do something similar.

Each story card should contain the full text of your story; reserve some space for adding notes. Figure 9-2 is a photo of an example card.

As you create a group of epics and stories, you can organize your stories into hierarchical maps. When placed in a shared space, this can be extremely helpful for your whole team to know what's going into the product. It also helps illustrate the relationship between each feature and uncover potential dependencies.

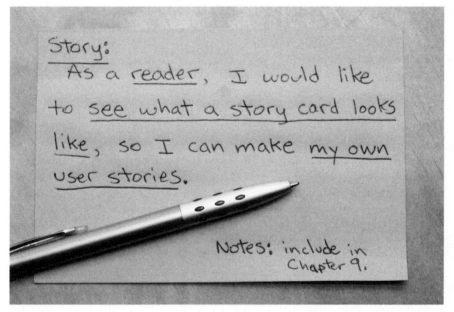

Figure 9-2: Story Card

Story Creation Games

Writing stories can be fun and creative. It's also a great way to crystallize your ideas. However, you can also run into roadblocks. The following items are a bunch of ideas that you can use to prime your creative juices or make changes that could produce a better result.

Games with Player Narratives

Your narratives are about the big-picture ideas and vision for your product. This is a good place to stress-test some of the ideas and explore alternatives, which are outlined in Table 9-1. Any of the questions may give you new insights about your story, or provide a new viewpoint that helps you overcome your own creative blocks.

Table 9-1: Narrative Brainstorming Ideas

Idea	Description
Cliffhangers	Think of yourself as Scheherazade. Inject something into your story where the players have to wait for more than a day before continuing. Would this keep them coming back for a longer period of time? Might it simply aggravate them?
Different Perspective	How would you describe the game differently if you played from the villain's perspective?
Sharing with Friends	Try rewriting any of your user stories from the standpoint of players who are sharing the game with a friend. Is this a feature they'd want to talk about? How would they describe it?
Use *Journey for Games* metaphors	Use metaphors from the *Hero's Journey for Games*. Is each element present in your story? If so, what would happen to your game if you took one out? What if one element were made larger and more important than the rest?
Use different archetypes	What happens if you rethink your player narrative from the standpoint of a totally different mythical archetype? Use any of the ones listed in the *Mythmaking Game* in Chapter 4.
Game addictiveness	Imagine a story in which an investigative journalist is exposing your game as "too addictive." How would she describe the game from her standpoint?
Combining narratives	Try combining two parts of your player narrative into one. Are there cases in which two ideas might actually be one idea in disguise?
Beware of getting "stuck"	Are there places in your narrative where it seems like the players could get stuck? If so, how do you make it so that they can get unstuck? Or is there a clever way you can use the fact that they're stuck to drive some form of social interaction?
Map your game	Draw a *mind map* of your narrative by writing the key concepts on a whiteboard or a sheet of paper. Free associate by creating new branches from your idea by listing related concepts. Keep free associating from each of these branches for as long as you'd like. Do any of these branches uncover a better idea?
Use pictures	Try to describe your player narrative using only pictures and symbols. It doesn't need to be a work of art—only a tool for ideas. Does this inspire any new thoughts?

Idea	Description
Replace luck with skill	In every case where your narrative discusses something that depends on luck, try rewriting it to be based on skill. Then try the opposite. How does this change the way you think about your game?
Tell a five year old	Try to explain your narrative to a five year old. Do they get it? If there's no handy five year old, you might need to pretend a bit. Or just try a dog—they're great listeners.
Read your narrative aloud	Does it sound exciting enough? How would you feel about delivering this narrative in front of a room of 100 people?
List exciting elements	Make a list of the most exciting things about your narrative. Then, try and imagine something that's opposite but equally fun. How might this change your narrative?
Delete social elements	Rewrite your narrative description without any social elements whatsoever. Does it still sound fun?

As a fun exercise, find a social game you like on Facebook. Write up your own version of a narrative for it. Then, try any of the preceding brainstorming tips to see what type of new ideas you come up with. Try it again on a game you hate, with the objective to make a better game.

Games with User Stories

Although user stories occur at the more formal end of the process explained in this chapter, there's no need to insist that formality means lack of fun. The following items are some ways you can play with your user stories:

- **Card-from-the-hat game.** After you write your epics on story cards, toss them into a hat and pull one out. What if the epic you pulled out was the main idea of your game? How would that change things? Is it fun enough? What would happen if you created the game without it?
- **Another card-from-the-hat game.** Pull any user story (not just an epic) from the hat. What would the experience be like if this were the first part of the game that a player saw?
- **Shuffle a deck of your story cards.** Imagine yourself explaining the assembly of your game to a brand new team member, using the order that the cards randomly appear in.

- **Supporting a card goal.** For each story card, try to identify other reasons to support each goal. Can you think of any better reasons? How does a change in the reasoning change how someone might approach the feature?

Based on your experiences with the preceding tips, you might find yourself returning to your player narrative or reprioritizing some of the stories.

Chapter in Review

This chapter began with the broadest definition of a story, addressing the elements of drama, myth, and symbolism that contribute toward good storytelling. You can use the ancient tools of myth and story structure to think about the ways in which your game can invoke the sense of excitement and engagement that stories have generated throughout the ages. This type of broad story, which can be used to capture the vision for a game, is called a player narrative.

Player narratives can be broken down into other elements. Epics are the major goals and important themes within the game; user stories define specific goals and objectives. When used iteratively, these three layers can provide both the definition and structure for any project that employs the player-centered design process introduced in Chapter 3

Choose Your Path

The following list gives areas of the book you might want to visit next.

- If you'd like to think about how the player narratives and user stories can turn into specific game systems such as rules, leaderboards, and so forth, that's the subject covered next, in Chapter 10.
- Because game mechanics, stories, and user interface are so intertwined in game development, you might enjoy thinking about the visual aspects of game design before you focus on the mechanics. If that's you, feel free to jump ahead to Chapter 12.
- If you'd like to discuss the brainstorming and creativity techniques that other people use to develop and refine their ideas, you can go online to www.game-on-book.com and enter **stories** in the secret code box.

10 Creating Compelling Game Systems

n this Chapter, you'll learn:

- How pace, flow, and fun work together to make compelling games
- How to design game systems that result in compulsive interaction
- How to deepen your own game design skills while having fun doing it

There's a huge difference between experiences that are simply fun activities and games that are fun over the long term. A fun activity might include any of the 42 types of fun covered in Chapter 5, but that's usually not enough. If you want people to keep coming back, you need to do more. You need story and engagement, and effective methods to communicate a player's progress within the game. This chapter introduces you to a number of game systems you can apply to any game or business environment to nurture long-term interactions with your customers.

To create enough fun to keep your players coming back, you need to create game experiences in which

- Each interaction is genuinely fun.
- The player has a combination of short-term and longer-term goals. The short-term goals satisfy the need for immediate enjoyment, whereas the longer-term goals persuade them to return.
- Challenge and skill are carefully balanced over time so that the experience doesn't seem too easy or too hard.
- Players are constantly told about their progress toward their goals.

Understanding Flow

Have you ever felt so engaged by an activity that time seems to slip away—yet at the same time you feel a constant sense of success and joy in what you're doing? You might have felt this way when playing a sport, performing on a musical instrument, solving a business problem, reading an interesting book—or playing a game. In sports, this feeling is sometimes called being *in the zone*.

Hungarian-born psychologist Mihaly Csikszentmihalyi (pronounced Mee-hye Cheek-sent-mah-yay-hye-ee) has pioneered a field called *positive psychology*, which seeks to understand why we have certain experiences such as "being in the zone." The concept of flow is that certain activities balance our perceived skills with the perceived challenge level of a given experience. When we feel skillful in our activity—and the activity is challenging enough—time can seem to blur by, and we feel deeply satisfied. This state of mind is called *flow*.

Flow explains why certain experiences are so enjoyable. Csikszentmihalyi defines eight elements that go into the most enjoyable experiences. People who experience flow:

- **Believe they can complete the tasks.** Examples include reading a book, cooking a special recipe, or finishing a level within a game.
- **Concentrate on the activity**. Activities done so passively that people don't even need to think about them usually don't create much enjoyment.
- **Receive clearly communicated goals.** When someone can't tell what the purpose behind something is, they often lose interest.
- **Receive immediate feedback during the experience:** Did you reach a new part of the story? Did the meal you just cooked taste good? Did you earn a new badge in a game?
- **Experience a deep involvement with the task.** This involvement means you can escape from the worries of everyday life.
- **Experience a sense of control.** Sometimes this is referred to as the *sense of agency*; you like to know that your actions have an impact on the world.
- **Lose a concern for the self.** In other words, your sense of self disappears during the activity because you focus on the activity itself.
- **Lose the sense of time.** The hours seem to fly by. Contrast this with Dunbar, a character from Joseph Heller's novel *Catch-22* who sought to make his life seem to last longer by only doing activities he disliked: "Dunbar loved shooting skeet because he hated every minute of it and the time passed so slowly." In real life, there aren't many Dunbars—and a good indication that you're enjoying something is the speed with which time seems to pass.

Balancing Challenge versus Skill

Perception is an important consideration in game design. It doesn't matter what the player's real skill level is—they'll have their own idea about how skilled they are. Likewise, it doesn't matter what the game designer feels is challenging; it matters only if the player feels the game is challenging. Figure 10-1 illustrates the various mental states that can be experienced based on your perceived skill and challenge levels.

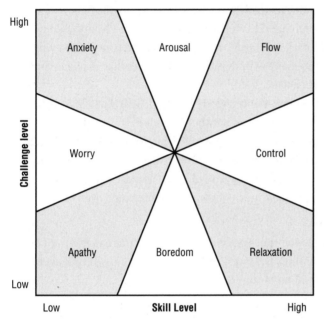

Figure 10-1: Challenge versus Skill

First consider some of the other positive states that can exist in the upper-right portion of the Figure 10-1:

- **Flow:** The ideal state of mind for a game; The player's skill and challenge are in perfect balance, leading to deep engagement and satisfaction. Although good games make it possible for players to enter a state of flow, no game can achieve this state 100% of the time, which leads to some of the other positive states of arousal, control and relaxation.
- **Arousal:** The mental state in which players feel that a particular activity is slightly beyond their current skill level, but that with enough practice they'll soon master it. Some amount of arousal is necessary within a game because players need to be presented with novel challenges that they need

to overcome to feel a sense of accomplishment—and to later allow them to enter a state of flow. However, a constant state of arousal could lead to exhaustion, which is why games need to vary the type of experiences they offer.

- **Control**: When players feel a moderate challenge is involved in an activity, and they don't need to push themselves much to enjoy success. Players in this state report that they feel in total command of the game. People like to feel in control, but eventually this feeling can shift to one of boredom as they feel so masterful that the activity becomes effortless. Many good game experiences swing back and forth between arousal and control, enabling the players to experience periods of flow during the times that challenge and skill fall into perfect balance.

- **Relaxation**: The state experienced when players believe that a high skill level is required to perform an activity but don't feel at all challenged by it. Periods of relaxation within a game can allow players to catch their breath and enjoy a sense of total domination, but eventually, things need to rise in challenge level again, or the players will grow bored. By their nature, relaxing activities don't ask much of the players and could even be sleep-inducing.

A mix of any of these mental states can create a positive game experience. The left portion of Figure 10-1 contains the states that you must avoid—or risk alienating players, who will quickly abandon your game:

- **Anxiety**: The feeling that players will have when the challenge of a game is so great that their current skill level isn't even slightly close to matching it—often causing them to feel that they'll never achieve mastery. Players who experience anxiety will look for easier challenges, perhaps by adjusting the difficulty level of the game or trying different content—but will quickly abandon the game if all they can find is anxiety-producing experiences. Nobody wants the feeling of helplessness or desperation that accompanies anxiety.

- **Worry**: The opposite of control; the players feel as if the game is playing them instead of them playing the game. They perceive that the game's challenge level is only moderate, yet their skills are simply not adequate to succeed, and their lack of success may make them feel as if they may not get better.

- **Apathy**: Occurs when both the game's challenge and the players' skill level are low. For example, consider the game of tic-tac-toe: Most people learn that it is possible to cause a stalemate 100 percent of the time by placing the right moves. Thus, the only way you can get better at it is to learn to make your moves even faster. Who cares? The game mechanic is too obvious and too easily mastered, so most people don't care enough to improve their skills. This general disinterest and lack of engagement could be considered the opposite of flow.

- **Boredom**: Occurs when the activity requires moderate amounts of skill but the challenge is too simplistic. The difference between boredom and relaxation is that boring activities simply don't use enough of your skills to maintain your interest.

Sources of Challenge

It's okay to have periods of relaxation in a game, but the only games that stay interesting in the long run are those that present the players with challenges. Games are largely about learning: They give players new things to do and then ways to adapt through experimentation. You can use any of the following areas to introduce new challenges to players:

- Interactions
- Tactics
- Strategies
- Complexity
- Physical skills

Learning New Interactions

Have you ever learned to play chess? If so, you might remember the surprise you experienced when you were shown how the knight moves, jumping in an L-shaped pattern over other pieces on the board, whereas all the other pieces move in straight lines. As soon as you learn how the knight moves, it gets you thinking about new tactics and strategies for winning the game.

Players feel challenged when they are introduced to new ways of interacting with the game. In chess, you need to learn all the basic moves during your first game, but computer games have the capability to dole out new types of interactions as you get immersed with them. Examples of new interactions include the following:

- **A new way of winning**: A game can start with a clear overall objective (beat the level, beat the boss, earn the most money, or collect more points than your friends) but can then introduce other subobjectives along the way: opportunities for earning badges, alternative ways of competing, and opportunities to create your own content.

- **A new move, magical spell, or ability you gain when earning a level**: For example, in *World of Warcraft*, players earn new spells that enable them to defeat opponents in new ways (which is balanced against harder-to-defeat opponents that will become easier to defeat as soon as you use your new ability).
- **A new rule**: Additional conditions are placed on certain situations to increase the difficulty to keep pace with the player's knowledge of the game. For example, when players learn how to perform well in *Bejeweled*, they can pit themselves against the clock, which increases the difficulty by introducing time pressure.
- **A new way to move within the game's environment**: Imagine an immersive 3D game in which you start out by walking through the environment but later the game involves you by showing you how to climb, swim, or fly.
- **A new way to view the game environment**: Perhaps you started out by seeing a 2D map of a strategy game, but now you have a special report page that helps you understand what's going on within the game in a new way.

Learning Tactics

In the military, the study of tactics largely involves the positioning and movement of units. An understanding of tactics guides what should be done in a situation in real-time. This is different from strategy, which is the overall plan used to win. In the course of executing a strategy, players need to respond to uncertainty and apply a variety of different tactics.

When first playing a game, players don't know enough about it to formulate a strategy. Instead, they gain an appreciation for the tactical moves of gameplay, learning how to respond to particular situations. As they gain access to an increasing number of interactions, they can learn how the right combination and sequence of these interactions produce better outcomes.

When the combinations are interesting and open to differences of opinion on what's regarded as best, the tactical understanding of the game opens up a whole new realm of challenges. Good tactical systems require the player to think about trade-offs, and the best games avoid having tactical combinations that are best 100 percent of the time.

TACTICS IN CHESS

Chess offers a good understanding of the basics of tactical gameplay. Beginning players of chess tend to focus on reacting to situations as play progresses—moving pieces into valid positions, taking and trading pieces, and hoping that their opponent isn't moving with much forethought. However, after a few games, they'll notice that certain pieces can be arranged in patterns that provide for distinct advantages. There is so much variety in chess that thousands of books have been written about its tactical patterns and opening moves. One of the more popular books on this subject, *The Oxford Companion to Chess*, features more than 1,000 openings.

Most social games lack the complex turn-by-turn tactical complexity of chess. Nevertheless, they still offer the opportunity for tactical development. Consider how this is done in some of the social games already discussed:

- **Energy tradeoff:** *Mafia Wars, Vampire Wars,* and *Gods of Rock* tactics involve deciding how to spend your energy and stamina. Is the payoff great enough for a particular job that it is better to do than others?
- **Damage output/control:** In *World of Warcraft,* tactics involve using the right sequence of events to maximize damage output and mitigate the damage received. It also includes things such as deciding which quest to do next, or whether you'd like to collect certain resources to sell in the auction house.
- **Scheduling:** Many social network games involve tactical decisions about maximizing the amount you can get done in a particular amount of time, or on a particular schedule. For example, *FarmVille* tactics involve deciding what crops to place on your map, and whether you'd like to focus on crops that yield faster or slower harvests.
- **Character movement:** In *League of Legends,* each character you can purchase has different individual moves, but it is the combination of the moves in the right situation that leads to success or failure. In addition, you need to decide which items to equip your character with through the course of each game.

Learning Strategies

After players gain an appreciation for the tactical elements of a game, they'll get more interested in strategy. This is the most mature stage of play, when people enter into a game experience with a particular plan of how they're going to win. For your players to enter a state of flow, you want to make it possible for them to adopt strategies and execute them, which can provide the satisfaction of thinking through moves, setting goals, and experiencing the benefits of a good strategy or the failure of a bad one.

Chess, again, provides you with a good demonstration of strategy. One basic chess strategy is "I'm going to play conservatively and defensively, waiting for my opponent to make a bad move. After I have the advantage, I will aggressively begin exchanging my weaker pieces for my opponent's stronger ones, opening up a path for a pawn to transform into a queen." Advanced chess players begin with an opening set of moves and plan through some of the likely outcomes—sometimes twenty or thirty moves or more, each involving a variety of tactical patterns.

The key to providing strategic gameplay is to offer players the ability to form plans. Returning again to some of the games already discussed in this chapter, players can change:

- **Character energy:** Strategy in games such as *Mafia Wars* center around how you are changing your character over time. In *Mafia Wars*, do you want to increase your energy (which will let you do more jobs) or increase your stamina (to attack other players more often)?

- **Character-building options:** In *World of Warcraft*, strategy involves a broader set of character-building options—the choice of mutually exclusive skills and combinations. It can also include the overall strategy employed to beat certain bosses, such as which characters to bring to the battle with their sets of equipment and individual tactical capabilities.

- **Goals:** In *FarmVille*, you can decide how you'd like to play: Do you want to earn the ribbons (the *FarmVille* version of achievements), earn the most money, or increase your level quickly? Deciding on your priority, the strategy you employ will be different.

- **Item/ability sequence:** In *League of Legends*, your personal strategy usually involves the sequence of abilities and items you choose during the course of a game. As players become more experienced, they'll form teams with other players where the strategy also involves a plan for which players will focus on certain activities given their relative strengths and weaknesses.

In social games, strategy can occur within at least two layers: the personal strategy an individual player brings to a game and the group strategy that friends have when playing together. Although these two layers can affect each other a great deal, keep in mind that players usually start out focused on their own plans before they are willing to work with other people to develop group strategies. When there are opportunities for creating and executing strategies in a game, players can enjoy more advanced forms of challenge.

Emergent Complexity

As the number of tactical and strategic variations increase, complexity rears its head. Complexity can alienate players when they aren't ready for it, but people crave complexity because it makes them feel they're solving interesting problems. It is the job of a good game to hide much of this complexity from the player and introduce people to more advanced forms of play as they become ready for it.

Good games introduce complexity over time by creating opportunities in which combinations between all the new interactions enable the player to achieve new victories. In a game such as *World of Warcraft*, high-level players have the opportunity to mix and match a wide range of factors (equipment, glyphs, talents, and tactics) to optimize their play; however, most players would find the quantity of options overwhelming if it were forced upon you at first level. Social network games such as *Mafia Wars* have an increasing complexity level over time as well, as players get involved with a wider range of features: property ownership, robbing other players, and acquiring rare items to unlock special jobs.

You can quantitatively measure the complexity of a game by looking at the total number of moves at each turn of a game. In real-time games, the idea of a "turn" becomes all of the choices you could possibly make at a given point in time (which might vary throughout the course of a day, or even an individual session). Creating a branching model that describes the increases and decreases in complexity over the lifetime of a game is called the *game-tree complexity*. Consider a few examples, starting from the simplest to the most complex:

- Rock, paper, scissors has three possible moves, and never changes over the course of a game until there's a winner.
- Tic-tac-toe starts with nine possible moves, which decreases over the course of the game; in other words, the most complexity you ever face is on the first move.
- Chess has 20 possible opening moves (any of the eight pawns can advance forward by one or two spaces, or either knight can hop right or left). During the course of the game, the number of possible moves increases until it reaches the endgame when far fewer moves are possible.
- In *Mafia Wars*, your "moves" fluctuate depending on where you are in the game. The first choice involves which part of the game you want to

use—shopping, attacking other players, performing jobs, or managing income-generating property are the main ones. From each of those, you have a number of different moves based on your level. At level 1, you have only one job you can perform, but this increases proportionate to your level.

- In *World of Warcraft*, at level 1 you only have a few moves at each point in time: You can move your character forward and backward, right or left; you can attack or use one or two starting abilities; and you can interact with other characters. All offer you the opportunity to accept quests or purchase items. As you level up, the choices you have increase dramatically: You need to choose where you want to adventure, how to outfit your character, and how to manipulate dozens of skills in real-time during battles. Add to this the fact that you also interact socially with other players, and it should be apparent that complexity results in a nearly infinite number of actions you can take at any moment during the game.

Try to map out the complexity of your game over time. Does it increase? Decrease? Reach a crescendo and then become simpler? Does it start fairly complex (referred to as *inherent complexity*) or is complexity something the player becomes comfortable with over time? You can manage the introduction of complexity by:

- Removing options when complexity isn't adding to the fun
- Delaying the introduction of new options until the player is ready to learn them
- Adding complexity by adding new features at stages where the player might be growing bored
- Adding stories or other user interfaces that help the player understand complexity as it is introduced

Knowing whether a game is too complex is part of the art of game design. Mapping out your complexity can provide some indication of extraordinary jumps in complexity; good designers sometimes have intuition about when certain features are too much. Excessive complexity may also be revealed through quantitative testing, because you can identify points in the experience where players are getting stuck or leaving the game. The latter subject is addressed in Chapter 9 during the discussion of the determinants of attention.

Mastering a Physical Skill

Many games require the player to by physically involved. This is most obvious in athletic sports, but it is also a huge element of the hand-eye coordination that occurs in action-oriented games. This isn't limited only to "hardcore" video games: In *Bejeweled Blitz*, the time-based competitions require players to quickly click the interface. *World of Warcraft* requires a significant amount of spatial awareness and comfort with the player's input devices.

Although physical interaction is not going to be a large part of many social games, it is another element of play that can't be ignored. For many games, this is a central source of challenge that increases over time.

Experiencing New Content

The content of a game can consist of items, characters, maps, visuals, stories, or anything else that comprises the experience of the game. At first blush, it might seem that this experience is passive but you're challenging the player to synthesize this new information whenever it is presented. The player needs to consider each new piece of content in the context of questions such as "How would I use this item?" or "Which part of this map do I want to explore?"

New content can gently increase the challenge of a game but also has the advantage of being its own reward: Players want novelty and surprise, and content is the way to do that.

Disrupting Flow

Much of this chapter is about placing your players into a state of flow while playing your game. Before moving onto that, it's worth identifying some of the ways in which flow can be disrupted:

- **Making the game too challenging**: One problem with designing a game is that you become accustomed to your own game mechanics, and you have a tendency to make things harder than they need to be. This is why testing is so important, which is discussed in Chapter 8.
- **Sudden, huge leaps in challenge**: Sometimes the challenge is fine in the beginning and things are going along well, but then a big leap in the challenge stops the player cold. You will learn some modeling techniques you can use to help predict this in advance, but it's another area in which playtesting is essential.
- **Decreases in challenge**: If the game doesn't continue to expose the player to new challenges, the game will become boring, and players will move on to something else.

- **Changing the fundamental nature of the fun**: A good game introduces new interactions, tactics, and strategy like the movements of a symphony. Each is introduced, adding layers of depth and challenge but not jarring the player. Continuing with the music analogy, imagine how an audience would feel if you start out with something that people thought was classical music, and just as they're enjoying it, it becomes rap. There might be some extraordinary talents out there that can pull this off, but in general it's a risky move. In games, the same holds true: You wouldn't start a game as a turn-based strategy, and halfway through the experience turn it into an action game.

Designing Progress Systems

Whether overt, all games involve the idea of progress. Games that stop offering the player a sense of progress become stale and boring. Games that provide a clear idea of what the player can do around the next corner can keep them engaged for the long term and offer the combinations of arousal, flow, and relaxation that can maintain their attention.

One of the first things you need to think about when designing a game is how to manage, communicate, and measure progress and use the stage of progress as a means to decide when to introduce new challenges to the player. One of the reasons why the idea of a "level" is so compelling in many games is because it reduces progress to one simple number that makes it easy for the players to know how far they've progressed. Likewise, level provides an easier mechanism for the game designer to decide how much challenge is appropriate for that player.

Even games without explicit measurements such as levels have progress. In chess, progress can be measured in each individual game as the ebb and flow of individual moves and exchanges, finally resulting in the capture of one player's king. Players of chess also have an opportunity to always learn new tactics and strategies, a form of play that transcends the individual game and makes mastery of chess a lifelong pursuit for millions of people.

The following items illustrated a few ways that you can think about progress in your game:

- Advancing through multiple levels
- Earning badges
- Earning a specific prize for a group of people
- Gaining a form of recognition

- Completing a story
- Defeating a certain type of opponent

Many games contain more than one progress system. By overlapping them, you can provide the players with multiple ways to advance through the game at their own pace. One benefit of this approach is that you can gear the challenge level for different forms of progress to appeal to different player types, while simultaneously increasing the depth and variety of content for players. Another benefit of tracking multiple forms of progress is that the design can encompass a broader scope of interests, and the game designer can see which parts of the game are favored by most players. However, you need to be careful to avoid overwhelming the players with too many ways to measure progress, or you risk confusing them before they understand what the game is all about.

When designing your progress systems, you'll find it helpful to think about it as a linear path, identifying the new types of challenges you introduce along the way. This forces you to think about the increases in challenge level and also gets you thinking about the new things you'll introduce to the players along the way. It can also help you spot holes in your progression pathway, such as a series of levels where nothing new happens.

At each step of your progress system, you also need to determine the gate for advancing to the next stage. Most level-based systems use a point system for advancing to the next level, in which points are received for performing challenging actions. Other systems of progress might be based on discrete events, such as completing a puzzle, defeating an opponent of a given difficulty, or simply performing an interesting action.

Leveling Systems

A level-based system gives players a sense of control: With enough effort, they can advance through the game's experience. Each level can be accompanied by new abilities, content, or recognition. Most level-based systems:

- **Increase the requirements (for example, "experience points") as each level increases.** The requirement is typically nonlinear, to introduce a slowing of progress over time. This satisfies the player's need for immediate gratification early in the game, while slowing down progress when they're more experienced.
- **Increase the rewards players gain for activities at each level.** The rewards can be the perceived benefit of virtual items or abilities players receive at

each level, or simply the number of points received for completing actions at that level. The rate at which the points for rewards are gained is usually lower than the rate at which points required for each level increases, which may provide the perception that rewards are scaling up while actually decreasing the absolute rate of progress over time.

- **Clearly communicate level progress.** Level is so important that it is usually displayed throughout the game (often visible at all times), along with indicators of how close the players are to the next level.

Figure 10-2 illustrates how *Bejeweled Blitz* combines a level-based system along with the score you earn upon completion of each individual game. Levels provide a means for the player to measure progress that's separate from aiming for a new high score.

Figure 10-2: *Bejeweled Blitz* Levels

Note how each level is accompanied by several ways to communicate progress. In this example, you can see the following:

- The numeric level (3) associated with the player's current level
- A progress bar showing how far, in relative terms, players are to the next level
- An indication of how many total points players need to reach the next level
- A title ("Apprentice") associated with the player's level, which serves as a simple reward for achieving each new level

Badge and Achievement Systems

Badges and achievements provide a different way to track progress through a game for people who enjoy collecting things. Examples include the Xbox Live achievement system or the achievements within *World of Warcraft* and *Mafia Wars*.

Achievements and badges actually serve at least two purposes in a game:

- **They can provide a means of progress, but they're also subtle teaching tools.** By providing the players with goals that they might not have thought of, they inform the players about features and content they weren't aware of. With an achievement system, you should consider whether to use the system to compare progress between different games, or whether it is internal to only one game. In the case of Xbox Live, achievements all feed into an overall "GamerScore," which tracks every player's progress across the spectrum of games available. An advantage of this system is that players are motivated to constantly try new games. To make this system work, each game is allocated a fixed number of points it's allowed to give, which prevents individual games from unbalancing the whole scoring system.
- **They can provide opportunities for social play:** Certain badges can be awarded based on the ability for players to work together, or can be awarded to groups of players who achieve collective success within the game, such as defeating a certain opponent, reaching a combined level, and so forth.

In addition badges can be granted for performing certain actions. A good badge system often consists of several elements:

- A few easy-to-earn badges
- Some super-hard badges that might take the players a long time to gain, which act as long-term goals
- Badges tied to different features, intended to introduce players to different features of the game they might not otherwise try
- Individual achievements can be assigned a score, which enables players to think of the entire collection of achievements as feeding into one linear progression path

Leaderboards

A leaderboard (also called a ladder or ranking system) is a way for players to compare themselves to each other. Leaderboards are inherently competitive and can focus players on improving their skill relative to those closest to them in skill. These include the following:

- **Indirectly competitive leaderboards** that pit players against each other based on everyone's relative progress through the game. Players don't have a way to negatively impact other players' scores but can see how close they are to passing other people.

- **Directly competitive leaderboards** that invite players to take actions against another player. If one player wins, the other loses, and their ranks on the leaderboards are affected accordingly.

There are trade-offs in any competitive leaderboard. Adrenaline junkies and type-A personalities might relish the thought of "beating" other players on a directly competitive leaderboard, whereas other players might be driven away. How do you know which might be appropriate for your game? Go back to the personas you developed in Chapter 4 and consider the motivations behind the players of your game. Your user stories can also help you understand the experiences your players expect from the game.

The next question with a leaderboard is to decide who will be included. The simplest leaderboard compares all players of the game against each other, providing one absolute ranking system. However, this has the disadvantage of lacking relevance to the players and can include numbers that might boggle the mind. Imagine a game with millions of players: Would anyone care about moving up from rank 5,231,514 to rank 5,119,217? You can increase relevance by arranging leaderboards into logical groups. One example of this is a league-based system, such as the one employed by *Starcraft 2*, illustrated in Figure 10-3.

Figure 10-3: *Starcraft 2* Leaderboard

Although there are millions of *Starcraft 2* players, you're given the illusion of playing within a small community of players because each league is limited to only 100 similarly skilled players. You can have the hope of becoming #1 because you have only a few other people to compete against.

In many social games, leaderboards are based on your friend list. In this case, the relevance to you is because you know each other. A view of the *Zynga Poker* leaderboard demonstrates this in Figure 10-4.

Figure 10-4: Social Leaderboard in *Zynga Poker*

In the case of *Zynga Poker*, the leaderboard helps you know where you stand relative to your friends but also incorporates cooperative elements. By clicking the Send button, you can provide friends with some chips that will enable them to play in the game.

Time Series Comparisons

In addition to leaderboards, another means of competitive comparison is to use a time series. Any progress or scoring metric is graphed over time, comparing the player versus a friend. This can be used as a way for players to decide how they're doing—a digital game equivalent of keeping up with the Joneses. *Bejeweled Blitz* includes an example of this, as shown in Figure 10-5, where you can view how your weekly high scores compare against a friend's:

Figure 10-5: Time Series
Comparison in *Bejeweled Blitz*

Pacing

After you assemble a list of all the steps in your progression, a tool you can use to visualize your design is to create a graph depicting challenge versus progress. This is a way to understand the page of the game—the rate at which the players are exposed to new challenges relative to their perception of how far they've progressed.

Figure 10-6 shows a progress pathway that might be appropriate for a simple, story-based game with a distinct beginning, middle, and end. The diagram shows the change in challenge level as the game progresses:

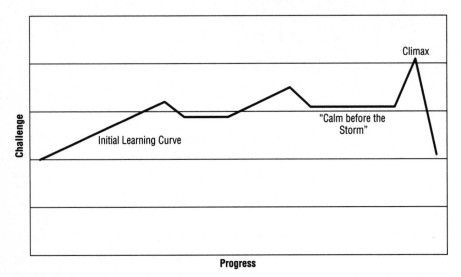

Figure 10-6: Pacing of a Story-Based Game

- **State of Flow:** Lines with a gentle slope imply that the player is entering a state of control or flow.
- **Greater Challenge:** Areas where the slope increases noticeably imply periods of greater challenge intended to arouse the players' interest in mastering the skills they need to advance further.
- **Relaxation:** Dips are the places intended to offer relaxation.

NOTE Because this is a graph intended to work within a story-based framework, you want to imply that the users are in a state of flow for most of the experience, punctuated by a few periods in which they need to master a new skill to advance.

- **Calm before the storm:** Toward the end, there's a period of relaxation—a calm before the storm—in which players can enjoy a sense of power for all their hard work.
- **Toughest Challenge:** The calm before the storm is followed by the toughest challenge of the game, after which players can relish their hard-won victory.

Graphing your challenge versus progress isn't a perfect science because there's no way to easily assign a *challenge value* to all the experiences you introduce to the player as they progress through the game. Playtesting can also reveal that some elements are far easier or harder than you expected. Nevertheless, creating simple models like this can give you a feel for what you want to accomplish in the game and guide you toward the different types of experiences you want players to encounter.

Social games are different from this simple story-based example in that they need to continue to reengage the player for a long period of time. To do this, you need to anticipate a longer progression pathway. Imagine what might happen with players given the shape of other progression curves. For example, Figure 10-7 shows an experience where challenge gently increases for the early and middle phases of a game but begins increasing exponentially toward the late stages of a game. The rapid and brutal increase in a challenge toward the late game is likely to make players feel that they can't keep up with the game's demands. (This difficulty curve is similar to that used by many arcade and action games, which were originally designed to get players to insert tons of quarters toward the later stages of the game.)

On the other hand, contrast this with Figure 10-8, which illustrates a progression curve that starts similarly but then dips in challenge. A game like this might be interesting while the players are first learning the game, but then it risks becoming boring. Because players find it less challenging after they master an initial set of skills, they might not stick with the game for the long haul.

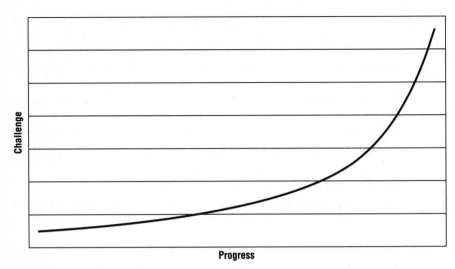

Figure 10-7: Pacing of Exponentially Increasing Challenge

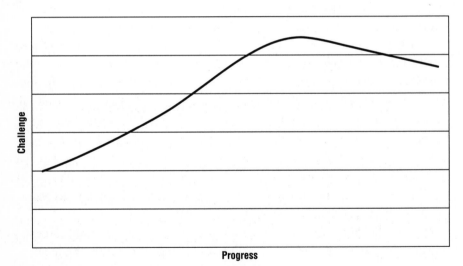

Figure 10-8: Pacing of Potentially Boring Game

Finally, consider Figure 10-9, which suggests a game that might have early play, but suddenly launches into a brutal midgame that is likely to turn away players.

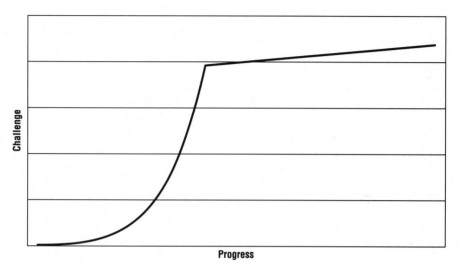

Figure 10-9: Excessive Midgame Challenge

Case Study: Pacing in *World of Warcraft*

World of Warcraft is a game that millions of players play years after its initial launch. Its model for challenge, progress, and pacing illustrates how you might engage players for a long period of time. It's as close to a perfectly-paced game as currently exists.

Players experience a very small but gradual increase in challenge as they increase in level (which may require hundreds of hours for a new player). The highest-level players then experience a dramatic increase in challenge, focusing more on learning to work together to defeat the most powerful opponents in the game; at this point, players have spent so much time in the game that they're willing to commit to the added difficulty.

Consider some of the phases a player experiences in *WoW*, shown in Table 10-1.

Table 10-1: *World of Warcraft* Game Phases

Level	Label	Description
1–9	Introductory	Can be completed by many new players in an hour or two. (Experienced *WoW* players can complete it even faster because they know exactly what to do.)
10	Talent points	Players are exposed to strategic play for the first time in the form of a *talent point*, which can be used to define their character's long-term direction.
15	Group play	Players can begin entering dungeons, which require cooperation with other players. Players need to coordinate their tactics to complete dungeons successfully.
20	First mount	With a new mount, players can now get from place to place faster than they could before. Earlier, travel through the maps might have been a challenge, but at this stage of play, some people begin to find it tedious. This is a change to the challenge level that feels like a reward for the effort the player has invested—and may encourage some players to explore more.
25	Glyphs phase 1	Players are introduced to *glyphs*, which are another way for players to modify their character strategy by applying bonuses to certain abilities.
50	Glyphs phase 2	Players earn their second set of glyphs.
60	Flying mount	Players earn a flying mount, which transforms the way people experience travel within the game.
70	*Burning Crusade* heroics	Players can access certain dungeons at the *heroic* level of difficulty. Players play through some of the same dungeons they played before, but now they are much harder. (And rewards are a little better.) The level of tactical cooperation needed to succeed is much greater.

Level	Label	Description
80	*Wrath* heroics	Players gain access to additional heroic dungeons (from the *Wrath of the Lich King* expansion).
85	*Cataclysm* heroics and raids	Players reach the maximum level allowed in the *Cataclysm* expansion, and may now work their way through a series of endgame dungeons and raids.

Furthermore, players gain access to new abilities every few levels; a character at level 1 has only a few abilities but earns dozens by the time they reach 85. Each of these abilities represents a new form of interaction with the game and a new opportunity for tactical combinations. Players also encounter other people while playing, which leads to participation in guilds, which adds another layer of social interaction at the point players are ready for it.

WoW also features hundreds of achievements that players can collect: Each is a badge for completing certain difficult, obscure, or interesting actions within the game. This provides an alternative set of goals that overlap with the goals of character development, exploration, and dungeon conquests.

Imagine if *WoW* required all new players to master all the skills, tactics, and strategy when they first entered the game: The result would be a game that would be only of interest to a small number of people who are willing to invest in the massive learning curve—and who would rapidly be bored with the absence of new and interesting things to do.

Case Study: Pacing in *Mafia Wars*

Mafia Wars is a much simpler game than *World of Warcraft*, yet has also managed to maintain a large number of players for long durations. Both systems are heavily based on level-based progression, yet both target different demographics. Each game provides a virtually limitless arena for advancement as well as player-versus-player and player-helping-player interaction for those seeking greater glory or notoriety.

Part of *MW*'s advantage is that it is played in small chunks of time. Because there's no immersive content to experience, the player consumes less of the game in each brief session. On the other hand, its model requires that it enables players to advance forever. The top players of *MW* have levels numbering in the thousands. As you advance in *MW*, the challenge increases by only small amounts—but you are exposed to constant new content to keep you interested. As player-versus-player conflict emerges, the challenge of the game shifts toward social coordination with your friends. Table 10-2 shows the various phases of the game:

Table 10-2: *Mafia Wars* Game Phases and Features

Level	Description
1–2	New players of *MW* can earn the first several levels before they run out of energy, which ensures that players learn enough to get hooked on the experience.
3–99	At these levels, players can easily advance at the rate of one level per play session by returning daily, which provides an ongoing sense of progress.
Frequent jobs	For almost every level of the first 100 levels of *MW*, players need to perform a new job. This keeps players focused on a simple goal that always seems just within reach. As players achieve higher levels, they are also introduced to certain jobs that require items looted from previous missions, which provides players with a network of simple subgoals.
Achievements	In addition to the character advancement goals, *MW* also features a set of achievements for completing actions within the game.
Player-versus-player	This aspect enables people to attack each other. The ability to succeed in attacks as you level gives you an alternative sense of mastery over the game.
Group Play	The size of the player's mafia (that is, the number of friends they play with) serves as another metric of comparison—spurring players to introduce their friends to the game. Larger groups are also more effective in player-versus-player conflict, spawning a whole community of cooperation and competition that exists outside the actual game.

Honing Your Game Design Skills

Creating games is a craft. To get good at it, you need to do more than read this book; you need to actually try your hand at creating or modifying some games. This might seem daunting due to the complexity of so many modern games, but you can do a few things to start down the road—all of which are tons of fun and require minimal investments of your time and money. Better yet, if your goal is to energize your business with games, you now have a real business reason to try things such as playing or designing a game. Maybe there's even a business expense deduction you can make for the purchase of a game or two!

Great games are almost always made by people who have a passion for games. I play more than a hundred new games per year—some for only a short amount of time, others for hours and hours. Some people I know play far more than that. You *won't* need to dedicate your life to playing games, nor will you need to play this many if you're interested in understanding how they work, but it's extremely helpful to identify some games that you enjoy and use them as a learning tool for teaching yourself what works and what doesn't. Great writers need to read a lot; great artists get better by studying techniques from other masters. Likewise, game designers need to spend time playing games. This chapter explains some of the systems employed by games, and there's no better way to understand how they work than by experiencing these systems in some games you enjoy.

Experiment with Board Games

Although the social games discussed in this book are limited in budget compared to the large multimillion dollar games the computer game industry has become known for, they're still full-blown games, and as such, creating them can be a bit intimidating. If you're new to this, you can practice game design techniques in ways that will cost you almost nothing.

Board games are a great Petri dish for experimenting with your own game design ideas. Almost every home has at least one or two, and you can pull those off the shelf to attempt several of the following ideas. In addition, almost every board game is actually a social game; they are designed to play with other people, and as such depend on some of the same motivators that you'll find in much larger games. Classics such as *Monopoly*, *Life*, and *Risk* can show you some of the tried-and-true systems that work well. If you have young children (or know some) games like *Candy Land* and *Chutes and Ladders* can also show you a great deal. For older groups—or for experimenting with more advanced game mechanics—you can also try some of the less well-known but more sophisticated board games from companies such as Fantasy Flight Games (*Talisman: The Magical Quest Game*), Mayfair Games (*Settlers of Catan*) and Rio Grande Games (*Carcassonne*).

After you play some games using the critical game design skills recommended here, try experimenting with changing games you are familiar with. When you feel you're ready, you can even try creating entirely new games by borrowing some of the pieces that might be floating around your home. The following are some ideas to get you started:

Table 10-3: Creating New Games from Other Board Games

Idea	Description
Create a metagame	Games such as *Monopoly* are not intended to have any continuity from game to game. Imagine you're creating a league, and challenge yourself to create special game mechanics that work across multiple games. You'll want to create something more than simply a ranking of who has won the most; for example, what type of badges could you create for performing certain actions in *Monopoly*?
Try changing the story	What happens to the way you imagine the gameplay when you completely change the narrative? For example, can you recast *Monopoly* as a game about galactic conquest without changing the underlying rules? How far from the original story can you get before the rules no longer make sense to people?
Design a game for children	If you have young children, this can be a great deal of fun, because kids love playing—and might even want to help out. Even when kids don't understand the nuances of the rules, they're often amazingly good judges of fun. For example, chess has a great deal of complexity to it, which might make it too hard for most young children, yet many will still be fascinated by the ideas of chess. The same goes for many other games. You can learn a lot from kids and what they think is fun.
Change a single rule in the game	Addition and subtraction are powerful tools for observing the impact of game design decisions. For example, how does a game of *Monopoly* feel if you remove the Go to Jail rules and just treat it as an empty space with no rewards? Alternatively, how does the game change if you create a new rule, such as giving each of the play pieces a special bonus. (Maybe the top hat gives you a slight bonus to rent, and the car always adds +1 to the dice you roll when moving.) Before designing entire games, this can show you how the mechanics of the game work. In many cases, you can gain new respect for the tried-and-true rules; in others, you can create a cool idea that makes for a new and interesting game.

Idea	Description
Try inventing your own board game	Board games teach so much about games because they need to be economical with their use of space, rules, and play pieces; they lack the infinite possibilities of computer games. You can borrow pieces from your other games and reassemble them into your own new concepts. Invent a story, create some basic rules, and decide how the game will proceed. Try it out with friends and family. Start simple, and add more rules and complexity over time to see how things work.
Create a brainstorming game	In brainstorming settings, people are often uncomfortable with making some of the nonlinear leaps in thinking that could produce new ideas and combinations. Games can help remove peoples' inhibitions by giving them a structured means to adapt their ideas. Use the play pieces or cards from a popular game as props within a brainstorming exercise. For example, you could use the letter words from *Scrabble*, telling the people in a brainstorming setting to use the letters to form a word and then use the word in a sentence to describe a product idea. Give each participant a point for each idea that uses a unique word. By combining structure and creativity at the same time along with a system of rewards, you may be surprised at the new results you'll receive!

Playing Games Critically

Critical gameplaying is going to be a bit different from the type of gameplaying you might normally do. The goal is to identify the fun, understand what the designers tried to accomplish, and assess the choices the designers made. It doesn't mean that you won't enjoy the game while you do it; actually, you might find that critical gameplaying opens up a whole new way to enjoy games. The overall goals of critical gameplaying are to:

- Understand the game designer's purpose.
- Analyze the effectiveness of the techniques used to achieve the purpose.
- Compare and contrast the systems used in the game to other similar games.

To do some critical game playing, do the following:

1. **Find some reputable, popular games and play them.** Don't just skim the surface looking for neat ideas. Truly get into them. Any of the games mentioned

in this book are good starting points, but the game market is changing all the time. Check out the top social network games on AppData.com and find some game design bloggers that discuss the latest games across the market.

2. **Keep a notepad handy.** Jot down your reactions as you're experiencing the game.

3. **Identify the systems that make the game feel fun.** Think about ways you might change the game to be more fun. If it isn't fun, try to explain why.

4. **Imagine yourself as the various types of people who would play the game.** Remember that the things that are fun for you might not be the same for others. Pretend that you don't know some of the more advanced features of the game, and try to think of how hard or simple the game might be for someone without all that advanced knowledge. Of course, this is hard to do because your experience will keep changing as you learn more about the game. That's why jotting down some notes as part of your first experiences can explain so much.

Critiquing Social Elements

If you try a social game on Facebook, invite a couple of friends to play with you. Do you feel a bit weird about that? If so, what does that tell you? Try to make some new friends who play as much as you do. Note not only what you went through to accomplish that, but also how you felt during the process. The following are some questions to help you consider the effective of a game's social game systems:

- Did you engage socially within the game? If yes, what were those experiences like and how did you feel about them?
- Did you ever feel loyalty, disdain, apathy, or love toward your in-game friends? What brought on these feelings?
- Try to be a great in-game friend to someone. Were you able to? How hard was that to do? Did the other player even notice?
- Did your social interactions add to your enjoyment? Did you feel pressured to act socially, or was it a natural part of the experience?

Critiquing the Fun

Social elements are often fun on their own, but there usually needs to be more to the game than social interaction alone. Sometimes, a game is going to want you to do something you don't think is fun. Do it anyway; really get into it. If you run into technical difficulties, try to open a support incident. Were you able to? How did their support and customer service make you feel?

The following are some other questions you can ask yourself to help understand what makes a game fun:

- Is there more than one source of fun? If so, what are they? Is the game better because of the multiple sources of fun, or do you wish they'd have focused on one?
- If the game has a story, did the story contribute to the feeling of fun? Was it helpful? Confusing? Relevant? Distracting?
- What emotions seem most related to the main source of fun?

Winning

Almost every game needs to give you a way to "win." Sometimes that is because the game gives you a specific goal. (For example, "Get the most points by finding combinations of three colored gems.") Or it might be more abstract. ("Complete the story the way you want to.") At a minimum, record specifically what you think the victory conditions of a game are and try to decide why you think the designers chose those particular conditions. The following are some questions to consider about the victory conditions:

- Did you feel you understood how to win at all times? If not, did the game do anything to help you understand what you ought to be doing?
- How did the game communicate to you that you were making progress? Was it clear, confusing, vague, excessive, or what?
- How did the difficulty of the game feel to you? If it were too easy, did you discover any ways to play at a harder skill level; if too hard, were there ways you enjoy the game in spite of the challenge?

Value

Games need to provide value for the players' time, or the games will be abandoned quickly. Consider the aspects of the experience that made it seem valuable to you:

- Did you ever feel like you were wasting your time? If so, note when and try to understand ways the game could have been improved to avoid these feelings.
- Did you ever have a feeling of regret after purchasing virtual goods in the game?
- How does the value (in time, money, or both) compare to other games you've played?

Why Did You Stop Playing?

Understanding why someone stops playing a game is one of the most important aspects of game design. Games that are chock-full of great experiences can be abandoned for a number of reasons. A few of the most common include game-stopping bugs; the sense of being "stuck" or game design choices that leave you with a sense of being unable to advance; being too easy; and being too hard. Consider the following:

- Why did you stop playing?
- Do you feel you want to continue to play at another time? Pay attention to this feeling carefully; note if you actually do return to the game in the future.
- Did you "complete" the game? If so, do you feel there's any way to replay the game in a new way, or are you done?

Sometimes there are good games hiding inside bad ones. If you can isolate the problem areas, you might be able to create something great. The same thing goes for products, websites and almost any business.

From Games to Websites

Many websites are already putting systems in place intended to create fun for their visitors. Examples include leaderboards, point systems, badges, and channels for social status. Make a list of your favorite websites to see which of them do this. Thinking about them critically, how much impact do you feel their game systems add to the engagement of their sites? In many cases you'll find that they don't do much at all—or even get in the way. Here's an interesting thought experiment you can use when looking at either websites or games:

- For a website, what could it do to be more game-like? How would that change the way you engage with it? Would you spend more time and come back more often?
- For a game, how could it be more Web-like? How could it adapt user interface techniques and access to information that has been refined within the online world?

Visit Toy and Hobby Stores

It's amazing how often I speak with people who haven't seen the inside of a toy store or hobby store since the time they were kids. Try and stop by one, and look at the games on the shelves; and take one home with you. The better hobby shops have some of the more avant-garde games and often have staff who can make some great suggestions based on your interests.

Network with Game Designers

You can attend a number of online and real-life venues to gain greater knowledge about how games work and what makes them effective. You'll also meet other people who share an interest in the craft and business of game design, which can help you hone your understanding.

The *International Game Developers Association*, or *IGDA*, is open to anyone who considers themself to be a game developer. You can join for a modest membership fee and take part in a variety of events and participate in an online forum where you can discuss everything from product engineering to the business issues surrounding games. Most IGDA chapters also hold local *post-mortems* where members of the local gaming community meet to discuss learning experiences from the game development process—and also network with other game developers. You can find a list of local chapters by visiting the IGDA website at `www.igda.org`.

A number of online resources exist to help you learn more about game design. One of these is `game-on-book.com`, where you can discuss this book with other readers, as mentioned in the "Choose Your Path" section at the end of most chapters. Another is `GamaSutra.com`, where you can go to read articles from game designers and executives from the industry. It is a good way to keep abreast of new developments in technology and business model and design methodologies.

Several colleges now offer game design programs. Check with your local schools to discover what programs they offer, and whether they have seminars or workshops open to the public. Some of these schools might also offer internships or cooperative education programs for students to apply their knowledge within industry.

You can find a variety of online networking resources and the educational programs in gaming in Appendix B.

Chapter in Review

In this chapter you learned that social games need to provide a mix of short- and long-term challenges for players to stay engaged over the long term. Short-term challenges provide immediate fun; long-term challenges keep people returning across several play sessions.

A helpful way to think about the engagement within games is Csikszentmihalyi's model of flow, which is based on the idea that people have the most enjoyable experiences when their skill level is balanced with the perceived challenge of an activity. Challenge can be gradually introduced to a game by adding to the number of interactions, tactical options, and strategic depth over the course of a game. Players also need a way to measure their progress if they're to achieve flow. This can be done using leaderboards, time series, leveling systems, and badges.

Designing good game systems requires more than points and progress systems. Games use stories and interesting game mechanics to involve players emotionally. To refine your ability to design games, you'll find it helpful to play a lot of games: Try to play games critically, identifying the aspects of fun within the games you like, and try modifying existing games to understand the impact of design choices.

Choose Your Path

The following list gives areas of the book you might want to visit next.

- Game systems need to be communicated through interfaces that add meaning and simplicity to the experience. That is the next subject, covered in Chapter 11.
- Virtual goods are a central element of many social games. To understand the virtual economies and currency systems that control how they work, you can skip ahead to Chapter 12.
- Any of the game mechanics and progress systems mentioned in this chapter are driven fun. You might find it helpful to review any of the 42 types of fun covered back in Chapter 5.

11 Designing Game Interfaces

n this Chapter, you'll learn:

- How different user interfaces address different challenges in game design
- How interfaces give you a way to tell your story
- Ways to take your player narrative and user stories and turn them into an interaction map

Every game is a world. The purpose of an interface is to enable the player to step through a magical doorway that they can enter for a time. An adequate interface is one that enables a player to move around in this world in an efficient manner—but a great interface considers the whole experience.

This chapter explains how to take some of your previous thinking—the development of user stories and the creation of prototype game mechanics—and take them into the realm of tangible interfaces that players can use to experience your game. As you explore the creation of these interfaces, you'll discover new things about your game: areas of unforeseen complexity, areas in which the interface alters the way you think about the game mechanics, or ways that the interface might change the way you think about the story of your game.

Doorways to a World

One of the major ways in which game development is so different from other types of software and websites is the way in which the interface might change the entire definition of the game. Consider a few examples:

- **Touch-screen:** If it weren't for the touch-screen interface, games such as *Godfinger* and *Angry Birds* wouldn't exist. Similar rules could be created, but the gestalt of the game experience actually involves physically touching and dragging objects on an iPhone or iPad.

- **3D graphics:** Although games such as *World of Warcraft* were the successor to earlier, text-based game experiences (MUDs), the graphical interface wasn't just a new coat of paint on top of an old design: 3D graphics made it possible to introduce entirely new game mechanics that used position and orientation in space.

- **Player interaction:** Game systems such as the Wii and Microsoft Kinect made it possible for players to involve themselves physically within the game experience in a way that wasn't possible with a simple handheld controller; this made possible a whole new category of game experiences.

- **Asynchronous play:** Social games such as *Mafia Wars* and *Gods of Rock* take advantage of asynchronous play in a way that adapts to players' expectations of how asynchronous news feeds and electronic mail systems work, changing the entire way a game is experienced.

As you think about your game experiences, you need think about interfaces not simply as a means of accessing the game, but also as a way to rethink the possibilities of the game.

Levels of Abstraction

All games are an abstraction of reality. Some occur entirely in your mind, whereas others seem a lot closer to being real. Regardless of the model you use, games are a collaboration: Your game design and rules work in cooperation with the player's imagination. Until you reach the point of holodecks or immersive virtual reality, you are stuck needing to decide how to present your world through symbols, metaphors, and interfaces that convey meaning to the player.

Purely Imaginative

You can have games that occur entirely in the imagination without the aid of models or images. That's exactly what happens within tabletop role-playing games, such as *D&D*. Players record information about their pretend selves on character sheets and the Dungeon Master has a set of notes and maps that they refer to, but those are just tools to facilitate the group's agreement on the rules that make up the shared imaginary world.

Players have a set of *virtual items* they possess and make their way through stories based on the fantasy they share with each other. A plethora of books can provide source material and rules, and dice to generate random numbers (Figure 11-1); however, the actual field of play exists within the imagination.

Figure 11-1: Major Equipment for *D&D*

Books are another form of media in which the contents exist entirely in your imagination; the words on the page are just a vehicle for the authors to project their thoughts into your mind. Your brain synthesizes the words into meanings, shapes, and characters.

For your game, ask the following questions:

- What areas of my game are best left to the imagination?
- Can I use text to deal with areas of pure imagination?
- How much will my game's development budget require me to rely on imagination for conveying certain experiences?

Symbolic Representations

The most ancient games use symbols to represent concepts. The classic pieces from chess (Figure 11-2) are a good example: The knight, which looks like a horse's head, is only slightly suggestive of the idea of a knight. The rook, which typically looks like the tower of a castle, has an interesting history: Originally, it was a chariot in Chinese and Indian interpretations of chess. When the game made its way to Europe, it transformed into the shape it has today, perhaps because the Sanskrit word for chariot sounded like the Italian word for tower. Despite the changes, chess pieces share a common theme: They are an abstraction of military conflict.

Figure 11-2: Chess

 OTAKU When you think of the rook as a chariot rather than a castle or tower, *castling* in chess make more sense. The king in his hurry to escape makes a fast retreat by the quickest conveyance available.

By taking stories of war and translating them to a game grid with pieces symbolizing characters with particular capabilities, chess made it possible to create a board where tactics and strategies can play out. Without these pieces, you couldn't keep track of all the positions of each piece.

What do *D&D* and venerable *Monopoly* have in common? Miniatures and game grids help players manipulate a layer of tactical complexity that makes the game fun. As you think about your interface design, ask the following questions:

• Are there specific symbols I'll need to create to represent concepts within the game?

- Do I need a symbol, or might it be best left to the imagination?
- Will my symbol be manipulated in some way, such as patterns, puzzles, tactical confrontations, and so forth, where the human mind needs me to present information in a way that demands use of a symbol?

Perspective Views

Computer games have made it possible to take the symbolic representations of playing pieces and translate them directly to environments that seem more real. For example, the farm you manage in *FarmVille* is represented by a grid of crops, but the individual crops also grow and wither over time. Characters move through the landscape and the environment changes, as shown in Figure 11-3.

Figure 11-3: *FarmVille* Grid

A symbolic representation of the objects are also in the game, but the level of detail afforded the designer has increased because this interface can contain far more variables: Not only are the individual symbols tracked, but they also morph over time. Space becomes more fluid because the resolution of movement has changed from the coarseness of a grid to as fine as the designer cares to make it, down to the level of a pixel. Real-time action and movement works here as well: Everything from early arcade games such as *Pacman* to modern real-time strategy games depend on some form of graphical perspective to illustrate movement and action.

It's more expensive to build interfaces with perspective than it is to use the player's imagination or more simple symbolic representations. Here are some questions to pose to yourself:

- Do I need an interface with perspective to provide the easiest way for players to interact with my game mechanics?
- Can a perspective interface provide opportunities for action that I wouldn't otherwise have?
- Am I prepared for the large amount of content development necessary to populate a perspective interface with the content it needs?

Immersive 3D

The least abstract games currently available use immersive 3D technology; they place the player right into the action, either viewing the world through the eyes of the character (first-person) or through a nearby vantage point (third-person). The advantage of this interface is the capability to handle motion in every dimension and to render things the way they might look in real life. This immersive experience enables for certain types of gameplay that wouldn't otherwise be possible.

However, even 3D games usually don't place all their interface elements within the 3D environment. For example, as shown in Figure 11-4, the content of your backpack in *World of Warcraft* is managed using a simpler, symbolic interface because it is easier than the alternatives. Imagine an interface in which you have an actual 3D backpack containing various objects, but you don't like sorting through piles of junk to find something. (Just as you might avoid the junk drawers in your home, which are actually places for you to lose something rather than store something.)

3D interfaces are the most expensive form of user interface to build. This is what has driven the cost of traditional game development into the millions of dollars. They also have another disadvantage in that they're harder to enter and exit; these games are synchronous by nature, which perhaps explains why all the big successes on Facebook thus far have depended on more highly abstracted interfaces.

If you're thinking about 3D, challenge yourself with these questions:

- Does the player actually need an immersive 3D interface to experience the game I have in mind?
- Are there ways I would use 3D technology to add new elements of gameplay that wouldn't be possible otherwise?
- Am I prepared for the huge expense to develop content for a 3D world?

- Are there cases in which I could use a simpler, more abstract interface to achieve certain user stories?
- How will I impact the ability for players to enjoy small, quick bursts of entertainment if I require them to enter into a complex 3D experience each time?

Figure 11-4: 3D Perspective in *World of Warcraft*

Other than the cost, there's another serious problem involved with 3D; the graphics created for a 3D environment tend to age rapidly. Images that seem photorealistic today can look silly a few years after the game is released (if not sooner; some games have taken so long to develop, that they've suffered from archaic 3D technology by the time they release). *World of Warcraft* overcame this by creating a more cartoonish (and decidedly non-photorealistic 3D) design. Creating graphics of this type is harder than it seems because it requires very talented art direction.

From 3D to Hypertext

A vital area of *WoW* is also handled almost entirely within the realm of text—meaning that it happens within the imagination of the player. This is the auction house, a feature where players can buy and sell items between each other (see Figure 11-5). Again, this is to make things easy: An auction house could have been made available through an immersive 3D interface, but the large amount of sorting and searching would have been annoying to deal with. In addition, the text-based interface could be easily translated to the Web; in 2010, *WoW* connected the auction house to the outside world, providing players with a means to play with the virtual economy even when they can't log in for an immersive experience.

Figure 11-5: Web-Based Auction Interface in *WoW*

3D Web Browsing

I'd like you to think about your game as a physical space, even if it isn't a 3D immersive game. We exist in physical spaces. Our minds are great at conceptualizing spatial relationships, and we prefer to think about things that we can organize in this manner. By going through the thought experiment of imaging your game occupying three dimensions, you may think of new ways your game could be organized.

In the early days of the World Wide Web, some people had all kinds of ideas about creating 3D web browsers. They imagined entering a metaverse of information where you'd travel between sites, and information would be rendered onto the walls of 3D rooms. Hyperlinks would be represented by windows and doors in the interface.

The worst thing about these interfaces is that they made the experience more cumbersome by adding time and steps to the process of doing things that were simply easier with text. However, they weren't completely crazy. The Safari web browser (Figure 11-6) takes the idea of your most-frequently visited websites, and renders them into a 3D wall displaying the screen shots of your favorite sites. There's even 3D effects such as reflections that makes the information take on the feeling of a real, physical space.

The Safari top sites interface is more pragmatic than many of the earlier 3D web browser ideas, but it is also more game-like. It uses 3D graphics in a way that makes it more memorable and easier to recognize information, without becoming obtrusive. As the web absorbs more and more game technology—and website designers strive to make the web more of an experience—you'll see more sites that look and feel more like places and spaces.

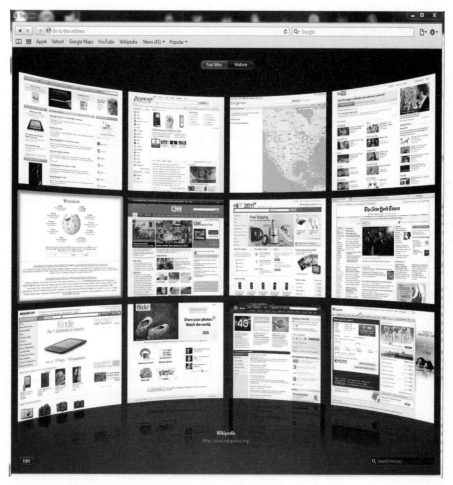

Figure 11-6: Safari Top Sites Interface

> **ARTISAN** Whether your game is 3D immersive or ASCII art-based, the challenge of the UI often comes down to one thing: location, location, location…
>
> After you know what players need to do, you must decide where on their display screen they should do it. Immediately you are challenged to find a way to fit whatever interface best enables the players to accomplish their play goals without stomping all over some other goal, such as the players wanting to see the world they are in or have fun. Before you know it, you'll be adapting the rules and behaviors of the game to fit the real estate. This is to be expected. The interface is the game. After you start making an interface, your game will change—probably for the better, but the process can be agony. Using some method of prototyping can enable you to minimize the pain and reap the benefits at the lowest cost possible.

MAGIC Game Interfaces

The celebrated science fiction author Arthur C. Clark once stated that "Any sufficiently advanced technology is indistinguishable from magic." Clarke might as well have been a user interface designer: After all, a great interface hides complexity and makes it easy for you to do what you want. When an interface is truly great, the user doesn't even realize it exists. With a nod to Clarke's vision, I've created a set of five elements to think about when designing a game interface; you can remember them using the mnemonic MAGIC. The elements of MAGIC are what you want to give your players through the user interface:

- **Memories**: Make a lasting impression on the players.
- **Attention**: Command and provide attention.
- **Goals**: Communicate and facilitate the creation of plans and objectives.
- **Intuitions**: React in a way the players expect.
- **Control**: Give the players the sense that their actions have an impact.

Memories

Imagine what would happen if people needed to completely relearn your user interface every time they returned to it. They'd become frustrated—and maybe not come back.

Memories are strengthened when they are connected to an emotional experience. This is where games have a decided advantage—they're fun! Games use stories, mythical symbols, and visual imagery to make things more engaging. The heightened emotional state of the player can actually contribute toward helping the player learn more.

Games are also exploratory experiences, which is a boon to memory. You remember things better when you explore, rather than when you're guided. A certain amount of education is usually necessary to get the player to understand how to manipulate an interface, but too much hand-holding can lead to the player failing to retain any useful information.

This too-much-hand-holding-is-bad principle was illustrated by researchers led by Eleanor Maguire. The team studied activation in the brain as people learned to navigate within a virtual reality town. When people were required to find their own way, there was increased activation in the hippocampus—the part of the brain intimately linked to memory formation. People who were simply shown a path to follow had no such activation and did not learn how to get around on their own. The conclusion: If you can encourage exploration through your interface, you'll engage the parts of your player's mind that strengthen memories.

Another way that interfaces can be memorable is through repetition and consistency. The game's interface should behave in a similar way regardless of context. The interactions a player needs to make—the specific sequence of clicks, gestures, or incantations—should be the same for performing the same action, obtaining the same information, or evaluating the same goal throughout the system. For example, if you have virtual goods in your game, you might need to provide a pop-up interface that enables players to inspect and learn more information about a particular item. If you deliver this information via a tooltip that displays automatically when the players move their mouse over an item, you shouldn't later require them to click to get the same information elsewhere.

Interface components that represent one type of interaction or information should be identical (or close to it) throughout the interface. For example, if you have a calendar in two parts of your game, it should look the same in both places.

Ask these questions to determine if there are ways you could make your interface more memorable:

- Do my tutorials and explorations promote exploration and experimentation within the interface or are they blocking it?
- Can I introduce new parts of the interface at periods of emotional engagement within the game?

- How can I heighten the emotional connection to interface components by using powerful, stimulating imagery?
- What do I do to reward the player for learning parts of the interface?
- Where can I reduce text and replace it with visual content?
- Am I consistent in the ways I repeat user interface elements?

Attention

Attention is bidirectional in a game; on the one hand, you need to command the players' attention or they'll get distracted and move on to something else. It's also important to give the players attention to make them feel as if they're the center of the universe.

Games are always asking the players to make decisions. If the experience becomes passive, and the players could just as easily go off and refill their coffee, their attention will wane. There's a constant flow of information in games that keeps the player focused. However, too much information and the opposite will happen: The players will feel overwhelmed. Some ways to balance the two are discussed when information channels are covered later in this chapter.

Another way that games command attention is by looking good. You could have the best game mechanics in the world, but if your interface is ugly or cluttered or contains misleading labels, people are going to look away. Aesthetics isn't simply a subject for art history majors and philosophers; things that are attractive are looked at longer. Much of this has to do with the way our brains have evolved. The next section will discuss some of the neuroscience behind beauty, which might help you think about the organization of your interfaces—and might inspire a few new game ideas.

Just as you appreciate beauty, you're also grabbed by novelty. The interface should contain visual characteristics that make it appear new to the players so that you can stand out from every other game or website that exists. (This will also make your game more memorable.) However, don't make it so new that it seems so unfamiliar that the players don't know what to do.

The following are some questions to ask to decide whether you're doing enough to capture and deliver attention:

- What do I do in the game to make the player feel like the center of attention?
- How can I use beauty in my interface to grab the player's attention?
- What do I do that is new and differentiated, yet doesn't obstruct the interface with the unfamiliar?

Goals

Whenever players take an action in the game, it is for the furtherance of some particular goal. If goals dry up, the players might take some actions to determine whether they can find some new goals, but if that fails, they'll soon give up and leave.

Figure 11-7: Active Quests in *Ravenwood Fair*

This is perhaps the largest area of improvement that many user interfaces in nongaming applications could learn from games. People almost always use software with a set of goals in mind; yet software rarely enables users to identify and establish their goals.

Because I'm using a word processor at this moment, it strikes me that there are so many simple game-like improvements that could be made: Why not make it so the outlining mode enables me to see a progress bar that lets me know how close I am to finishing a particular section? Why not offer me some words of encouragement for hitting certain milestones? How about giving me a summary of current word processing projects when I log in, with a comparison to my progress across different projects? Project management software certainly exists to do some of these things, but they exist on the periphery: outside my applications, or managed by another person—not where they should be, as an integrated part of my experience while using the application.

Goals can be either immediate (*I want to get the hell away from this tiger!*) or longer term. (*I want to reach level 85 so that I can kick the crap out of these tigers.*) Immediate goals are visceral; you'll present them right in front of the players so that they can act quickly. Longer-term goals, if they're important enough, might also be a persistent part of your screen's real estate. An example is the experience point bar present in many role-playing games.

To support the player in setting and acting upon goals, you need to provide information. Does the interface convey the right information for the players to make progress on their goals? It's easy to get carried away with data. Information is not data; data is a set of facts without sufficient context or organization to make it meaningful, and too much data can overwhelm and distract your players. The most important information the players need can help them take actions to advance a goal. (*There's a tiger in front of you—do you want to attack or flee?*)

To make your interface more goal-centered, ask the following questions:

- Do I give the player enough information to help take actions that further their goals?
- Do I expose the right mix of short-, mid-, and long-term goals?
- What is the most important reason my players are here, and can I provide them with a clear way to advance toward that goal throughout my interface?
- Considering all the purposes and reasons behind my various user stories, which of them could be turned into a clear goal and presented within the interface?

Intuitions

An intuitive interface is one in which the players have a hunch about what to do, even before they do it. Elsewhere in this book you can find some of the things that your mind seems to be hard-wired for, and you might wonder whether there might be certain user interface components that simply work with the way your brain works. Maybe someday that will be the case—and you'll have interfaces that somehow feed sensory stimuli directly to your mind, enabling you to control machines with your thoughts. Until then, there's a huge gulf between your machines and your minds. How can you overcome that gulf and make things intuitive?

To make something intuitive means, first and foremost, to make it familiar. Don't reinvent the wheel. Every experience people have is viewed through the filter of all their prior experiences. User interfaces are no different: Buttons appear on computer screens because you already had buttons in the real world. You use keyboards to enter text into computers that are virtually identical to the QWERTY typewriters manufactured by Remington in 1873.

If inventors had found a way to mass-produce the Hansen Writing Ball (shown in Figure 11-8) which was invented before the modern typewriter, you might have used this to access your computer today.

Figure 11-8: Hansen Writing Ball

In hardcore gaming, intuitiveness explains a lot of why first-person immersive games have become so popular: People navigate the world exactly as they'd expect—by moving and interacting just as they do in the real world. Their actions are directed by inputs that control movement and direction in real-time. The recent explosion in social media games may also be partially explained by the widespread use of web-based, hypertext interfaces within games—the exact type of interface that people had already become familiar with.

You can use metaphors for things that are borrowed from the real world that match the player's mental model for how things are expected to work. For example, you can control the volume on your computer by clicking an icon that looks like a speaker. Volume could have been expressed any number of different ways: perhaps a dial icon, an up-and-down arrow, the Chinese character for volume, or a random doodle. However, these lack the solid connection to what you already know and they suffer from being ambiguous. A speaker is familiar, unambiguous, and has a clear connection to the idea of how loud you volume will be.

Some of your interface will be new to the players. That's normal in any game and important if your players are to have the sort of exploratory experiences that will also be memorable. The trick is to make it so that the learning process is so transparent that they don't even realize they're learning something new. Adapt each piece of new knowledge from things they might already know. Techniques such as tooltips, help text, or even voiceovers can help explain how the player can perform actions, while making the players more comfortable with exploring the possibilities. Labels for some of the most important actions can also be helpful, although you should be cautious about having too much text.

Ask these questions to decide if you've done as much as possible to make your interface intuitive:

- Where have I gotten carried away with making things cool at the expense of making them familiar?
- Can I find objects from the real world that would be familiar to players, and use that as the way to perform actions and obtain information?
- What metaphors can I leverage within icons and symbols?

Games must give players a sense of agency—that the actions they take will have an impact. If they don't have a sense of control, then they'll feel passive, maybe even hopeless—and they'll never enter that state of flow discussed in Chapter 10.

The interface needs to enable players to perform actions in the easiest way possible. Most of the time, players shouldn't even have to think about the existence of the interface—when they want to perform an action, they just do it. And when they perform their action, they need to receive feedback immediately so that they know they've done something that had an impact.

You can provide immediate feedback by rewarding players. A reward can be a simple acknowledgment that things are working—like the hum of the engine when you turn the ignition in your car—or more elaborate—like points or badges. For the most part, simply observing a consistent reaction to the players' actions is enough to give the players a sense that they control things.

The following are some questions to ask to decide whether your interface is doing enough to give the player enough control:

- Do I provide a reaction to every action?
- Are the most important verbs from my user stories (described in Chapter 10) represented within the interface so that players can initiate them at any time?
- Do I make it safe for the players to probe the interface to see what actions are possible?
- Are there places I could cut down on the number of steps required to perform important actions?

How Beauty Engages Customers

Art is important for business not because it is nice to look at, but because it is so important for engaging customers. Before you can understand its role within interfaces in general and social media games in particular, you need to grapple with an age-old question: What is art? Why are things beautiful?

Debates over the definition of art and beauty have raged for at least as long as written history. Game designers have been forced to think about several aspects of beauty because it is so central to the creation of entertaining experiences. The aesthetics of a game can be beautiful in themselves: Many three-dimensional, immersive games place the player in detailed, spectacular worlds. Simpler games might use more campy graphics, but the whole must come together in a way that appeals to the artistic sensibilities of many customers.

Well-organized objects, maps, interfaces, and designs can seem "beautiful" in their own way. Indeed, some games such as the *Rubic's Cube* are entirely about converting something messy and disorganized into something beautiful and ordered. If you could understand why the human brain thinks certain things are beautiful, you'd have an easier time designing compelling game experiences.

Recently, the field of neuroesthetics has emerged to help explain what happens in your brain when you think something is beautiful. V. S. Ramachandran, the director of the Center for Brain and Cognition at the University of California in San Diego, outlined a set of ten *artistic laws* that appear to be based on neurological structures:

- Peak Shift Principle
- Grouping
- Perceptual problem solving
- Isolation
- Contrast
- Symmetry
- Abhorrence of coincidence
- Metaphor
- Repetition, rhythm, and orderliness
- Balance

These principles are outlined in greater detail in the following sections.

Peak Shift Principle

The Peak Shift Principle is a fairly technical name for a simple concept. In short, it's the idea that people react favorably toward art that exaggerates a certain feature. In a scientific experiment, rats were taught they'd receive cheese when they saw a rectangle. They would respond with excitement when the shape was shown. Later, when the same rats were shown an exaggerated rectangle—one even more stretched out in comparison to a square—they responded even more strongly.

Many types of art are about interpreting the environment in novel ways that exaggerate certain features. For example, impressionist paintings emphasize the interaction of light. Peak shift also explains the modern fascination with silicone implants and other fashion modifications that further exaggerate the human form. This principle is also behind the tendency to amplify or celebrate older forms of art within new ones: Recognizing and drawing out the elements of art you want to hold out as important.

The experiment with rats didn't show that the rats simply prefer larger objects; they were learning a rule about the association between certain types of rectangles and gaining food. In other words, they were playing a game about the *rule* of rectangles. Most games are about players learning or discovering an underlying rule system. By allowing players to discover rules on their own, you're using a form of fun based on neural circuitry that all animals share.

Grouping

Imagine yourself as a stone-age hunter: If you can see through an animal's camouflage, it might mean you'll eat dinner that night—and also notice the lion lurking in the tall grass. Grouping visual information together can help you learn to recognize patterns, overcome camouflage, and detect hidden objects. If you're good at it, you might notice that lion before it's too late.

A lot of art depends on displaying groupings that don't make sense until you've stared at it for a bit. Likewise, many games depend on your ability to unravel visual information and reorganize it into something easier to see. Because this is a skill that helps your survival, your brain rewards you when you succeed at it—in other words, it's fun. Games that challenge the player to find hidden objects (such as *Where's Waldo?*) or identifying certain patterns (such as *Bejeweled*) use the parts of the brain involved in grouping.

Perceptual Problem Solving

Even when you can't see a complete object, your brain is good at filling in the details you miss. For example, you don't have any difficulty realizing that an animal is a lion even when a lot of its body is hidden by other objects. Your ability to fill in missing visual details is called *perceptual problem solving*. Games such as jigsaw puzzles and first-person shooters take advantage of this neural circuitry. Here's a simple test: Are you able to read the following?

Y cn rd ths sntnc, vn thgh t dsn't hv sngl vwl

Isolation

Antoine de Saint-Exupéry, best known as the author of the *Little Prince*, wrote that "Perfection is achieved, not when there is nothing more to add, but when there is nothing left to take away." This is a good way to think about the artistic law of isolation—that the artist can remove all the extra information and leave you with the content that emphasizes a certain image. For example, a silhouette can often be sexier and more alluring than a completely revealing nude. Again, this is a feature of the brain that enables you to work with incomplete information, spurring you on to a goal that you must envision in your minds.

Contrast

If you ever saw an episode of *Sesame Street*, you couldn't have avoided the *One of These Things is Not Like the Other* game. The brain is good at identifying things slightly different than others and then categorizing the specific way in which they are different. This helps to detect new objects in your environment that could either be helpful or dangerous. Because your brain is curious and loves to identify new things, these contrasts can be experienced as pleasing.

Symmetry

Your brain is particularly good at detecting symmetry because of its value in identifying predators and prey (who are almost always symmetrical). In addition, we know from experimental evidence that people prefer potential mates who look more symmetrical. (Perhaps because asymmetry suggests disease or genetic disorders.)

The *Golden Ratio* refers to a naturally-occurring symmetry between forms that occur in biology; for example, the spirals of a nautilus shell grow according to the Golden Ratio. Artists and architects have learned that this ratio, approximately 1.618, helps create forms that are pleasing to the eye.

Abhorrence of Coincidence

Human brains are excellent at detecting patterns, but you are naturally distrustful of coincidences. Depending on the artistic impression you try to create, you can use the brain's abhorrence of coincidence in a number of different ways. A commonplace coincidence that has become popular in movies is the convenient use of furniture, plants, or other foreground objects to cover up the naughty bits of actors during love scenes. The result is a visual experience unintentionally absurd (and used to comic effect in the *Austin Powers* movies).

Another use for this principle is avoiding visual scene composition that looks artificial: For example, trees and bushes positioned so evenly that they seem unnatural. In addition, many puzzles and optical illusions depend on the brain's abhorrence of coincidence to creating surprising visual outcomes that are also fun.

Metaphor

William Wordsworth wrote that poets frequently draw upon "the pleasure which the mind derives from the perception of similitude in dissimilitude." Much of the enjoyment derived from art, poetry, and games is grounded in the ability to identify the hidden connections between things, the underlying rules that unify different objects.

Like the pleasure that comes from the Peak Shift Principle, metaphors are about identifying rules. We congratulate ourselves (and our brain provides a small burst of pleasure) when we can figure out a rule. This is a large part of the enjoyment of visual symbols and literary metaphors and is at the heart of the twin human fascination with both science and religion, which seek to explain the hidden connections and rules within the universe.

Repetition, Rhythm, and Orderliness

Throughout life, your brain is tasked with making sense of the environment. It begins at birth, when during the first six months of life you cannot differentiate between auditory, visual, and tactile senses. The brain's first job is to make sense of all these inputs, recognize patterns, and allocate the senses to different parts of your neural machinery. Next, you begin digesting language, which, like several other of the "laws of art" mentioned here, depend on learning rules and not simple memorization. Identifying rhythms was probably important for hunting, listening for the sound of predators, and other useful survival skills. Because all these neural features aid in your survival, the brain rewards you for exercising them. As a consequence, experiences that draw on these same skills are interpreted as fun: Recognizing patterns within visual art, hearing music, and learning the patterns that make games work.

Balance

The neurological basis for balance is still only speculative, but the premise is simple: Humans seem to have a preference for "balanced" works of art. (It is also possible to create unbalanced works of art in which the intention is to create discomfort or anxiety.) A number of principles exist in a variety of art forms that reflect the concept of balance:

- **The *Rule of thirds* in photography and painting:** This teaches that images are more pleasing if you divide the visual space into equal thirds, both vertically and horizontally. The image usually looks better if you place key parts of the image so that they appear centered at the intersection of the thirds. (Compare that with overly staged vacation snapshots, like Aunt Sally's trip to India in which she's obtrusively centered in front of the perfectly centered Taj Mahal in the background.)

- **The ancient Chinese art of Feng Shui (風水):** This is largely about creating harmony in the physical environment by balancing the placement of certain furniture, plants, and other objects.

- **The *Rule of three* in writing:** This teaches that words and ideas are often more prominent, pleasant, and potent when grouped into threes. ("Ready, set, go!")

- **A balance exists between simplicity and complexity in most forms of art:** Simplicity, in this case, refers to the ability to access and consume a work of art. Complexity refers to the art's ultimate depth. Most children quickly outgrow songs such as Barney the Dinosaur's "I love you, you love me" because the words and music are too simple. On the other hand, Beethoven's *Fifth Symphony* has enough complexity to have survived for two centuries, yet the opening notes are so simple and recognizable that they've transcended the symphony. Similarly, games need to be concerned with a balance between *inherent complexity* (the initial system of rules and interfaces you need to play at all) and its *emergent complexity* (that which grows naturally out of the process of playing).

NOTE Game balance is addressed in detail in Chapter 10, which covers how to create compelling play through good game mechanics.

Details: It Is about Perception

For the eye altering, alters all.

WILLIAM BLAKE, "THE MENTAL TRAVELLER"

The Spice Box is a restaurant located on the University of Urbana-Champaign campus where students are trained to prepare and serve a wide range of fine-dining experiences. Meals are offered on a prix fixe basis, as is the custom for certain upscale establishments.

Recently, the restaurant's guests were offered a complimentary glass of wine. Half of the diners were told that the wine was from California. The others were told it was from North Dakota. In fact, the wines were identical and diners were participating in a psychological study of behavior.

Apparently, people don't consider the wines from North Dakota to be legendary. Their opinion was so low that they liked the "North Dakota" wines less—entirely on the basis of where they thought it was from. As if this weren't enough, researchers found that there was also a spillover effect: People not only disliked their North Dakota wines, but they also ate less food.

Your experiences are colored by your beliefs and expectations. Not only do you believe something might be better based on how it is described, packaged, or presented, you truly do like them more. The reason why wine producers now invest significant sums in creating and testing the packaging for their bottles is because perception and the aesthetic properties that focus on your perceptions are important. Even a word or label can have a huge impact on how much fun you expect to have with something.

Every perception you create in a game has the potential to alter the player's level of fun. Even subtle choices in labeling can have large consequences. When we tested one of Disruptor Beam's social games with a focus group, we found that in one of the starting screens for a game we told the player they'd receive their "first item free." We thought the word "free" would be received favorably, but instead it set the expectation that only their first item would be free, and they'd be forced to purchase any extras. When we removed any discussion of free or money, we increased engagement. This is also a lesson in why talking to customers is often more valuable than relying on quantitative testing alone; we learned more in a few conversations than we'd have learned in a substantial amount of A/B testing.

Creating an Interaction Map

Remember the user stories introduced in Chapter 9? These provide a perfect starting point to create a MAGIC interface. That's because each user story has three elements to it:

As a game's designer you need to identify...

- **Which player persona is going to be performing a given action:** This informs you as to the things this player is likely to be familiar with already. This knowledge can help you create an intuitive experience with the use of familiar interface metaphors.
- **What actions a player will want to take:** This tells you what the player will need to gain a sense of control.
- **Why a player wants to perform each action:** This implies the specific goals that player will have in mind.

Knowing all this is a major accomplishment; however, you won't yet know the best way to organize all this information into an actual interface. To do that, you need to create an interaction map.

If you've already written out all your user stories on index cards as suggested, you'll find that this facilitates sorting your user goals into different categories. You'll even find it helpful to tape them onto the wall, or on whiteboards, where you could draw lines between them or rearrange them as needed. If you don't like to work with index cards, or if you're team is too distributed to take advantage of them, software tools such as Protoshare (listed in Appendix B) can help you capture and organize this information.

After you organize your user stories into a form that makes it easy to manipulate them, you can assemble lists of information by sorting your user stories in different ways:

- Identify all the objects the player will interact with.
- Identify all the information channels a player will need.
- Identify the various contexts the player will interact from.

Identifying Objects

An object is anything that a player acts upon within a user story. To identify and classify objects, follow these steps:

1. Go through all your user stories and extract the list of objects into a separate list, including things such as the following:
   - The player himself
   - Other players

- Virtual items
- Missions/quests/jobs/gigs
- Maps

Each of these objects need to exist within the user interface.

2. Identify all the attributes that can describe each object. For example, the players might have the following attributes:

- Name
- Level
- Points
- List of virtual items they own
- List of badges they have earned
- Number of times they've visited the game
- Amount of virtual currency they have to spend

For a virtual item, it might be the following:

- The item's name
- Minimum level required to use the item
- Purchase price of the item
- Category of the item
- Rules that the item will modify or impact
- The date the item was purchased

3. Now, you can move onto another order of analysis: looking for the ways that attributes relate to each other. For each attribute, you can compare each to itself and all other attributes in the game. Ask the following question for each attribute:

- Does this attribute relate to progress toward one of the player's major goals? If so, highlight this. It will be important in the next steps.
- Is it possible to rank or compare a list of information in this category? For example, you could compare all the players based on level to create a leaderboard that tells all players how they compare against each other. Comparison on any of the other attributes could also be interesting to players depending on the particular game.
- Which attributes will be most memorable to a player?
- Which attributes will grab the player's attention best?

Identifying Information Channels

In the steps in the previous section, you developed lists of attributes relating to all of the objects in your game. In the cases where some of these attributes are directly related to a player progressing toward a major goal, you need to identify potential channels for information.

A *channel* here is just like a television channel. It's a useful analogy because a player can pay attention to only so much information at once. Consider the following information channels that exist on the main page of Facebook:

- **News feeds:** These contain the aggregated statuses and public conversations you're having with all your friends. They contain the actual messages from friends, along with who posted them, the comments on each message, and date stamps. This supports your goal to maintain social contact with your friends.
- **Friend notifications:** The list of recent notifications you've received from your friends. It provides information about what things your friends are doing on Facebook that directly involves you so that you can react. Again, this supports a goal to maintain and deepen social contact.
- **Private messages:** The list of private messages you've received from other Facebook users, which also supports social contact, but with information people wouldn't want to share publicly
- **Applications:** The list of applications and games you've installed. This helps you return to applications that are deepening your social contact with friends on Facebook.
- **Birthdays:** These are birthdays celebrated by your friends, and they provide you with a reason to initiate or reinitiate social contact with a friend on Facebook.
- **Information:** Information about people on Facebook so that you can know the identity of people you interact with; in particular, the friends you share in common

There are countless ways that each of your objects could potentially be organized into channels. At this stage, focus on capturing some of the ideas; later you can eliminate redundancies and pare it back to the minimum necessary for your game. The purpose here isn't to design the interface itself—that'll happen soon enough—but rather to play with the various ways in which information could be presented so that you've explored several options for displaying the information that will advance your player's goals.

Sorting Opportunities

What's the most meaningful way a player would interact with an information channel containing a lot of data? For example, a list of friends could be alphabetically sorted, or it could be based on the friends who have played most recently. Each method provides a different way to think about the same information that could relate to a different goal.

Rankings

Sorting lists of information in an information channel based on certain values can increase the sense of competition, if that's one of your goals. A leaderboard containing the top players based on level is a type of information channel, but you could come up with many other forms of comparison simply by looking at the attributes of your objects.

Feeds

Another way to sort information is to organize it based on time, such as the news feed on Facebook. This can be a great way to deliver information that's time-relevant: For example, the list of your friends who have recently been awarded badges in the game might provide you with some incentive to earn the badges yourself—or might simply make you aware that they exist.

Intersections

These can sometimes provide information that could give you motivation or progress relating to a major user story: For example, Facebook always tells you which friends you have in common with someone else, which gives you a common ground for conversation, and increases the likelihood you'll have social contact.

Context

Objects exist somewhere. You need to decide where players live, where virtual items live, and where the actions of the game are performed. Content is the relationship between the environment and the objects within that environment.

There are likely to be many possible contexts for a given action on an object in your game. A virtual good could be purchased from within a shop, delivered in a mailbox, given to you by another character, or picked up from the ground in a graphical landscape.

The following are some questions you can challenge yourself with to think about potential contexts:

- If my game were a board game (such as *Risk*, *Monopoly*, and so on) how would I design the board? What sort of regions and maps would I depict?
- What's the best metaphor for a given context in my game? Is there a real-world place that can provide a good frame of reference for the objects and actions I'm offering?
- If I were designing a theme park based on this idea, what areas would I have within it?
- If this were a 3D immersive role-playing game, what sort of places would I include in it?
- How would I organize a museum exhibit to show the information I need?
- How can I utilize already existing metaphors as potent illustrations within my product? Make a short list of the most potent metaphoric symbolism you can think of. Examples include: An eagle, a cross, golden arches, a dove, a flower, a heart.

Everything in your interface exists in the imagination of the player. Your challenge is to identify the best containers to represent these ideas. After you can identify all the possible contexts, you can play with various ideas, asking questions like the following:

- Which goals will they have in mind for each context?
- Which actions would a player want to perform from a given context?
- What information do I need to prepare the players with so that they can take actions and advance their goals?

Common themes will emerge; multiple actions will make the most sense when approached from a given context. It is from this that you can assemble a map of the various interactions that happen within your game. As you work your way through this process, the most important question you need to answer is this: What is the main arena for action that occurs within my game? Consider how this is done in other games, shown in Table 11-1.

Table 11-1: Game Actions

Game	Main Arena	Action	Goal
FarmVille	Visualizing your farm	Plant and harvest crops.	Build a bigger farm.
World of Warcraft	A 3D immersive interface	Explore landscapes and battle opponents.	Become a more powerful character who can explore more exotic landscapes and battle harder opponents.
League of Legends	The maps where players battle each other	Battle other players.	Become a top-ranked player.
Mafia Wars	The login page, which summarizes all the recent activity	Acquire items or form social relationships that improve your standing.	Grow your criminal empire.

You can perform the same analysis on nongaming websites. For example, on Facebook and LinkedIn, the main arena is a news feed that tracks what all your friends and associates have been up to. These real-time updates are intended to spur you to perform all the deeper interactions available within the site.

Creating a Context Map

When you identify the main context for your game, you can assemble a map of all the other contexts a player will need to enter to conduct the various subgoals and actions associated with all the user stories you've developed. Each node on your map represents one context that a player can reach, and the lines between nodes indicate the pathways someone would need to traverse to get to a particular context.

At each node in your map, you need to indicate which information channels will be important for each context and the actions that players will perform.

In Disruptor Beam's game *True Pirates,* a social game about conquering the high seas during the Golden Age of Piracy, the theme centered around a pirate world rich in real history and lore—something different from all the cartoony games found all over Facebook, and from all the Johnny Depp-inspired games that exist already. In the course of defining what would be important in our game, we arrived at the list of major contexts presented in Table 11-2:

Table 11-2: Major Contexts for True Pirate

Context	Description	Action	Goal
A map room	Where players could chart their course to various adventures through an aesthetic inspired by 17th-century cartography	Perform missions.	To live by the "no rules, no mercy" mantra of pirates
A log book	A realistic book containing individual pages and hand-drawn illustrations	Review progress, see prior adventures, and learn more about pirate lore.	To feel a connection to history and identify possibilities for collecting artifacts that would lead to further adventures
A sea chest	Collection of your plunder	Look at your plunder, give gifts to your friends, and design your pirate flag.	Establish a distinct identity as a pirate.
A hideout	This appears as a customized pirate's cove.	Upgrade equipment; recruit crew.	Decide on your longer-term strategy for upgrades, propelling you toward becoming the scourge of the high seas.
A shop	A listing of items you can purchase	Buy virtual goods.	Identify the items that could set you apart from other players.
Your ship	A screen showing what your ship looks like	Review all your equipment and statistics.	Investigate ways you could improve your ship.

Based on this, we developed the map shown in Figure 11-9.

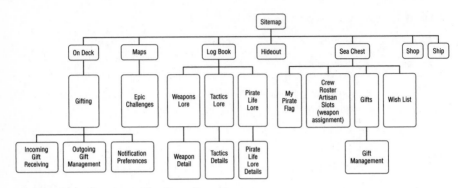

Figure 11-9: Interaction Map from *True Pirates*

At Disruptor Beam, we use a web-based product called Protoshare to develop our maps and design concepts. You might also find it productive to use white boards, post-it notes, and index cards. It's most important that your team communicate, rearrange, and try different ways to organize information.

Returning to Story

At this stage you might learn that some of your objects or user stories don't fit, might be too complex, or get buried. Don't look at this with frustration; it's a good thing to find the elements that are difficult or don't quite make sense. Be willing to cut back; games are different than many other forms of software in that the overriding goal for any project is to craft a fun experience. You might find that some of the user stories you developed early on, although well-intentioned, simply don't live up to that implicit promise. The design process is intended to be iterative, not linear, so if you find yourself returning all the way to rework your original player narrative, you're probably building a better game.

Overly complex game mechanics can also become exposed at this stage. As you look at the various objects, you might find previously unknown interdependencies or attributes that simply don't matter to the player. In either case, you need to revisit their importance and trim them if necessary. In the case of dependencies, sometimes this can be a good thing when it unfolds as part of emergent gameplay, especially for a more advanced player but run the risk of confusing new players who are just beginning to learn the game.

Adding Social Elements to Your Interface

A game isn't social simply because it is delivered on the Web or through a social network. To become social, the game must also include elements that facilitate interactions between players. The benefit of these actions is that players will spread the game to their friends and reengage people who have played in the past.

As you design your interface, you need to sprinkle it with various social actions that players can perform that spread the influence of the game beyond its confines. Ideally, some of these were already a part of the user stories you developed before you ever began the interface design process. However, when you have a map of the interface, you'll find that there are numerous opportunities for social interaction that you hadn't previously thought of. Use this point in time to decide whether you need to reiterate your story-creation process, and create new user stories to handle these cases. You might find that some of this social interaction even changes the way you think about game mechanics.

The following sections show ways you can add social interfaces to Facebook to several areas of your game.

Sharing

Many of the events that happen in a game are interesting enough to players that they might want to share them with their friends. The key to making a good sharable piece of content is something that is just as interesting to the sharer as the recipient. It's been common to share things such as level-up events and new badges in the past, but this is also the type of content people are most likely to ignore because it doesn't place them at the center of the attention. On the other hand, limited-time opportunities, chances to receive a gift, or novel ways the recipient could interact are more interesting.

Leverage Online Status

By tracking whether players are in the game at the same time as their friends, you can offer additional ways for them to interact with each other. For example, when you enter *Zynga Poker*, you are shown which of your friends are playing in real-time, which enables you to quickly join them in a game.

Activities are more fun when you do them with friends, so this can be an effective way to deepen the engagement in any online experience.

Commenting and Conversation

Games can provide players with a way to add their own messages to the game. When games contain distinct pieces of content—items, places, players—these are all opportunities where you could offer the players a chance to add their own messages. This engages some players in the same way that a blog does; it enables them to participate directly in the conversations happening within the game. You can even add a share feature to these commenting systems and make it possible for the conversation to extend outside of the game.

In addition to the static forms of conversation afforded by commenting, many games are beginning to offer real-time chat. Even games with asynchronous gameplay can offer a way for some players to interact directly with each other by having conversations in real-time.

Chat is best in environments in which players actually need to communicate in real-time to coordinate their activities. It is also helpful as a way to enable players to assist each other. However, beware of adding chat into a game prematurely, because nothing makes a game look abandoned and forgotten than an empty chat channel.

Reward Social Network Integration

Social networks provide a number of ways for any application to raise its profile throughout their service. On Facebook, this is done by liking an application and inviting your friends to play. These features can be so important that they appear persistently through the interface. As shown in Figure 11-10, *Zynga Poker* does an effective job to encourage the player to take social actions within the game that also fit into a simple story about blowing up a safe to earn more in-game currency.

Figure 11-10: Blowing up the Safe in *Zynga Poker*

Chapter in Review

In this chapter you learned about how the interface to a game enables the players to enter into a new world. You can use different levels of abstraction to achieve this: Everything from text all the way to immersive 3D interfaces. The right interface will be one that is affordable (from a development standpoint), supports the player's imagination, and enables your system of rules.

You can use MAGIC to identify the elements that make up the substance of your interface: Memories, attention, goals, intuitions, and control. Although created as a way to think about game interfaces, you may find it helpful to adapt MAGIC to any interface as a way to create a lasting, more engaging experience, leave customers with pleasant memories, focus attention, provide goals, interact intuitively, and offer a sense of control.

Use the techniques in previous chapters to refine the raw information that you can break into a map of interactions. This level of design is at the threshold of implementation; engineers and product developers could begin to actually build things, entering their own iterative development process with this information. However, the interaction map is also a way for you to iterate the design process: What sort of game mechanics and story holes does it expose? What opportunities for stronger interactions, better rules, or better stories does it invite? As with anything in an agile design process, the design of a user interface is an ongoing process, not a distinct point in time.

Choose Your Path

The following list gives areas of the book you might want to visit next.

- This chapter depends on the creation of user stories to identify the right content for your interaction maps. If you need to review that, turn to Chapter 9.
- Creating interfaces can change how you think about the rules of your game. For a treatment of that subject, go to Chapter 10.
- The next chapter discusses the element of social games that often makes them profitable and engaging: virtual goods. If you're ready for that, turn the page to Chapter 12.

12 Designing for Virtual Goods

n this Chapter, you'll learn:

- Who is buying virtual goods, and what they're buying
- How to manage the risks of a virtual economy
- Techniques for introducing and selling virtual goods in your game

In 2010, approximately 13 percent of the online population had bought virtual goods. By the end of 2011, consumers are expected to spend more than $2 billion on these digital products, mostly within games—and by 2013, some analysts see that amount nearly doubling again.

Virtual goods had trivial revenues only a few years ago. Why is it they've exploded to this degree? Who buys them, how do they buy them, and how do you go about designing a system to use virtual goods? These are the questions this chapter answers.

Why Do People Buy Virtual Goods?

Virtual goods are purchased by players for the same reason any real-world product is purchased: They have perceived value. Why does this value exist? As pointed out elsewhere in this book, games work because they engage your emotions. Virtual goods exist only in your imaginations, yet they offer advantages that you find emotionally satisfying.

Consider the popularity of pets and cute animals: Even *Mafia Wars* encourages you to build a menagerie of lions and other exotic, fearsome animals. Some games (*FishVille*, *Pet Society*, and *Zoo Kingdom*) are entirely about collecting pets. Pets pull on your heartstrings, and they've been a way for games such as *World of Warcraft* to add extra dollars to its subscription revenue; *WoW* companion pets have absolutely no impact on the game other than to look charming while they follow you around.

The emotion of impatience is also a strong motivator. For some players, time is their most valuable resource. Virtual items can short-circuit the path to other content, speed up the rate at which you can play, or remove obstacles.

Yet another emotion is the desire for individuality. Virtual items can provide players with unique ways to express themselves that other players lack. This can include ways for players to customize their appearance but may also include new ways for players to interact with other people.

Who Buys Virtual Goods?

Although the average player of a social network game in 2010 was a 43-year-old woman, you'll find that only some of these players are spending all the money that is driving the explosive growth of social gaming. When asked whether people would be willing to spend real money to get an item in a game that offered a temporary bonus, about one-third of players answered affirmatively (Figure 12-1).

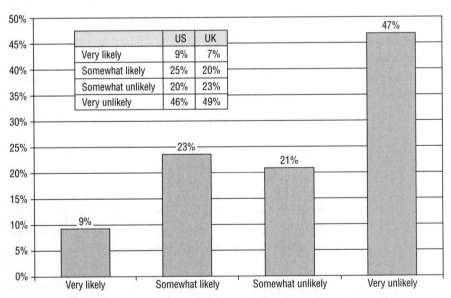

	US	UK
Very likely	9%	7%
Somewhat likely	25%	20%
Somewhat unlikely	20%	23%
Very unlikely	46%	49%

Q29: How likely would you be to purchase a virtual item with (real-world) money if it gave you a modest short-lived advantage in a game, e.g., power up special, bonus multiplier or special weapon or tool?

Information Solutions Group/Popcap, "2010 Social Gaming Research"

Figure 12-1: Popularity of Virtual Goods Purchases

Because I'm heavily invested in the success of the social games market, the optimist in me sees this as a great opportunity for social game designers: It means that there's still a chance to craft even better games that appeal to two-thirds of the market in ways that the current crop of products don't. Maybe you'll be similarly inspired by this incredible opportunity. On the other hand, you might be wondering whether all these purchases are being made by 43-year-old women, or whether there's a better way to slice up the market.

According to research from Frank N. Magid Associates, a research firm that looks at the broad computer game industry, people who spend the most money on virtual goods tend to be younger and male (see Figure 12-2).

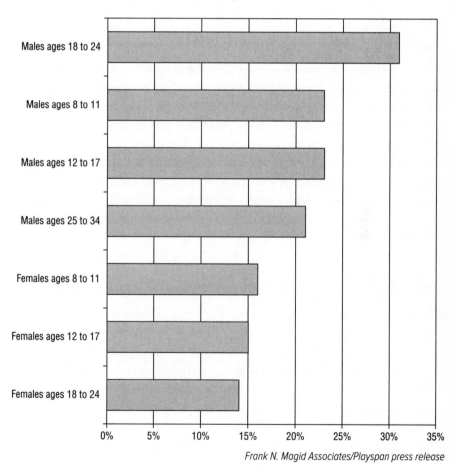

Frank N. Magid Associates/Playspan press release

Figure 12-2: Most Frequent Buyers of Virtual Goods

Is this a surprise? Younger audiences will often be the most receptive to new types of products, new distribution channels, and new ways to pay for content. However, averages can be very deceiving—it is actually the buyers of particular products that matter. For example, more than 50 million virtual gifts have been exchanged on Dogster (an online community for dog lovers), where the majority of buyers are between 35 and 50 years old. On the opposite extreme, you have products such as *Club Penguin* and *Webkinz*, which are targeted at young children. (Although the ultimate buyer is a parent.) Don't be fooled by averages into thinking that you need to build products only for 43-year-old women if you want to earn the most revenue—there are opportunities everywhere in the market for the right product.

Where Do People Buy Virtual Goods?

Virtual goods are purchased across a wide range of online experiences. Free, web-based games (from outside of social networks) lead the way—some of these products have had a few more years to optimize their processes. Social networks and games within social networks and other free-to-play online games round out the remainder of the top, as shown in Figure 12-3

Virtual goods are not a phenomena limited to one class of games in one particular distribution channel; they're powering a wide range of products throughout everyone's online experience, which suggests that people are becoming more accustomed to virtual goods. That's a big part of why the growth expected in the virtual goods market is so easy to believe.

How People Pay for Virtual Goods

Originally, the developers of online games would need to create and implement their own billing and payment systems so that they could conduct an online transaction. Back in 1992, I recall just how hard it was to even explain what we did to some of the credit card processing companies–and got lumped along with adult telephone services and other seedy businesses, simply because they couldn't figure us out. Fortunately, those days are long past, and there's a wide range of ways that customers can pay for virtual goods—and a wide array of companies you can partner with to establish a payment system within a matter of days, if not hours.

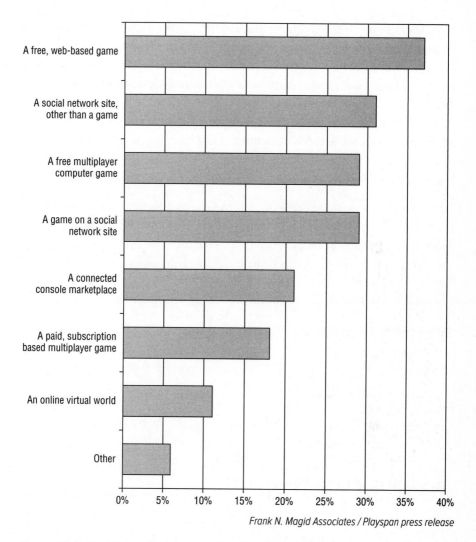

Frank N. Magid Associates / Playspan press release

Figure 12-3: Most Frequent Places to Buy Virtual Goods

Credit Cards and Payment Aggregators

Credit card payments can be added to an online game today with little effort: Simply go to the website for a third-party payment aggregator such as Trialpay or Super Rewards, and all you need to do is go through a quick approval process, and your company can process credit card transactions for a nominal fee. If your transaction volume ever becomes enormous, you might find it's more profitable to deal with a bank directly—but don't even think about it until you're doing millions in fees. Even the larger social game companies almost entirely depend upon third parties for this service.

In addition to credit cards, most of the third-party payment aggregators support all the other payment methods mentioned in this section.

Facebook Credits

One of the largest developments in 2010 was the emergence of Facebook Credits (shown in Figure 12-4), which is an online currency built into Facebook. Credits can be purchased by users of Facebook and then exchanged for items within the games they play on Facebook. All that developers need to do is implement a Facebook API. Although still considered "in beta" at the close of 2010, it was clear that the currency was gaining significant momentum.

Figure 12-4: Purchase Facebook Credits

Initially, many developers felt that Facebook Credits was an imposition on them; after all, Facebook wants 30 percent (which is surprisingly similar to what Apple charges for applications to be distribution via the AppStore). However, many developers who had chosen to work with Facebook exclusively quickly found that it removed so much friction from the purchasing process that their net revenue actually increased.

If you offer virtual goods in your product, Facebook Credits is something you need to seriously consider. Focus on net profits, not simply the total revenue. As of the time this book is going to print, it's still new, yet promising.

Paypal

Paypal has been conducting Internet payments longer than almost anyone, so it's no surprise that it also established a strong position in the online game market. You can integrate with Paypal directly, using its APIs, or you can get it as part of a package offered by a third-party payment aggregator.

Mobile Phone Payments

It's been possible to purchase online services via your mobile phone for a number of years. Typically, that has been used for content such as ringtones, entertainment services, conference calls, and premium SMS. However, mobile phones are now used to make purchases for nonmobile products, simply by using the phone as a payment device.

Currently, the costs for mobile payment transactions can be fairly high because of the many middlemen involved in the process. Zong (shown in Figure 12-5), one of the major mobile payment providers that works with web-based companies, charges approximately 40 percent of any transaction—which makes Facebook Credits seem cheap in comparison.

Figure 12-5: Zong Purchasing Interface

Game Cards

A game card is a disposable, single-use card for obtaining currency within an online game. Some of the larger social game companies including Zynga have created their own game card products, which are distributed at thousands of retail outlets throughout the world (as shown in Figure 12-6). Game cards enable people to pay for a card using cash or any other acceptable form of payment accepted at the establishment. Players take the card home, and enter a code from their card into their computer, and the currency is deposited into their online game account.

Figure 12-6: Game Cards for Sale

An advantage of game cards is that they give people a new way to pay, including hard cash. The physical presence of the cards in retail also acts as an additional form of promotion and distribution for your games. For most companies smaller than Zynga, manufacturing and distributing your own game cards isn't a viable option; fortunately, a number of companies have emerged to help you out. This includes the Ultimate Game Card, created by Playspan, and GMG Entertainment. Both of these companies are included in Appendix B.

Categorizing Virtual Goods

Virtual goods exist in a wide variety of forms, each appealing to different emotions or different game mechanics. Read on to learn which might be appropriate within your game or social media business.

Gifts

One of the most common types of virtual goods is a gift. These work well for the same reason gifts work in the real world: They enable people to express emotion and gratitude toward someone in a form that's more thoughtful than simply giving them money. Furthermore, a virtual gift carries with it a feeling of reciprocity; people are more inclined to send back a virtual gift after they've received one.

Facebook was one of the pioneers with virtual gifts, although it has discontinued the service to focus on creating Facebook Credits as a platform to assist a wider range of companies to take part in virtual gifting (see Figure 12-7).

My Sent Gifts

From: **Angela Bull Radoff (gifts)**
When: February 12, 2008

This is a private gift. Delete it | View Gift on Profile
Others will see the gift, but not the message or who sent it.

" Sweety-pie Valentine-jin. "

Figure 12-7: Facebook's Obsolete Virtual Gifts

Virtual gifts include those that are always purchased for real money and others that simply exist to increase player-to-player engagement and interaction. Today, gifting is one of the most popular ways to drive engagement between players Inside Social Games. As this section describes the other types of virtual items, realize that any of them could also be packaged as gifts.

Boosts and Power-Ups

Many games provide a basic set of items that you can use for free and entice you to buy premium items for real money. These items can be distinguished in a number of ways:

- **Attractiveness:** They can look more interesting than other items.
- **Customization:** You can send/purchase items that customize the appearance of the player's avatar. This can be especially potent when players are showcased in a way that enables other players to look at them.
- **Power enhancement:** They can have better statistics that make it easier to win the game. Examples: special weapons in *Mafia Wars* and special fashion accessories in *Gods of Rock*.
- **Power boosts:** They can enable you to perform one-time interactions with the game that allow for more advanced gameplay. Example: the special boosts offered inside *Bejeweled Blitz*.

The primary game design concern when offering items like this is that they can't compromise the integrity of the gameplay. You need to balance the advantages they offer against the need to engage nonpaying customers: You don't want them to resent the game, thinking of it as simply a game about paying to win. It's important to provide pathways for customers who want to invest a lot of effort to reach the same results as paying customers. This way, you give everyone two alternatives: Sweat or cash, but everyone can still win.

Personalization and Creativity

Some games offer virtual goods as a way to customize your appearance to others. In products with particular game mechanics, where an advantage is offered to the player, these items might also double as boosts and power-ups. However, some forms of social media use virtual goods entirely as a way for the player to express their uniqueness to other members.

Second Life is one of the best-known examples of a virtual economy based on the creativity of its members (called residents in *Second Life* parlance). The major items acquired by its residents include real estate and items to customize their character appearance. Other social media environments such as instant messengers have made use of avatar technology to enable members to present themselves uniquely.

 OTAKU Although *Second Life* is more of a virtual world than a game in its own right, many of the residents have crafted their own role-playing environments within it. In one case, the *Bloodlines* game within *Second Life* enables members to assume the role of vampires and bite other residents. Vampirism spreads virally as players bite each other; various items such as a nightshade potion are sold to remove the "curse" from players who don't want it. These curses have no real impact on players other than what they believe it to be.

Two specialized forms of personalization include:

- **Themes.** Just as players are willing to purchase boosts or customizations, many people are willing to make purchases that customize the aesthetic experience they have within the game. This includes new skins, graphical themes, and sets of icons that enable players to choose how they perceive the game.
- **Emotes.** These are expressions that players can make within a game. They enable players to act out or show feelings to other players. These began in multiplayer text-based games like MUDs, appeared next in massively multiplayer games like *World of Warcraft* (where it is implemented as dances and other animations players can express), and now it is emerging within other online games as well. Whereas customizing a player's avatar enables players to change how they appear to other players, emotive content can enable them to develop certain token expressions that other players can't perform. This will probably be another area of growth within social network games.

Play Accelerators

Another class of virtual goods is those that provide an increase in the rate with which you play the game. Like boosts and power-ups, these give you an edge within the game—but are focused on making it possible to experience the game more quickly. These are often some of the most effective ways to monetize a game because people are naturally impatient, and some of them will be inclined to spend real money if it means they can continue playing. Examples include purchasing a good that enables:

- **More moves:** For example, you can purchase energy in *Mafia Wars* or *Gods of Rock.*
- **Speed-ups:** This makes certain in-game actions happen faster. For example, you can speed up the completion of a building in *Kingdoms of Camelot.*
- **Bonuses:** These improve the rate at which you can progress through the game. For example, you can purchase an experience-point booster in *League of Legends* that allows you to level up your character more quickly

Collectibles

Collecting things is already a compelling game mechanic on its own. When combined with virtual goods, it can be turned into a revenue-generating event. You can provide some items that are found for free in the game and allow the collection to be completed with items purchased for real currency—or traded as gifts. Sometimes collections are completed just for the fun of it or for an in-game bonus received upon turning over the collection.

Expansions

Entire sections of games can be offered as part of an expansion or sequel that can be unlocked only upon purchase. This is a common model outside of social network games, including downloadable content on the Xbox—or entire new stories and maps in games such as *World of Warcraft: Cataclysm.*

This type of virtual good isn't popular within social media games today, but that likely has to do with the limited content offered within these games as of 2010. As production values rise, expect to see entire expansion sets offered as a virtual purchase.

Transmedia Content

Virtual goods are now used to package other types of content from additional forms of media. An example is the way *Rock Band* and *Guitar Hero* sell music through downloadable content; the music becomes a new way to interact with the game—and also resonates with the player as a song they've probably heard elsewhere.

Music and other types of media are appearing in social media games as well. For example, Crowdstar worked out a deal with Bon Jovi in which the band's greatest hits will be made available in *Happy Aquarium*.

Managing Virtual Economies

Any time you have a set of scarce goods, you have an economy. When the scarce goods are virtual, you have a virtual economy. In games, this often means a set of items that players may acquire using an in-game currency that symbolizes money (such as gold in *World of Warcraft*). However, a virtual economy can exist any time there's a scarcity of rewards that can be redeemed for specific benefits. For example, on certain social media websites such as Slashdot, users are rewarded with a limited supply of *karma points*, which can be used for voting on the quality of other messages. Although karma points were not intended as a currency, they're scarce, which causes them to operate within their own economy.

Understanding Virtual Markets

The purpose of virtual currency is to purchase any of the virtual goods outlined earlier in this chapter. The most basic way this can be done is by providing a store that players can use to acquire items from your game directly. However, games can also implement markets that enable players to trade with each other. The following are a list of such trading media:

- **Gifts:** The simplest form of a market is a system that enables players to give gifts to each other. Players send gifts because it feels good or because they want to show a friend that they're having a great time in your game. Gifts were discussed as a type of virtual item earlier in this chapter.
- **Barter:** Barter economies can also emerge within games, in which players send gifts to each other with the expectation of receiving different items in exchange.
- **Currency:** When you allow players to exchange virtual currency with each other, you've entered new territory: With or without an explicit marketplace

(such as the auction house in *World of Warcraft*) you'll have created a real market economy. Players can engage in transactions with each other for the in-game currency.

Market economies in games are exciting for game designers because they can add a whole new element of engagement between players. Buyers and sellers emerge, people communicate with each other about transactions, and some players can specialize—just like in a real economy. The virtual economy can become a form of emergent gameplay even more compelling than the underlying game itself. Some games even feature elaborate crafting systems in which players buy and sell virtual goods to construct more complex virtual goods that they offer back to other players. However, virtual economies are challenging to manage and have their own set of risks.

Money Supply

Like any real economy, money needs to be created. In the real world, the money supply is limited by the actions of central banks, which can add or remove money from the economy. In this case, money remains a limited resource because someone who wants to buy one good needs to earn the money from someone else. Contrast this with how most games essentially mint new currency any time it needs to be given to a player—imagine if the central bank printed new money every time you received your paycheck!

Games introduce new currency into the virtual money supply a few different ways:

- **Rewards:** By directly rewarding virtual currency to the player for performing certain jobs (quests, missions, and so forth).
- **Stipends:** Through a regular stipend for logging into the game. An example of this is in *Zynga Poker*, where you are awarded with some in-game currency after returning to the game after an absence.
- **Sell backs:** By paying the customers virtual currency when they sell virtual items back to the game.
- **Purchases:** By enabling players to purchase virtual currency with real money.
- **Bugs and exploits:** These may lead to ways for players to generate unintended amounts of virtual currency. For example, imagine what would happen if players figured out a way to duplicate their items and sell the copies back to the game.

Problems in Virtual Economies

After you open the door to a market-based virtual economy, you can experience some of the same problems as a real-world economy. Any of the items in Table 12-1 can have disastrous effects on the game, resulting in discouraged players and a distinct lack of fun and may result in players becoming bored and leaving the game. The solutions mentioned in the third column of the table are discussed in the next section.

Table 12-1: Various Virtual Economy Problems

Problem	Description	Solution
Hyperinflation	Inflation is normal in a game as in the real world. But hyperinflation, when prices rise out of control, is totally destructive, causing players to perceive little value in any virtual good and destroying the integrity and trust players have for the game. This can occur when the virtual money supply greatly exceeds available money sinks.	Reduce money supply or increase money sinks.
Depressions	Occur if players cannot earn virtual currency at an adequate rate to continue enjoying the game. Players feel that the more they play, the less they acquire. This can be due to a lack of content, game mechanic imbalances, or excessive cost structures that squeeze out what they can acquire. This causes a virtual depression where players get emotionally depressed.	Increase money supply; add more compelling content; increase diversity of the economy by providing more item variety.

Problem	Description	Solution
Perceived inequities	Because some players learn ways to advance at a faster rate than others, it's almost impossible to perfectly balance a game. However, if players discover that other players have substantial advantages—due to when they joined the game or the early decisions they made—this can lead to resentment, especially if players feel there's no way for them to catch up.	You might find it desirable to offer a mix of strategies in which some players are economically advantaged because it leads to players investing time in learning and discussing the game.
Black markets	If you create virtual goods or currency, people will look for ways to circumvent your controls. *World of Warcraft* suffered from secondary markets when *gold farmers* entered the game for the sole purpose of collecting and selling gold to other players. *WoW* has no real-money currency and is based on a subscription. If player1 purchases currency from player2, player2 decreases the potential amount of time he needs to play; this potentially decreases the length of player2's subscription, which costs Blizzard money. Players have even been known to hire other players to level up their characters for them, known as *power leveling* services.	Implement a dual currency system, monopolize the sale of your own virtual currency, implement policies against secondary market trading, and defend vigorously. If you want to allow players to trade, then create the trading market yourself and consider collecting a transaction fee.

Mitigating Problems with Virtual Economies

The right time to think about mitigating the risks in your virtual economy is before problems like black markets or hyperinflation have taken hold. When they begin, you might have no choice but to take bold corrective action such as banning certain players or forcibly removing virtual currency. You can also implement some virtual tools.

Fortunately, the tools that can manage your economy may also have the effect of increasing the engagement of your players. The following methods have been employed by various game designers to mitigate risks:

- Dual currency systems
- Effective currency sinks
- Restricting certain item transactions
- Reset buttons
- Measuring economic activity (covered in Chapter 8)

Dual Currency Systems

World of Warcraft is an example of a game that has only a single currency because players acquire gold by playing, and almost all the items purchased in the game are bought using it. (Although *WoW* now provides certain services or items, such as companion pets, which are purchased directly from Blizzard with real currency.)

Under a dual currency system, one type of currency is rewarded for performing actions in the game, and another currency is purchased only with real money. For example, *League of Legends* has a dual currency system in which Riot Points are purchased with real money, and Influence Points are earned by playing the game. Some items in *LoL* may be purchased with either currency, but certain premium items may be acquired with Riot Points only.

The advantage of a dual currency system is that you mostly limit the risk of inflation to the currency earned within the game, excluding the real-money currency.

Some dual currency systems might offer small amounts of the real-money currency for performing certain in-game behaviors. *Mafia Wars* is one example: You earn Godfather Points for doing certain things, like earning a level, but for the most part you need to purchase them if you want to buy the snazzy items. If you create a hybrid system such as this, you need to be cautious about creating exploits in the gameplay that might enable some players to earn more currency than you expect; Be careful about allowing players to transfer the real-money currency between each other. If you do, the following are the risks:

- **Decreased sales:** You'll have decreased currency sales because players can give the currency to their friends when they quit playing.

- **Loss of players:** Players who quit playing and give their currency to a friend will be less likely to return because there's no stored value in their game account.
- **Discounted currency:** If you have a hybrid dual currency model such as *Mafia Wars*, where players can earn some of the real-money currency for in-game activity, they may transfer and sell excess currency to others at a discount to your price (which deprives you of revenue).

Currency Sinks

Games that add currency into the money supply in an unbounded manner will also need ways to remove money from players. This includes the following:

- **Selling items to players from an in-game store.** When purchases are made, the currency is effectively deleted, rather than transferred to another player.
- **Providing single-use, consumable items.** Such things as healing potions, energy refills, and short-term accelerants can be especially effective at removing currency for items that enjoy steady demand.
- **Transaction fees:** A percentage of a market transaction can be deducted when players sell an item to each other, which permanently reduces the sum total of currency existing between the two players.
- **Item decay:** Items can decay over time or with use, which requires payments of virtual currency to maintain them.
- **Recurring fees and expenses:** These can be levied on players to reduce income in exchange for in-game benefits.
- **Offering upgrades:** Items can have upgrades or certain improvements made to them for additional payments of virtual currency.

Transaction Restrictions

Certain virtual items can be marked as nontransferrable. *World of Warcraft* calls these *soulbound* items, which is a term that has been adopted by a number of other games. After a player uses certain items for the first time, he or she cannot give it to anyone else.

When an item is soulbound, it can also be thought of as a currency sink: An item could be sold once (which removes a certain amount of currency) but it can never be salvaged for more than a nominal percentage of its original value.

Reset Buttons

When a game features rules that enable players to progress along long pathways, some players make choices that they later regret. Some games offer players the ability to reset their state—enabling them to remake certain previous decisions. When virtual currency is charged for this, it can be an effective currency sink, but it can also be a good way to enable players to try different strategies, which can reduce the risk that players perceive inequities in how other players have played the game.

Pricing and Merchandising Virtual Goods

One of the most important things for you to determine is the price elasticity of demand for your virtual products. Because virtual goods have no marginal cost, your goal should be to maximize your revenue at the price players are willing to pay. To do that you need to experiment with a variety of price points and measure purchase volume.

Besides price, you have a number of ways to influence the demands for your virtual goods. The perceived value of a virtual good is based on the emotional and game mechanical advantage that players associate with an item. Still, you can increase demand further by using the bag of tricks employed by retailers for thousands of years. To increase demand for your goods, consider trying to offer:

- **Different virtual items for sale in different places in your interface:** To do this, you need to learn which points in time the player is most likely to want to buy.
- **Different ways to display the price:** Some research suggests that the best way to show a price is to simply show the number—dollar signs, decimal points, and words might cause people to buy less.
- **A display of groups of three products at once:** With this group, you show one low price option, one medium price option, and one higher price option. Some research suggests that players are driven toward buying medium-priced options. This can be used as a means to drive average purchase price up by positioning middle options as a "great deal."
- **Bundles:** This is as simple as packaging products together into similar groups.
- **Limited editions of certain products:** Players will feel they're in competition with other players to acquire something unique.

- **Limited time offers:** You can create sales by offering a discount for currency and certain virtual goods for a limited period of time.
- **Specials:** These are special events as well as seasonal and holiday items.

Chapter in Review

In this chapter you learned about virtual goods, which are items sold within online games. Virtual goods are often symbolic of real-world equivalents, such as a sword you might buy in an online role-playing game—but may also include other types of content such as new features, media, expressions, or personalization options.

When you allow players to trade with each other, you go beyond virtual goods and enter the more complex realm of virtual economies. In a virtual economy, you need to be concerned with inflation, depressions, perceived inequities, and black markets. Fortunately, techniques such as currency sinks, dual-currency systems, and transaction restrictions can be applied to manage these risks.

Like the real world, you can create added revenue from virtual currency and virtual goods by testing different pricing strategies. You can also increase demand through sales, limited editions, and bundles.

Choose Your Path

The following list gives areas of the book you might want to visit next.

- If you'd like to learn more about techniques that help you measure how well your virtual economy is working, you can read Chapter 8, which covers the metrics you use to measure a virtual economy.
- This is a good time to review the ways in which you can create added demand for virtual goods through the use of compelling game mechanics. That subject was covered in Chapter 10.
- If you'd like to discuss some of the latest research and knowledge about virtual goods and economies, head to http://game-on-book.com and enter **economy** in the secret code box.
- If you've reached this chapter because you've read the entire book, then award yourself the Social Game Energizer achievement. You've made it the whole way through! The following pages in the Coda will sum up the major themes that I've covered.

13 Coda

Games are a reflection of humanity. Each game glints with certain values, truths, and recollections of your evolutionary past. Games show you who you are and invoke your imaginations.

Games have been around for at least as long as human memory, and there is a lot to them—and you. Although I don't propose to have created the Grand Unified Theory of Fun, I've nevertheless attempted to weave together a number of unifying themes regarding social games throughout this book.

Anything Can Be a Game

Wouldn't the world be a better place if things were more fun? Fun is the feeling you get when you experience flow—that sense of deep engagement, timelessness, and satisfaction that comes from doing the things you enjoy. This enjoyment makes you smile and laugh, actually affecting your brain chemistry in positive ways—increasing your brainpower and good health. Fun isn't just about entertainment; it can sharpen your interest, engrave your memories, and keep you returning time after time to any experience.

Gamification has emerged as a term for applying the principles of game design to everyday life. Although the goals are admirable, too many people miss the point. Games aren't a collection of point systems, achievements, levels, or any of the other cognitive devices that games employ to provide feedback and reward. That's just one part of an effective game system. Chapter 2 explains how games and experience making impacting way business is conducted. Chapter 6 discusses the way games can turn many tasks into fun experiences and explores cases from a range of social games and social media websites.

Games Are a Mathematical Art Form

In this sense, games are similar to music, which would not exist without the numeric basis of specific pitches, rhythms, and meter. Most of the rules of games can be easily reduced to numbers. Games are worlds in which physics and economics come to life.

Chapter 7 introduces what goes into the games that appear on popular social networks such as Facebook. Chapter 8 explains the business model for social games—how to convert attention into dollars. This mirrors the values of your experience economy, in which memories and personal transformation have become more valuable to you than most physical goods. Of course, math is used to model the game mechanics that define the rules within games, as touched upon in Chapter 10.

Games Are Stories

Games touch on the same elements that make myths so enduring. Each game is a hero's journey; each player is on a path of transformation. Characters, archetypes, and heroic motifs are potent tools for thinking about experience—and should be considered equal to systems that reveal progress and achievement.

The idea of the hero's journey is first mentioned in Chapter 4 where the concept is presented as a way to think about how your customers envision themselves. Chapter 9 discusses this subject in greater depth by explaining how you can use myths and storytelling techniques to explore design challenges. These techniques are part of the player-centered design process, which creates user stories for guiding the design of game systems discussed in Chapter 10. Next, Chapter 11 expands on bringing worlds to life through the different user interface techniques. Lastly, Chapter 12 discusses populating these worlds with interesting virtual objects.

The introduction to this book mentions that you've embarked on a hero's journey simply by reading this book. Maybe you want to create your own social game with epic fantasy stories, electronic casinos, or gem-encrusted puzzles; or maybe you want to learn about the magic of game design so that you can bring it into your own business. Whatever your motives are, your journey is only at its beginning. This book can be the mentor that gives you that slight push, sending you on your new adventure. The next steps are up to you.

The Future of Social Games

Games can expand your imagination, act as collaborative storytellers, and create new opportunities for social interaction. However, the truth is that the industry still has a long way to go.

The future holds amazing possibilities for social games. Inventors will create new game mechanics that will use social interactions between players in new ways. In the future, when you look back to our current state, these innovations will probably seem obvious, as many great inventions often do. But you'll also sense that we're on to something different—that social media isn't simply a term for a category of websites, but also a fundamentally new way that people are interacting. Everywhere that people have interacted throughout history, they have also found new classes of games. Whether the creation of polo in ancient Persia as a form of military training, the emergence of game shows on television, or the creation of interactive digital games—shifting culture and new forms of media bring with them new ways to have fun and new opportunities to grow businesses.

Glossary, Resources, and More

A Glossary

achievement

An accomplishment in a game for performing an action or combination of actions successfully. Achievements are a means to communicate progress and success to a player. Achievements often come with badges or other rewards that players may collect and display.

ad network

A business that connects the sellers of advertising inventory (publishers, such as game creators) with the buyers of ads (marketers and advertising agencies).

agile development

The creation of working software through rapid iteration, focused on customer collaboration and self-organizing teams.

alief

Automatic belief-like behavior that may be in conflict with observable facts.

archetype

In the model of recurring character themes presented by Joseph Campbell, called the monomyth, as well as dreams studied by Carl Jung, an archetype is one of the recurring character types—such as a rebel, a mother, a hero, etc.

ARPU

Average Revenue per User, determined by dividing total revenue (for a particular period of time) by the number of active users. When this refers to the average revenue per paying user, this is sometimes also referred to as ARPPU.

asynchronous

A system in which events can occur in any order, such as a game where different players can place their moves without being concerned about the order that other players are moving. Contrast with synchronous.

CAC
Customer Acquisition Cost, the total expenses spent on acquiring new customers divided by the actual number of customers acquired.

context map
A set of pathways between contexts (often metaphorical environments) that a player accesses part of the game from. An example of a context would be a shop within a game; the context map lists all the interactions possible within the shop and the paths taken to get to the shop.

cooldown
A period of time that needs to elapse before a player is allowed to repeat a particular action in a game.

CPA
Cost per Acquisition. A pricing model for advertising in which the advertiser pays when a user takes a particular action, such as making a purchase or providing contact information.

CPC
Cost per Click. A pricing model for advertising in which the advertiser pays anytime a user clicks an advertisement.

CPM
Cost per Thousand. A pricing model for advertising in which a fixed price is paid for every 1,000 times an ad displays.

currency sink
The opposite of the money supply; this is the removal of money from the economy. In a virtual economy, this is performed by charging players for virtual goods and services that cause the virtual currency they spend to be removed.

DAU
Daily Active Users. The number of users who use a game or application in a particular day.

dual currency
The creation of two currencies within a virtual economy: one that is given for performing actions within the game, and another that is typically acquired only with real money.

EdgeRank

A ranking formula used by Facebook to determine whether individual stories should appear in a user's news feed.

emergent complexity

Complexity that emerges naturally out of a game experience. Emergent complexity is typically absorbed by players at their own pace and requires little or no learning in advance. Contrast with inherent complexity.

endowment effect

The psychological tendency to value things you already own more than you'd be willing to pay to acquire them. Compare with Loss Aversion.

epic

(1) A wide-ranging user story that explains overarching goals and design objectives. An epic typically needs to be broken down into additional user stories according to the INVEST principals; (2) as a colloquialism in games, epic is an adjective often applied to something that's hard to achieve or particularly valuable to the player

experience economy

The theory that the modern economy is shifting toward experience industries (those that produce memories as their product or transform the customer in some way) and away from physical goods and services.

flow

A theory of enjoyment proposed by Mihály Csíkszentmihályi, suggesting that optimal experiences are those in which the participant is in a state of high concentration and engagement. States of flow are typically enabled by providing experiences with a high degree of immediate feedback, control, instant reward, and clear goals. Effective games make use of flow to keep players absorbed.

freemium

A product that starts for free but includes premium options a customer may want to pay for.

frequency cap

A limit on the number of times a user may be shown an advertisement. Typically combined with CPM pricing models, this limits an individual user from seeing an ad an excessive number of times.

game-tree complexity

A model of a game's complexity determined by recursively quantifying the number of moves that can occur based on all possible moves in a game.

gamification

The process of adding game-like features to a game. This book argues that to properly *gamify* something, you need to consider not only the functional elements of game design (leaderboards, achievement systems, and points) but also the emotional elements of story and experience.

Hero's Journey

A set of plot elements that recur within the monomyth structure proposed by Joseph Campbell.

hyperinflation

The state of prices increasing out of control. Hyperinflation is a risk in poorly controlled virtual economies.

information channel

A set of similar information that appears within a user interface. For example, a feed within a game that reports on the activity of your friends is a particular information channel.

Inherent Complexity

The complexity built into a game from the beginning. Players typically need to learn the rules resulting from inherent complexity when they first start playing a game. Contrast with emergent complexity.

INVEST

A mnemonic intended to capture the principals of user story design: Independent, Negotiable, Valuable, Estimable, Small, and Testable.

K-Factor

A term borrowed from epidemiology that refers to the number of people who are, on average, *infected* by a marketing program. For example, if a game has a K-Factor of 2.0, it means that each player who tries the game will get two other friends to play it.

leaderboard

A comparison that ranks players against each other. Leaderboards may be directly competitive in nature or may simply compare progress between multiple players.

loss aversion

The psychological tendency to avoid losses, even when they might be good for you. Compare with Endowment Effect.

LTV

Lifetime Value; the average amount of revenue that you expect to receive from a customer.

MAGIC

A mnemonic for a set of user interface principles relevant to game development, standing for memories, attention, goals, intuitions, and control.

MAU

Monthly Active Users, the total number of users who interact with a game or social application during the course of a month. Compare with DAU.

metagame

A game about games. An example is the achievement system on Xbox Live, which provides a system of badges that players can collect from across multiple games.

minimum viable product

The minimum set of features in a product that enables it to be accepted by a customer.

MMO

Massively Multiplayer Online. A category of social games that operates independent of social networks, featuring interaction between large numbers of players.

MMORPG

Massively Multiplayer Online Role-playing Game. A role-playing game featuring interactions between a large number of people, such as *World of Warcraft.*

money supply

The creation of new money in an economy. In a virtual economy, this function is provided by the game system, which may generate new currency whenever a player purchases virtual currency with real money or performs certain actions within the game environment.

monomyth

A theory proposed by Joseph Campbell that certain stories contain a common set of mythic elements that may be found throughout history.

open source

Software provided with all the source code available, enabling developers to contribute changes. Most open software is available for free; although, many companies also license commercial software on an open basis.

player-centered design

An iterative design method introduced in this book adapted from user-centered design that includes envisioning the product, moves to persona development, the creation of user stories, and the development of user interfaces. After interface development, principal software development commences followed by ongoing testing and measurement. Each stage may produce information that can cause an iteration back to a previous step.

player narrative

A story that explains the experiences a player should receive when playing a game; a first step in developing the ideas behind a game concept. These can be broken down into epics and user stories.

price discrimination

Charging different customers different prices for an item with little or no difference, or little underlying difference in the supplier's cost.

progression

The system of advancement that a game uses to communicate how far the player has progressed in the game, and how far they are from their next milestone. This includes systems such as levels and achievement systems.

social channel

An information channel on a social media website that enables applications to communicate updates. Social channels are often used to conduct viral marketing programs. An example of a social channel is the news feed inside Facebook.

social game

A game played by more than one person; a form of entertainment for thousands of years.

social media

A form of online media featuring significant participation by users. Examples include social networks, blogs, forums, and online review sites.

social media game
A game or game adaptation within social media. Includes social network games but also applies to websites such as LinkedIn that use game mechanics.

social network game
A social game primarily distributed through social networks such as Facebook.

standard deviation
A measure of how distributed the values of a probability curve are, relative to the average.

story card
A small card, usually stored on an index card or Post-it note, containing a user story.

synchronous
Events that happen in time dependent upon a particular sequence, such as individual turns in a game. Contrast with asynchronous.

time on site
The average amount of time that users spend on a particular website.

time per session
The average amount of time that users spend inside an application or game.

user experience
The sum total of the experience of using a particular technology product, including the impact of brand and the emotional state of the user.

user interface
The input and output devices and on-screen gadgets that make it possible for a human to interact with technology.

user story
A short narrative that explains who wants something to happen in a piece of software, what they want, and why they want it.

viral marketing
The acquisition of new customers that occurs when your customers spread your product to new customers on your behalf.

virtual currency

A unit of account and store of value within a virtual economy. An example is the gold used in *World of Warcraft* or the Godfather Points used in *Mafia Wars*.

virtual economy

An economic system consisting of the exchange of virtual goods and virtual currency, such as occurs within online games.

virtual gift

A virtual good intended as a gift to another player.

virtual good

An item that exists only in the mind of the user, such as currencies, gifts, or other objects that exist within online games. *See also* virtual currency, virtual economy, and virtual gift.

wireframe

A loose design for a user interface intended to show the major interface elements, interactions, and proportionate use of real estate—but not the actual visual design of the interface.

B Resource Guide

The following list includes companies, websites, and products mentioned in this book. For an up-to-date listing, visit http://game-on-book.com and enter **resources** in the secret code box.

Game Studios

Game studios are companies that build social game products that they either self-distribute, or work with other partners or publishers to market and distribute. Details of each are presented in Table B-1.

Table B-1: Game Studios

Game Studio	Description	Website/Contact Information
Blue Fang	Blue Fang was the creator of *Zoo Kingdom*. It used its experience in animal-themed games to create *Zoo Kingdom*, a popular social network game.	Website: www.bluefang.com
Disruptor Beam	The author's company. Disruptor Beam creates some of its own products, including *Gods of Rock*, but also partners with publishers and other creative companies to develop great social game products based on its Thorium platform.	Website: http://disruptorbeam.com Contact: info@disruptorbeam.com 831 Beacon Street #105, Newton Centre, MA 02459

continues

Table B-1: Game Studios *(continued)*

Game Studio	Description	Website/Contact Information
Kevan Davis	Independently developed *Chore Wars* (mentioned in this book) and *Urban Dead* (one of the original online social games about the impending zombie apocalypse).	Website: `kevan.org` Contact: `kevan@kevan.org`
Rovio	The creator of *Angry Birds*. It also created games for Electronic Arts, Nokia, Namco Bandai, and other publishers.	Website: `http://rovio.com` Contact: `contact@rovio.com`
Simutronics	The creator of *Gemstone*, the game that hooked the author on social games over two decades ago.	Website: `http://www.play.net`
Wonderland Software	The creator of *Godfinger*.	Website: `wonderlandsoftware.com` Contact: `hello@wonderlandsoftware.com`

Social Network Game Publishers

The game publishers in Table B-2 include companies that either self-publish their own products or fund the development of outside game studios.

Table B-2: Game Publishers

Publisher	Description	Website/Contact Information
6waves	Develops, publishes, and distributes a range of social game products. It also offers distribution to games that have been developed outside of its network.	Website: `6waves.com.` Contact: `bd@6waves.com` (developer inquiries)
Ayeah	Publisher of *FanSwarm*, a celebrity collecting game (developed by the author's studio, Disruptor Beam).	Website: `ayeahgames.com` Contact: `info@ayeahgames.com`

Publisher	Description	Website/Contact Information
Crowdstar	The creator of social network games including *Happy Aquarium, Zoo Paradise*, and *Happy Pets*.	Website: `crowdstar.com` Contact: `partners@crowdstar.com`
GSN Digital	Publisher of the *Wheel of Fortune* social network game, `Worldwinner.com`, and other online games.	Website: `www.gsn.com`
Kabam	The creator of *Kingdom of Camelot*, mentioned in this book.	Website: `www.kabam.com` Contact: `corp@kabam.com`
Lolapps	Lolapps has created games including *Critter Island* and *Ravenwood Fair*.	Website: `www.lolapps.com`
Ngmoco	The publisher of a large number of social games, mostly with mobile components. It published *Godfinger*, which is mentioned in this book.	Website: `ngmoco.com` Contact: `gamemakers@ngmoco.com` (for independent developers)
Playfish	Now a part of Electronic Arts and the creator of social network games including *Restaurant City, Madden Superstars*, and *Pet Society*.	Website: `www.playfish.com` Contact: `info@playfish.com`
PopCap	The creator of enormously popular casual and social games including the *Bejeweled* franchise and *Plants vs Zombies*.	Website: `www.popcap.com` Mailing address: 2401 4th Ave, Suite 300, Seattle, WA 98121
Quickhit	Creator of social games based on an NFL football license.	Website: `www.quickhit.com`
Riot Games	The publisher of *League of Legends*, a popular social game for core gamers that plays in a standalone client.	Website: `www.riotgames.com`
SCVNGR	A game about doing challenges at places.	Website: `www.scvngr.com` Contact: `scvngr.com`
Tencent	The largest Internet service portal in China; now creating social game content for US and European audiences as well.	Website: `www.tencent.com`
Zynga	The largest social network game company as of 2010, it has created top games including *Mafia Wars, FarmVille*, and *FrontierVille*.	Website: `www.zynga.com`

Payment Processing and Monetization

Payment processing services included in Table B-3 provide the capability for social game companies to accept credit cards, PayPal, and mobile phone payments. They also include offer-based monetization, which enable companies to enable players to pay for virtual currency by participating in surveys and advertising.

Table B-3: Payment Processing Services

Service	Description	Website/Contact
Super Rewards	Enables players to earn rewards for engaging in incentivized offers and also provides payments through standard payment vehicles.	Website: www.superrewards.com
Tapjoy	Previously known as Offerpal, this company provides a wide range of payment and offer-based services. Although originally focused on social network games, it became more focused on mobile at the end of 2010.	Website: www.tapjoy.com Contact: info@tapjoy.com
TrialPay	Provides advertising and monetization services for social applications and game developers.	Website: www.trialpay.com
Peanut Labs	A company focused on providing surveys to social applications and games to provide a source of additional revenue.	Website: www.peanutlabs.com Contact: info@peanutlabs.com Mailing address: 114 Sansome Street, Suite 920, 950 San Francisco, CA 94104

Advertising Optimizers

Table B-4 includes companies specializing in placing ads on social networks, and can help you lower the cost of acquiring new customers.

Table B-4: Advertising Optimizers

Company	Description	Website/Contact Information
AdParlor	Promote Facebook products on a CPA (cost-per-acquisition) payment model.	Website: www.adparlor.com
Nanigans	Fully managed, pay-for-performance ad network for Facebook games and social applications.	Website: www.nanigans.com

Advertising Networks

An advertising network is a company that markets multiple publishers and game products to a number of advertisers, providers, and publishers with a source of revenue in exchange for a share of their ad revenue. Advertising Networks are listed in Table B-5.

Table B-5: Advertising Networks

Network	Description	Website/Contact Information
Appssavvy	Branded virtual goods are placed within social game products by appssavvy.	Website: www.appssavvy.com Mailing address: 594 Broadway STE 207, New York, NY 10012
Game Advertising Online	Advertising network focused on the promotion of online game products, mostly with web-based display ads.	Website: game-advertising-online.com
Mochi Media	Advertising network for social and casual games.	Website: www.mochimedia.com Contact: sales@mochimedia.com Mailing address: Mochi Media, Inc., 611 Mission St., 5th Floor, San Francisco, CA 94105

Social Media + Gaming

The companies mentioned in Table B-6 might not always be considered the creators of games, but they use some of the techniques of games to drive engagement. They've been discussed elsewhere, primarily in Chapter 6.

Table B-6: Social Media and Gaming Companies

Company	Description	Website/Contact Information
eBay	The largest online auctioneer in the world.	Website: `www.ebay.com`
Foursquare	A mobile application that enables you to earn points and badges for exploring your city.	Website: `www.foursquare.com`
LinkedIn	The original online business card collecting game, LinkedIn, makes use of progress bars, collections, and social status to drive engagement between business networkers.	Website: `www.linkedin.com` Contact: `business@linkedin.com` (business development inquiries) Mailing address: 2029 Stierlin Court, Mountain View, CA 94043
Livemocha	A social language-learning community that uses several gaming techniques to help people learn a new language.	Website: `www.livemocha.com`
MeYou Health	A subsidiary of Healthways, Inc., is a company committed to improving well-being. It created the Monumental stair-climbing game for the iPhone and is working on other fun and engaging ways to get people to think about health and wellness.	Website: `www.meyouhealth.com`
Practically Green	A website that enables people to make commitments to a more environmentally sustainable lifestyle.	Website: `www.practicallygreen.com`. Mailing address: 545 Boylston Street, 3rd Floor, Boston, MA 02116
YouTube	A Google subsidiary, this is the largest online video sharing community.	Website: `www.youtube.com`

Distribution Networks

Distribution networks provide alternative means to bring social game products to the attention of potential players. Some popular distribution networks are listed in Table B-7.

Table B-7: Distribution Networks

Network	Description	Website/Contact Information
Applifier	Provides a toolbar that increases the visibility of your game to millions of potential players. For each click that you send to another game, you earn credits toward inbound traffic.	Website: www.applifier.com
Viximo	Helps social game developers obtain distribution on international game networks—taking you beyond Facebook.	Website: www.viximo.com

Developer Support

The resources in Table B-8 can help you learn more about game development or introduce you to other developers.

Table B-8: Developer Support Resources

Resource	Description	Website/Contact Information
Gamasutra	Provides blogs and news articles of interest to industry professionals including game executives and designers.	Website: www.gamasutra.com
Game-on-book.com	Visit game-on-book.com to join the community that's talking about the contents of this book. Learn more about social game development and best practices, and meet others who share an interest in energizing their business with social games.	Website: game-on-book.com

continues

Table B-8: Developer Support Resources *(continued)*

Resource	Description	Website/Contact Information
International Game Developers Association	A nonprofit group that serves the interests of individuals who are involved in the creation of games.	Website: www.igda.org

Traditional Game Publishers

Almost every traditional game developer is now creating social games; therefore, it's somewhat artificial to place them in a separate category. The distinction with the publishers presented in Table B-9 is that they tend to be a bit older and also continue to develop a large number of games outside of the social gaming market.

Table B-9: Traditional Game Publishers

Publisher	Description	Website/Contact Information
Activision	One of the most venerable names in the computer game business, it owns world-famous brands with social-gaming elements including *Call of Duty* and *Guitar Hero*. Blizzard, the creator of *World of Warcraft* and *Starcraft,* is a subsidiary.	Website: www.activision.com
Bungie	The creator of *Halo*, one of the most popular games in history. Its use of agile testing and product improvement methods is discussed in Chapter 4.	Website: www.bungie.com
Electronic Arts	Creator of a wide range of social game content, including MMORPGs. Owner of Playfish, and also other studios focused on social games, such as *Lord of Ultima*, created at its Phenomic Studios subsidiary.	Website: www.ea.com

Publisher	Description	Website/Contact Information
Harmonix	The creator of *Rock Band*, a game that enables people to enjoy the feeling of being a rock star along with a group of friends.	Website: `www.harmonix.com`
Maxis	A subsidiary of Electronic Arts, it is the creator of *Spore* and the *Sims*.	Website: `www.maxis.com`
Microsoft Xbox Live	Microsoft learned the power of social gaming features when it added achievements and player matchmaking to the Xbox Live console gaming service.	Website: `www.xbox.com`
Valve	The creator of popular games such as *Half-Life*, *Portal*, and *Team Fortress*. Its Steam network is a distribution platform for downloadable game content. Valve was an agile game development pioneer with the creation of the cabal methodology discussed in Chapter 3.	Website: `www.valvesoftware.com`
Ubisoft	Publisher of popular console games including *Assassin's Creed*; the company is now venturing into social game development.	Website: `www.ubisoft.com`
Wizards of the Coast	Creates games for the hobby market including *Magic: the Gathering* and *D&D*. It also licenses its products for use within computer and console game systems.	Website: `wizards.com`

Creativity Tools

Creativity tools include products mentioned in this book that could help your team collaborate or create ideas together. These are presented in Table B-10.

Table B-10: Creativity Tools

Tool	Description	Website/Contact Information
IconiCards	The invention of Dr. Sharon Livingston. Each card contains a mythical archetype that you can use to inspire ideas for stories, customer types, and motivations.	Website: `iconicards.com`. Contact: `sharonl@tlgonline.com`
iRise	Visualize applications before building them.	Website: `www.irise.com`
Protoshare	A product for collaboratively brainstorming and developing wireframes for user interfaces.	Website: `www.protoshare.com`

Market Research

The companies listed in Table B-11 provide market research and data that you may find helpful to understand the game market.

Table B-11: Market Research Companies

Company	Description	Website/Contact Information
DFC Intelligence	DFC Intelligence provides strategic market research and consulting on the game industry.	Website: `dfcint.com` Mailing address: 12707 High Bluff Drive, Suite 200, San Diego, CA 92130
Inside Network	Creator of `InsideSocialGames.com` and also a creator of research reports of interest to social game and application developers.	Website: `www.insidenetwork.com`

Company	Description	Website/Contact Information
NPD Group	NPD provides market data on a wide range of retail products including automotive, games, software, and food.	Website: npd.com Contact: contactnpd@npd.com
Frank N. Magid Associates, Inc.	Frank N. Magid Associates provides strategic consulting and market research services with a focus on digital media and games.	Website: www.magid.com

C Book References

 his appendix gives a list of references used in this book.

Abrams, J.J. 2009. "J.J. Abrams on The Magic of Mystery." *Wired*, 17.05.

Agile manifesto: see www.agilemanifesto.org.

Alexander, Leigh. 2010. "Bejeweled Sales Hit 50 Million." *GamaSutra*. 10 February 2010. Web. 30 January 2011.

Arrington, Michael. 2009. "Mobile Payments Getting Traction On Social Networks, But Fees Are Sky High." *TechCrunch*. 13 January 2009.

Bartle, Richard. 1990. "Interactive Multi-User Computer Games." MUSE Ltd.

Bartle, Richard. 2005. "Virtual Worlds: Why People Play." *Massively Multiplayer Game Development: v. 2*. Ed. Thor Alexander. Charles River Media.

Birdwell, Ken. 1999. "The Cabal: Valve's Design Process for Creating *Half-Life*." *GamaSutra*. 10 December 1999. Web. 30 January 2011.

Bloom, Paul. 2010. *How Pleasure Works: the new science of why we like what we like.* New York, NY: W.W. Norton & Co.

Boven, L. and Gilovich, T. 2003. "To Do or to Have? That Is the Question," *American Psychological Association* 85.6: 1198. Figure reprinted with permission.

Calderón , Sara Inés. 2010. "Farmers Insurance Partners with Zynga's FarmVille, Protects Against Virtual Crop Withering." *Inside Facebook*. 15 October 2010. Web. 30 January 2011.

Campbell, Joseph. *The Hero with a Thousand Faces,* Third Edition. 2008. Novato, California: New World Library.

Chalk, Andy. 2010. "Beating Bejeweled: The Ultimate in Hardcore Casual." *The Escapist*. 29 April 2010. Web. 30 January 2011.

Charron, Sylvain and Koechlin, Etienne. 2010. "Divided Representation of Concurrent Goals in the Human Frontal Lobes." *Science* Vol. 328, No. 5976, 360–363.

Clarke, Arthur C. 1962. *Profiles of the Future: an Inquiry into the Limits of the Possible*. New York: Harper & Row.

Coleridge, Samuel Taylor. 1986. *The Rime of the Ancient Mariner*. Ed. Harold Bloom. New York: Chelsea House.

DeLeire, Thomas and Kalil, Ariel. 2010. "Does consumption buy happiness? Evidence from the United States.", *International Review of Economics* 57:163–176.

Doubloon. 2010. "Freemium Games are the New Music Stores." Web. 30 January 2011.

Edge Staff. 2008. "DLC Battle: Rock Band Vs Guitar Hero." *Edge*. 24 March 2008. Web. 30 January 2011.

Entropia Universe, "Entropia Universe Enters 2008 Guinness World Records Book for Most Expensive Virtual World Object." 18 September 2007. Web. 30 January 2011.

Fehr, E., Fischbacher, U., Gächter, S. 2002. Strong Reciprocity, Human Cooperation and the Enforcement of Social Norms. *Human Nature*, 13(2002): 1–25.

Field, Syd. 1979. *Screenplay: The Foundations of Screenwriting*. New York: Bantam Dell.

Florida, Richard. *The Rise of the Creative Class*. New York: Basic Books. 2002.

Florida, Richard. *The Great Reset*. New York: HarperCollins. 2010.

Gendler, Tamar Szabó. 2008. Alief and Belief. *The Journal of Philosophy*, 105(10):634–663.

Giant Interactive, "Giant Interactive Announces Fourth Quarter and Fiscal year 2009 Results," 4 March 2010. Web. 15 September 2010.

Gibson, William. "Modern boys and mobile girls." *The Observer* 1 April, 2001.

Gilmore, James and Pine, B. Joseph II. 2007. *Authenticity*. Boston: Harvard Business School Press.

Godin, Seth. *Unleashing the IdeaVirus*. New York: Hyperion. 2001.

Godin, Seth. *Purple Cow: Transform Your Business By Being Remarkable*. New York: Penguin. 2002.

Gullberg, Jan. 1997. *Mathematics: From the Birth of Numbers.* New York: W. W. Norton & Co.

Hamann, Stephen. 2001. "Cognitive and neural mechanisms of emotional memory." *Trends in Cognitive Sciences* 5:9, 394–400.

Harding-Rolls, Piers and Bailey, Steve. 2010. "Social Network Games: Casual Games' New Growth Engine." *ScreenDigest.* 9 July 2010. Web. 30 January 2011.

Harford, Tim. 2005. *Undercover Economist.* New York: Random House.

Hooper, David and Whyld, Kenneth. 1996. *The Oxford Companion to Chess.* Oxford University Press, USA.

Houghton, Arthur Boyd. 1865. Dalziel's "Illustrated Arabian Nights' Entertainments," depiction of Scheherazade. Thank you to George Landow for making a scan of the image available, which may also be viewed at www.victorianweb.org/art/illustration/houghton/1.html.

Information Solutions Group. *2010 Social Gaming Research.* 2010.

Jenkins, Henry. *Convergence Culture.* New York: New York University Press. 2006.

Johnson, Stephen. *Everything Bad is Good for You.* New York: Riverhead. 2005.

Kazemi, Darius and Triola, Scott. 2010. "Understanding Your Players Through Data." *Boston Post Mortem.* Web. 30 January 2011.

Kesmodel, David and Wilke, John R. 2007. "Whole Foods Is Hot, Wild Oats a Dud—So Said 'Rahodeb'." *The Wall Street Journal* 12 July 2007, front page.

Kincard, Jason. 2010. "EdgeRank: The Secret Sauce That Makes Facebook's News Feed Tick." *TechCrunch.* 22 April 2010. Web. 30 January 2011.

Knight, Cheryl. 2010. "New Global Initiatives Help Pfizer Inc. Save More Than $30M." *Fleet Financials.* July 2010. Web. 30 January 2011.

Krahulik, M. and Holkins, J. 2004. "Green Blackboards (And Other Anomalies)." Penny Arcade. 19 March 2004. Web. 18 October 2010.

Kruger, J., Epley, N., Parker, J. & Zhi-Wen, N. 2005. "Egocentrism over e-mail: Can we communicate as well as we think?" *Journal of Personality and Social Psychology,* 89:6, 925-936.

Lenhart, A., Kahne, J., Middaugh, E., Macgill, A. R., Evans, C., & Vitak, J. 2008. Teens, video games, and civics. Pew Internet & American Life Project.

Levitin, Daniel. *This is Your Brain on Music.* New York, NY: Penguin. 2006.

Levy, Ari and Galante, Joseph. 2010. "Facebook Games May Lead Payment Startups to $3.6 Billion Market." *Bloomberg Businessweek.* 3 February 2010.

Lundmark, Torbjorn. *Quirky Qwerty: A Biography of the Typewriter.* New York: Penguin. 2002.

Mad Men. Prod. Matthew Weiner, AMC. Bethpage, New York. 18 Oct 2007.

Maguire, E., Burgess, N., & O'Keefe, J. 1999. "Human spatial navigation: cognitive maps, sexual dimorphism, and neural substrates." *Current Opinion in Neurobiology.* 9:171–177.

Magic: The Gathering player types: Rosewater, 2006.

McLuhan, Mashall. *Understanding Media: the Extensions of Man.* Critical Edition edited by W. Terrence Gordon. Corte Madera: Gingko Press, 2003.

Meggs, Philip and Purvis, Alston. 2005. *Meggs' History of Graphic Design, Fourth Edition.* New York: John Wiley and Sons.

Meloni, Wanda. 2010. "The Brief – 2010 Ups and Downs." *M2 Research.* 5 January 2010. Web. 30 January 2011.

Mitchell, J. P., Banaji, M. R., & Macrae, C. N. 2005. "The link between social cognition and self-referential thought in the medial prefrontal cortex." *Journal of Cognitive Neuroscience,* 17, 1306–1315.

Tatsuya Nogami and Jiro Takai. 2008. "Effects of Anonymity on Antisocial Behavior Committed by Individuals." *Psychological Reports* 102:1, 119–130.

Norton, Michael I. 2009. "The IKEA Effect: When Labor Leads to Love." *Harvard Business Review* 87:2 (February 2009): 30.

Nutt, Christian. 2009. "Q&A: Valve's Swift On *Left 4 Dead 2*'s Production, AI Boost." *GamaSutra.* 12 November 2009. Web. 30 January 2011.

Odean, Terrance.1998. Are Investors Reluctant to Realize Their Losses? *The Journal of Finance,* Vol. 53, No. 5, 1775–1798.

Ogline, Tim. 2009. "Myth, Magic, and the Mind of Neil Gaiman." *Wild River Review,* October 2009.

PlayNoEvil. 2006. "The World of text MMOs / MUDs – An Interview with Matt Mihaly, CEO of Iron Realms Entertainment." 8 September 2006. Web. 30 January 2011.

PlaySpan and Magid Associates. 2010. "Magid Associates and PlaySpan Release 2nd Annual Survey on Virtual Goods Market Penetration and Growth in North America." *PlaySpan* press release. 27 May 2010.

PQ Media. 2010. *Global Branded Entertainment Marketing Forecast 2010–2014.*

Pruitt, J. and Grudin, J. 2003. "Personas: Practice and Theory." Association for Computing Machinery.

Radoff, Jon. 2008. "Megatrends in Video Gaming." Edinburgh Interactive Festival. 11 August 2008. Web. 30 January 2011.

Ramachandran, V.S and Hirstein, W. 1999.The Science of Art: A Neurological Theory of Aesthetic Experience. *Journal of Consciousness Studies,* 6(6–7), 15–51.

Ramachandran, V.S. *A Brief Tour of Human Consciousness.* New York, NY: Pearson Education. 2004.

Reiss, Steven. *Who Am I?: the 16 basic desires that motivate our behavior and define our personality.* New York, NY: Penguin Putnam. 2000.

Ritchey, M., Dolcos, F. & Cabeza, R. 2008. "Role of Amygdala Connectivity in the Persistence of Emotional Memories Over Time: An Event-Related fMRI Investigation." *Cerebral Cortex* 18.11 (2008): 2494–2504.

Rosewater, Mark. 2006. "Timmy, Johnny and Spike Revisited." *Making Magic Archive.* Wizards of the Coast. 20 March 2006. Web. 17 October 2010.

Royal Tombs of Ur. The British Museum. N.d. Web.16 October 2010.

"SAP User-Centered Design Process, The." Design & Research Methodology, SAP User Experience, SAP. 10 December 2006. Web. 16 October 2010.

Schwartz, Barry. 2004. *The Paradox of Choice.* New York: HarperCollins. 2004.

Shiv, B., Loewenstein, G., Bechara, A., Damasio, H., & Damasio, A. 2005. Investment "Behavior and the Negative Side of Emotion." *Psychological Science,* 16(6):435–439.

Slater, Michael. 2009. *Charles Dickens.* Yale University Press.

Smith, Justin and Hudson, Charles. 2010. *The US Virtual Goods Market 2010–2011.* Inside Virtual Goods.

Suler, John. 2004. "The Online Disinhibition Effect." *CyberPsychology and Behavior,* 7, 321–326.

Takahashi, Dean. "Zynga's FarmVille social game partners with real-world farm to offer in-game crops." *GamesBeat.* 14 July 2010. Web. 30 January 2011.

Thompson, Clive. 2007. "*Halo 3*: How Microsoft Labs Invented a New Science of Play." *Wired,* 15.09.

Tromp, John. "Number of chess diagrams and positions." John's Chess Playground. Retrieved October 5, 2010. <http://homepages.cwi.nl/~tromp/chess/chess.html>.

Tuckman, Bruce. 2001. "Developmental Sequence in Small Groups." *Group Facilitation.* No. 3, Spring 2001.

Vale, Malcolm. 2001. *The Princely Court: Medieval Courts and Culture in North-West Europe.* Oxford University Press.

Wake, Bill. 2003. "INVEST in Good Stories, and SMART Tasks." 18 August 2003. Web. 30 January 2011.

Wansink, B., Payne, C., & North, J. 2007. "Fine as North Dakota wine: Sensory expectations and the intake of companion foods." *Physiology & Behavior,* 90 (5), 712-716 DOI: 10.1016/j.physbeh.2006.12.010.

Weber, Max. 1978. *Economy and Society.* Translated by Fischoff et al. Edited by Roth, Guenther and Wittich, Claus. Los Angeles: University of California Press.

Woodcock, George. 1944. "The Tyranny of Clocks." *War Commentary,* March 1944.

Wordsworth, William. 1800. Preface to *Lyrical Ballads.*

Wright, Don. Photo credit for the image of pieces on a chessboard, 2008 (Flickr image).

Yee, Nick. 2007. "Motivations for Play in Online Games." *CyberPsychology and Behavior,* 9, 772–775.

Index